S0-CMU-827

LIFE AND PUBLIC SERVICES

OF

HON. ABRAHAM LINCOLN

𝔚𝔦𝔱𝔥 𝔞 𝔓𝔬𝔯𝔱𝔯𝔞𝔦𝔱 𝔬𝔫 𝔖𝔱𝔢𝔢𝔩.

TO WHICH IS ADDED A BIOGRAPHICAL SKETCH OF

HON. HANNIBAL HAMLIN.

Engd by R S Jones from A Photograph by Brady

A. Lincoln.

LIFE AND PUBLIC SERVICES

OF

HON. ABRAHAM LINCOLN,

With a Portrait on Steel.

TO WHICH IS ADDED A BIOGRAPHICAL SKETCH OF

HON. HANNIBAL HAMLIN.

BY DAVID W. BARTLETT

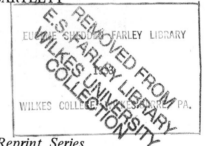

EUGENE SHEDDEN FARLEY LIBRARY

WILKES COLLEGE, WILKES-BARRE, PA.

REMOVED FROM E. S. FARLEY LIBRARY WILKES UNIVERSITY COLLECTION

Select Bibliographies Reprint Series

BOOKS FOR LIBRARIES PRESS
FREEPORT, NEW YORK

E 457
B 29

First Published 1860
Reprinted 1969

STANDARD BOOK NUMBER:
8369-5066-6

LIBRARY OF CONGRESS CATALOG CARD NUMBER:
78-95064

PRINTED IN THE UNITED STATES OF AMERICA

PREFACE.

But a single word is necessary. Every reader will easily understand that a "campaign" life of any man, got up with despatch, is like neither "Boswell's Johnson" nor "Lockhart's Scott." They were the work of years—this of days. But it is believed that this is an accurate life of Mr. Lincoln in every respect, and as such, we send it forth to take its share in the great work of making Abraham Lincoln next President of these United States.

D. W. B.

Washington, D. C., *June 1st*, 1860.

159517

CONTENTS.

PART FIRST.

EARLY HISTORY.

PART SECOND.

IN CONGRESS.

PART THIRD.

THE GREAT SENATORIAL CONTEST.

PART FOURTH

THE CONVENTION AND ITS NOMINATIONS.

LIFE AND SPEECHES

OF

ABRAHAM LINCOLN.

PART FIRST

EARLY HISTORY.

ABRAHAM LINCOLN is a native of the county of Hardin, Kentucky. He was born February 12, 1808. His parents came from Virginia, and it is said made no pretensions of belonging to " one of the first families." His grandfather, Abraham Lincoln, emigrated from Rockingham county, Virginia, to the State of Kentucky, about the year 1781. A year or two later than this, he was killed by the Indians, while at work in the forest. Mr. Lincoln's earlier ancestors were members of the Society of Friends, and went to Virginia from Berks county, Pennsylvania, where some of the family still reside.

Mr. Lincoln's father, at the death of his father, in 1783, was but six years old. He removed to what is now Spencer county, Indiana, in 1816. The early,

Indiana life of Mr. Lincoln is thus described by one of his friends :

" The family reached their new home about the time the State was admitted into the Union. The region in which they settled was rude and wild, and they endured, for some years, the hard experience of a frontier life, in which the struggle with nature for existence and security is to be maintained only by constant vigilance. Bears, wolves, and other wild animals, still infested the woods, and young Lincoln acquired more skill in the use of the rifle than knowledge of books. There were institutions here and there, known by the flattering denomination of "schools," but no qualification was required of a teacher beyond "readin', writin', and cipherin'," as the vernacular phrase ran, as far as the rule of three. If a straggler, supposed to understand Latin, happened to sojourn in the neighborhood, he was looked upon as a wizard, and regarded with an awe suited to so mysterious a character.

" Hard work, and plenty of it, was the order of the day, varied, indeed, by an occasional bear-hunt, a not unfrequent deer-chase, or other wild sport. Of course, when young Lincoln came of age, he was not a scholar. He could read and write, and had some knowledge of arithmetic, but that was about all ; and as yet, he had but little ambition to know more of what was to be found in books. His attainments otherwise were not to be despised. He had grown to be six feet four inches in stature, was active and athletic, could wield the axe, direct the plough, or use the rifle, as well as the best of his compeers, and was fully up to all the mysteries of prairie farming, and fully inured to hardship and toil.

Since he arrived at age he has not been to school. Whatever his acquirements are, they have been picked up from time to time as opportunity occurred, or as the pressure of some exigency demanded."

At the age of twenty-one he removed to the State of Illinois, which was thereafter to be his home. The first year he passed in Macon county, in hard labor upon a farm, where he and a fellow-laborer of the name of Hawkes, in the year 1830, split three thousand rails. He also, at one time, managed a flat-boat on the Ohio river. From Macon county he went to New Salem, now Menard county, where he remained a year. Then the Black-Hawk war broke out. A company of volunteers was raised in his county, and he was elected its captain. He served through the war, and gained much popularity. It may not be amiss to give a sketch here of the origin of this war, which engaged Lincoln's services at so early an age, and we make the subjoined extracts from *Brown's History of Illinois*, for that purpose :

THE BLACK-HAWK WAR.

Black-Hawk, the Indian chief, who has recently occupied a considerable space in the public mind, and cost, it is said, the United States more than two millions of dollars, was born, as it was supposed, about the year 1767, on Rock river, in Illinois.

At the time of which we are about to speak, the Winnebagoes occupied all that part of the Wisconsin territory bordering on the river Wisconsin and in the vicinity of Winnebago lake. Their population in 1820 was estimated at one thousand five hundred and fifty souls, of whom five hundred were warriors. White Tom was a conspicuous chief among them. He opposed General Wayne in 1794—fought at Tippecanoe in 1811—was active during the war of 1812 on-the side of the British, and treated with General Harrison at Greenville, in 1814.

The Menomonies resided 'still farther north, upon a river of that name, in the vicinity of Green Bay. They were estimated in 1860 at three hundred and fifty souls, of whom one hundred were warriors.

The Pottawatomies occupied the head waters of Lake Michigan ; they were estimated in 1820 at three thousand four hundred souls. The United States paid them, yearly, five thousand seven hundred dollars. The Pottawatomies were known to the French at an early day. In 1668, three hundred of these warriors visited Father Allouez at Chegaumegon, an island in Lake Superior.

The Sacs (or rather the Sauks) and Foxes—usually mentioned together (one nation, in fact), occupied the country west of the Pottawatomies, between the Illinois and Mississippi rivers ; they were estimated, in 1860, at three thousand souls. They were also known to the French, and Christianity was taught them by the Jesuits, in 1668. Keokuk was, for many years, a conspicuous chief among them, as also Black-Hawk, before referred to. The latter was a grandson of Na-na-ma-kee, or Thunder, and having taken the scalp of an enemy at the early age of fifteen, was admitted to the rank of " a brave." A short time afterward he joined a war party against the Osages, and became noted for his valor. On his return he was allowed to join the war-dance of his nation. He frequently led war parties against the enemies of his tribe, and, in almost every instance, was victorious.

On the 27th of June, 1804, a treaty was made at St. Louis, by General Harrison, with the Sacs and Foxes, and the lands east of the Mississippi were ceded to the United States. This treaty, having been executed, as Black-Hawk pretended, without the knowledge or consent of the nation, was the subject of much altercation and serious difficulty thereafter.

The territory of Illinois, in 1818, having been admitted into the Union, and peace between Great Britain and United States restored, emigrants from every direction repaired thither, and the country of the Sacs and Foxes was shortly surrounded by the settlements of white men. In order to hasten the departure of the Indians from the ceded territory, some outrages, it is said, and we have no doubt of the fact, were committed on their persons and effects.

On the 19th of August, 1828, a treaty was held at Prairie du Chien, with the Sacs, Foxes, Winnebagoes, Chippewas, Sioux, and other northwestern tribes, by William Clark and Lewis Cass, in behalf of the United States, for the purpose of bringing about a peace between the Sacs and other tribes. The United States undertook the part of mediators. However pure their motives, the effect was not such as could have been desired. Hostilities continued, and murders frequently happened. In the summer of 1821, a party of twenty-four Chippewas, on a tour to Fort Snelling, were surprised by a band of Sioux, and eight of their number were killed and wounded. The commander of Fort

Snelling caused some of the Sioux to be delivered to the Chippewas, by whom they were shot. Red-Bird, a chief of the Sioux, resented the affront, and determined to retaliate. He, accordingly, led a party against the Chippewas, and was defeated. On his return home he was derided as being "no brave." Red-Bird being disappointed of vengeance upon the Chippewas, determined to seek it among their abettors, the whites ; and on the 24th of July, 1827, two whites, in the vicinity of Prairie-du-Chien, were killed and another wounded, and on the 30th of July, two keel-boats, conveying military stores to Fort Snelling, were attacked, two of their crew killed and four wounded. Black-Hawk was charged, among others, with this last offence.

General Atkinson thereupon marched with a brigade of troops, regulars and militia, into the Winnebago country, and made prisoners of Red-Bird and six others, who were held in confinement at Prairie-du-Chien until a trial could be had. Red-Bird died in prison. A part of those arrested were convicted and a part acquitted. Black-Hawk, after a year's imprisonment, was discharged, not for want of guilt but for want of proof. Matters remained in this state for about three years. Though violence was frequently done punishment seldom followed.

A treaty, on the 15th of July, 1830, had been made, by which the Sacs and Foxes ceded all their country east of the Mississippi to the United States ; but Black-Hawk had nothing to do with it. Keokuk, or the Watchful Fox, at this time headed the Sacs, who made the treaty. Black-Hawk, when apprized of what they had done, disapproved of it, and was much agitated.

Keokuk was a friend of the whites, and Black-Hawk used to say, sold his country for nothing.

About the time of the execution of the treaty of Prairie-du-Chien, several outrages were committed on the Indians by the whites, which served to exasperate still more those already excited.

Black-Hawk, when he first learned that Keokuk had sold the Sac village, with the rest of the country on the east side of the Mississippi, remonstrated with him on the subject ; and " Keokuk was so well satisfied," says Black-Hawk, " that he had done what he had no right to do, and what he ought not to have done, that he promised to go to the whites and endeavor to get it back again." Black-Hawk agreed to give up the lead mines if he could be allowed to enjoy their old village and the little point of land which their wives had cultivated for years, undisturbed, and the graves of their fathers.

Relying on the promise of Keokuk, the Sacs set out on their winter's hunt, in the fall of 1830, as usual. Returning thence, in the spring of 1831, they found the whites in possession of their villages, and their wives and children, on the banks of the Mississippi, without a shelter. " This," says Black-Hawk, " is insufferable. Where is there a white man who could or would endure this ? None ! not the most servile slave. Their village they would," said Black-Hawk, " again possess." They acted in accordance with this resolution, and went and again took possession. The whites were alarmed, and, doubting their ability to drive them off, the Indians said they could live and plant together.

The Indians had been told, in the fall of 1830, that they must not come again east of the Mississippi. Soon afterward the lands they had occupied, or part of them, were sold to private adventurers, and the Indians were ordered to leave them. Black-Hawk and his band refused to go. The settlers thereupon exclaimed against *Indian encroachments*, and Governor Reynolds forthwith declared the State of Illinois invaded by hostile savages.

On the 28th day of May, 1831, Governor Reynolds wrote to General Gaines, the military commander of the western department, that he had received undoubted information, that a section of the State, near Rock Island, was invaded by a hostile band of the Sac Indians, headed by Black-Hawk ; that to repel said invasion and protect the citizens of Illinois, he had called on seven hundred of the militia of said State, to be mounted and ready for service ; and respectfully requested his co-operation. General Gaines, in reply, said he had ordered six companies of regular troops to proceed from Jefferson barracks to the Sac village, and, if necessary, he would add two companies from Prairie-du-Chien. This he considered sufficient ; but, continued he, if the Indian force should be augmented by other Indians, he would correspond with his excellency by express, and avail himself of the mounted volunteers he had tendered.

" The object," said Governor Reynolds, " of the State government, is to protect their own citizens, by removing said Indians, ' peaceably if they can, forcibly if they must.' "

General Gaines proceeded at once to the country in

dispute, and, by discreet and prudent management, succeeded in settling the most prominent difficulties, which amounted, on examination, to little or nothing. On the 20th of June, 1831, General Gaines wrote to the Secretary of War, as follows :

"I have visited the Rock River villages, to ascertain the localities and dispositions of the Indians. They are resolved to abstain from hostilities, except in their own defence. Few of their warriors were to be seen. Their women and children and old men, appeared to be anxious and none attempted to run of. I am resolved to abstain from firing a shot without some blood shed, or some manifest attempt to shed blood, on the part of the Indians. I have already induced nearly one third of them to cross the Mississippi—the residue say they will not cross, and their women urge their husbands to fight, rather to move and abandon their homes."

Thus matters stood till the Illinois militia arrived. On the 7th of June, Black-Hawk met General Gaines and told him he should not remove. On the 25th, the militia arrived. The Indians, to avoid difficulty, fled across the Mississippi, and, on the 26th, the army took possession of the Sac village, without firing a gun. On the 27th Black-Hawk raised a white flag to indicate his wish for a parley—a parley ensued and a treaty followed.

General Gaines thereupon wrote to the Secretary of War that the Indians were completely humbled as if they had been chastised in battle, and less disposed to disturb the inhabitants on the frontier. Govenor Reynolds likewise expressed the same opinion. In this, however, they were both mistaken. General Gaines promised the Indians corn, in lieu of what they had abandoned. The supply, however, was insufficient, and they began to feel the effects of hunger. In this state of things they went over to steal corn from their own land, and a new series of troubles began, which ended afterward in bloodshed.

In the spring of 1832, Black-Hawk recrossed the Mississippi and moved up Rock river. Governor Reynolds at once ordered out a thousand of the militia, who were armed and equipped for the service, and who came from the southern and central counties of Illinois. It was one of the companies of this force which young Lincoln commanded, in the course of the war, which lasted for but a short time. In an engagement with the State militia, at "Stillman's Run," the Indians obtained an advantage over the whites which alarmed the entire State. The Governor called out three thousand more of the militia, and on the 2d of August a very decisive engagement took place at the mouth of the "Bad-Axe," the Indians experiencing a defeat, and Black-Hawk fled. He was afterward arrested and brought to Washington, where President Jackson set him free. In this war, as we have remarked, Mr. Lincoln served with faithfulness and success.

HIS PROGRESS UPWARD.

Returning to Sangamon county, Mr. Lincoln studied surveying, and prosecuted that profession until the financial crash of 1837 destroyed the value of real estate and ruined the business—the result of which was that young Lincoln's surveying apparatus was sold on execution by the sheriff. Nothing daunted by this turn of ill-luck, he directed his attention to law, and borrowing a few books from a neighbor, which he took from the office in the evening and returned in the morning, he learned the rudiments of the profession in which he has since become so distinguished.

Mr. Lincoln was in his youth known as the swiftest runner, the best jumper, and the strongest wrestler, among his fellows ; and when he reached manhood and his physical frame became developed, the early settlers pronounced him the stoutest man in the State. His abstemious habits and his hardy physical discipline strengthened his constitution and gave vigor to his mind. He improved every opportunity to cultivate his intellect, often studying his law-books far into the night by the reflection of the log-fire in his farm-home on the prairies. He was early distinguished for a disputational turn of mind, and many are the intellectual triumphs of his in the country or village lyceum selected by old settlers who remember him as he then appeared. His strong, natural, direct, and irresistible logic marked him there as it has ever since, as an intellectual king.

The deep snow which occurred in the winter of 1830–'31, was one of the chief troubles endured by the early settlers of Central and Southern Illinois. Its consequences lasted through several years. The people were illy prepared to meet it, as the weather had been mild and pleasant— unprecedentedly so up to Christmas—when a snow-storm set in, which lasted two days ; something never before known even among the traditions of the Indians, and never approached in the weather of any winter since. The pioneers who came

into the State (then a territory) in 1800, some of
whom are still living, say the average depth of snow
was never, previous to 1830, more than knee deep to
an ordinary man, while it was *breast high* all that winter,
not in drifts but over a whole section. " For three
months," say the old settlers, " there was not a warm
sun upon the surface of the snow." It became crusted
over, so as (in some cases) to bear teams. Cattle and
horses perished, the winter wheat was killed, the mea-
gre stocks of provisions ran out, and the most wealthy
settlers came near starving, while some of the poorer
ones actually did. It was in the midst of such scenes
that young Abraham Lincoln attained his majority, and
commenced his career of bold and manly independence.
It was this discipline that was to try the soul of the
future President. Communication between house and
house was often entirely obstructed for teams, so that
the young and strong men had to do all the travelling
on foot ; carrying from one neighbor what of his store
he could spare to another, and bringing back something in return sorely needed. Men living five, ten,
twenty, and thirty miles apart were called " neighbors"
then. Young Lincoln was always ready to perform
these acts of humanity, and foremost in the counsels
of the settlers when their troubles seemed gathering
like a thick cloud about them.

" About this time," says one of Mr. Lincoln's friends,
" the Whigs of this county conferred upon him a nomination for the Legislature. He was successful in this
and three succeeding elections, by triumphant majorities. While a member of the Legislature he first gave
indications of his superior powers as a debater, and he

increased, by frequent practice, his natural faculty for public speaking. He improved industriously the opportunities that were here offered of self-cultivation. From the position of a subaltern in the ranks of the Whig party, a position that was appropriately assigned him by his unaffected modesty and humble pretensions, he soon became recognized and acknowledged as a champion and leader, and his unvarying courtesy, good nature, and genial manners, united with an utter disinterestedness and abnegation of self, made him a universal favorite.

" During his legislative period he continued his law studies, and removing to Springfield he opened an office and engaged actively in practice. Business flowed in upon him, and he rose rapidly to distinction in his profession. He displayed remarkable ability as an advocate in jury trials, and many of his law arguments were master-pieces of logical reasoning. There was no refined artificiality in his forensic efforts. They all bore the stamp of masculine common sense ; and he had a natural easy mode of illustration, that made the most abstruse subjects appear plain. His success at the bar, however, did not withdraw his attention from politics. For many years he was the ' wheel-horse' of the whig party of Illinois, and was on the electoral ticket in several Presidential campaigns. At such time he canvassed the State with his usual vigor and ability. He was an ardent friend of Henry Clay, and exerted himself powerfully in his behalf, in 1844, traversing the entire State of Illinois, and addressing public meetings daily until near the close of the campaign, when becoming convinced that his labors in that field would be unavailing, he crossed over into Indiana, and continued his efforts up to the day of election. The contest of that year in Illinois was mainly on the tariff question. Mr. Lincoln, on the whig side, and John Calhoun on the democratic side, were the heads of the opposing electoral tickets. Calhoun, late of Nebraska, now dead, was then in the full vigor of his powers, and was accounted the ablest debater of his party.   They stumped the State together, or nearly so, making speeches usually on alternate days at each place, and each addressing large audiences at great length, sometimes four hours together.   Mr. Lincoln, in these elaborate speeches, evinced a thorough mastery of the principles of political economy which underlie the tariff question, and presented arguments in favor of the protective policy with a power and conclusiveness rarely equalled, and at the same time in a manner so lucid and familiar, and so well interspersed with happy illustrations and apposite anecdotes, as to establish a reputation which he has never since failed to maintain, as the ablest leader in the Whig and Republican ranks in the great West."

PART· SECOND.

IN CONGRESS.

IN 1846, Mr. Lincoln was elected to Congress from the central district of Illinois.

He took his seat in Congress on the first Monday in December, of the year 1847. It was the Thirtieth Congress, and the House of Representatives to which he was elected was presided over by Mr. Winthrop of Massachusetts. The House was composed of 117 Whigs, 110 Democrats, and 1 Native American. Illinois then had seven representatives, and all were Democrats but Mr. Lincoln. He alone from that State held up the old Whig banner. With him, from other States, were associated such well-known names as the following : Collamer, Marsh, Ashmun, Truman Smith, Hunt, Tallmadge, Ingersoll, Botts, Goggin, Clingman, Stephens, Toombs, Gentry, and Thompson. Opposed to him in politics were men like Wilmot, Brodhead, Boyd, Bocock, Rhett, Brown, Linn Boyd, Andrew Johnson, etc., etc. In the Senate were Webster, Calhoun, Dayton, Davis, Dix; Dickinson, Hunter, Hale, B·ll, Crittenden, and Corwin. It was a Congress full of the most talented men—crowded with the real statesmen of the country, and such a one in these and other respects as the country rarely elects to make its laws. It turned out to be one of the most excited, agitated, and agitating ever convened.

HARBOR AND RIVER BILL.

One of Mr. Lincoln's first votes was given, December 20, 1847, in favor of the subjoined resolution :

"*Resolved*, That if, in the judgment of Congress, it be necessary to improve the navigation of a river to expedite and render secure the movements of our army, and save from delay and loss our arms and munitions of war, that Congress has the power to improve such river.

"*Resolved*, That if it be necessary for the preservation of the lives of our seamen, repairs, safety, or maintenance of our vessels-of-war, to improve a harbor or inlet, either on our Atlantic or Lake coast, Congress has the power to make such improvement."

A motion was made to lay the resolution on the table, and Mr. Lincoln voted with the other Whigs then in the House against the motion, and it was defeated. The resolution was laid over after this test vote to another day for debate.

SLAVERY IN THE DISTRICT OF COLUMBIA.

The next day the slavery question was agitated in the House. Mr. Giddings presented a memorial from certain citizens of the District of Columbia, asking Congress to repeal all laws upholding the slave-trade in the district. Mr. Giddings moved to refer the memorial to the Judiciary Committee, with instructions to inquire into the constitutionality of all laws by which slaves are held as property in the District of Columbia. A motion was made to lay the paper on the table. Mr. Lincoln voted *against* the motion. The result was a

tie vote, and the Speaker voted in the negative. Mr.
Howell Cobb stated that he wished to debate it, and it
lay over under the rules.

On the 22d of December, Mr. Wentworth of Illinois
moved the following resolution :

"*Resolved,* That the General Government has the
power to construct such harbors, and improve such
rivers as are necessary and proper for the protection of
our navy and commerce, and also for the defences of
our country."

A motion was made to lay on the table, and then
withdrawn. An exciting contest ensued on the demand for the previous question. It was sustained, and
the House came to a direct vote on the resolution,
passing it by 138 ayes to 54 nays, Mr. Lincoln voting,
of course, with the ayes.

THE MEXICAN WAR.

On the same day Mr. Lincoln offered the following
preamble and resolutions on the Mexican War :

"Whereas, the President of the United States, in
his Message of May 11, 1846, has declared that ' the
Mexican government refused to receive him [the envoy
of the United States], or listen to his propositions, but,
after a long-continued series of menaces, have at last
invaded *our territory,* and shed the blood of our fellow-
citizens on *our own soil ;*'

"And again, in his Message of December 8, 1846,
that ' we had ample cause of war against Mexico long
before the breaking out of hostilities ; but even then
we forbore to take redress into our own hands until
Mexico basely became the aggressor, by invading *our*

soil in hostile array, and shedding the blood of our citizens ;'

"And yet, again, in his Message of December 7, 1847, ' The Mexican government refused even to hear the terms of adjustment which he (our minister of peace) was authorized to propose, and finally, under wholly unjustifiable pretexts, involved the two countries in war, by invading the territory of the State of Texas, striking the first blow, and shedding the blood of our citizens on *our own soil;'*

"And whereas, this House is desirous to obtain a full knowledge of all the facts which go to establish whether the particular spot on which the blood of our citizens was so shed, was or was not, at that time, *our own soil :* Therefore,

"*Resolved, by the House of Representatives,* That the President of the United States be respectfully requested to inform this House—

"1st. Whether the spot on which the blood of our citizens was shed, as in his memorial declared, was or was not within the territory of Spain, at least after the treaty of 1819, until the Mexican revolution.

"2d. Whether that spot is or is not within the territory which was wrested from Spain by the revolutionary government of Mexico.

"3d. Whether that spot is or is not within a settlement of people, which settlement has existed ever since long before the Texas Revolution, and until its inhabitants fled before the approach of the United States army.

"4th. Whether that settlement is or is not isolated from any and all other settlements of the Gulf and the

Rio Grande on the south and west, and of wide uninhabited regions on the north and east.

" 5th. Whether the people of that settlement, or a
majority of them, have ever submitted themselves to
the government or laws of Texas or of the United
States, of consent or of compulsion, either of accepting office or voting at elections, or paying taxes, or
serving on juries, or having process served on them,
or in any other way.

" 6th. Whether the people of that settlement did or
did not flee at the approaching of the United States
army, leaving unprotected their homes and their growing crops *before* the blood was shed, as in the message
stated ; and whether the first blood so shed was or was
not shed within the enclosure of one of the people who
had thus fled from it.

" 7th. Whether our *citizens* whose blood was shed,
as in his message declared, were or were not, at that
time, armed officers and soldiers sent into that settlement by the military order of the President, through
the Secretary of War.

" 8th. Whether the military force of the United
States was or was not so sent into that settlement after
General Taylor had more than once intimated to the
War Department that, in his opinion, no such move-
ment was necessary to the defence or protection of
Texas."

These resolutions were laid over under the rule. We
have quoted them entire because one of the false charges
of Mr. Lincoln's political opponents is, *that he voted
against the supplies* to the army. He was a Whig,
and took the position of the Whigs of his day, many

eminent Southern men included, which was opposition
to the declaration of war with Mexico, by the President, so long as that opposition would accomplish any
purpose, which it would not when Mr. Lincoln was in
Congress ; and always, as these resolutions of his prove,
objected to what he considered *a false statement as to
the origin of the difficulties.* No circumstances, in his
opinion, would justify falsehood in reference to the
history of that or any other war, and so he on every
proper occasion criticised the language of the President,
which repeatedly declared that the war was begun by
the act of Mexico.

SLAVERY AGAIN.

On the 28th of December Mr. Lincoln voted to
sustain the right of petition. Several citizens of
Indiana petitioned Congress for the abolition of slavery
in the District of Columbia, and Mr. C. B. Smith
moved to refer the petition to the Committee on the
District. Mr. Cabell moved to lay the memorial upon
the table, which motion was carried, Mr. Lincoln voting
against it and in favor of according to it a respectful
consideration.

On the 30th of December, a similar memorial against
the slave-trade was presented to the House, and on a
motion to lay upon the table Mr. Lincoln voted again
in the negative.

January 17, 1848, Mr. Giddings introduced a resolution in the House, reporting certain alleged outrages
against a colored man in the District, and calling upon
the Speaker to appoint a select committee to inquire
into the expediency of repealing such acts of Congress

as sustained or authorized the slave-trade in the District. The resolution caused considerable excitement, and a motion to lay on the table was made and lost by one vote. Mr. Lincoln voted against the motion. The resolution was now before the House, but the previous question was pending. Questions of order arose and the House was in great confusion. Mr. Giddings claimed the right to modify his resolution, and the Speaker decided that he had that right. Mr. Stephens, of Georgia, appealed from the decision of the Chair. In answer to a question, the Chair stated that if the resolution was modified, a second motion to lay on the table would be in order, whereupon Mr. Stephens withdrew his appeal. Mr. Giddings modified his resolution, and it was again moved that it be laid on the table. This time the motion was successful—ayes 94, nays 88—Mr. Lincoln voting no.

VOTE OF SUPPLIES FOR THE WAR.

On the 17th of February, Mr. Lincoln gave a vote which effectually destroys the assertion of some of his political enemies of this day, that he voted against the supplies for the war in Mexico. The Committee of Ways and Means reported a Loan Bill to raise the sum of sixteen millions of dollars to enable the government to provide for its debts, principally incurred in Mexico. This bill passed a Whig House of Representatives ; ayes 192, nays 14, *Mr. Lincoln voting for the bill.* This vote alone disposes of the slanderous charge that he voted against the supplies because of the war with Mexico.

PUTNAM'S RESOLUTION.

On the 28th of February Mr. Putnam moved the following preamble and resolution :

"*Whereas,* In the settlement of the difficulties pending between this country and Mexico, territory may be acquired in which slavery does not exist ; and whereas, Congress, in the organization of a territorial government, at an early period of our political history, established a principle worthy of imitation in all future time, forbidding the existence of slavery in free territory : Therefore,

"*Resolved,* That in any territory which may be acquired from Mexico, over which shall be established territorial governments, slavery or involuntary servitude, except as a punishment for crime, whereof the party shall have been duly convicted, should be forever prohibited ; and that, in any act or resolution establishing such governments, a fundamental provision ought to be inserted to that effect."

Mr. Putnam moved the previous question.

Mr. Brodhead moved to lay the resolution on the table.

The motion to lay on the table was decided by yeas and nays.

After the roll was called through, Mr. C. J. Ingersoll rose and asked leave to vote. Mr. I. said he was not within the bar when his name was called, but came in before the following name was called. Mr. I, said, if allowed to vote, he would vote aye. His vote was not received.

Mr. Murphy rose and said he was not within the

bar when his name was called, but he asked leave to vote. It being objected to—

Mr. C. J. Ingersoll moved to suspend the rules, to allow Mr. Murphy and himself to vote. Disagreed to.

The result was then announced, as follows :

Yeas.—Messrs. Green Adams, Atkinson, Barringer, Barrow, Bayly, Bedinger, Birdsall, Black, Bocock, Bowdon, Bowlin, Boyd, Boyden, Brodhead, Charles Brown, Albert G. Brown, Burt, Cabell, Cathcart, Chase, Clapp, Franklin Clark, Beverly L. Clark, Clingman, Howell Cobb, Williamson R. W. Cobb, Cocke, Crisfield, Crozier, Daniel, Dickinson, Donnell, Garnett Duncan, Featherston, Ficklin, French, Fulton, Gaines, Gayle, Gentry, Goggin, Green, Willard P. Hall, Haralson, Harris, Haskell, Henley, Hill, Hilliard, Isaac E. Holmes, George S. Houston, Inge, Iverson, Jackson, Jamieson, Andrew Johnson, Robert W. Johnson, Geo. W. Jones, John W. Jones, Kaufman, Kennon, Tho. Butler King, La Sere, Levin, Ligon, Lord, Lumpkin, Maclay, McClernand, McKay, McLane, Mann, Miller, Morehead, Morse, Outlaw, Pendleton, Pettit, Peyton, Phelps, Pilsbury, Preston, Richardson, Richey, Robinson, Roman, Sawyer, Shepperd, Simpson, Sims, Robert Smith, Stanton, Stephens, Thibodeaux, Thomas, Tompkins, John B. Thompson, Robert A Thompson, Toombs, Turner, Venable, Wick, Williams, Wiley, Woodward—105.

Nays.—Messrs. Abbott, Ashmun, Bingham, Brady, Butler, Canby, Collamer, Collins, Conger, Cranston, Crowell, Cummins, Dickey, Dixon, Duer, Daniel Duncan, Dunn, Eckert, Edwards, Embree, Nathan Evans, Faran, Farrelly, Fisher, Freedly, Fries. Giddings, Gott, Gregory, Grinnell, Hale, Nathan K. Hall, Hammons. James G. Hampton, Moses Hampton, Henry, Elias B. Holmes, John W. Houston, Hubbard, Hudson, Hunt, Irvin, Jenkins, James H. Johnson, Kellogg, Daniel P, King, Lahm, William T. Lawrence, Sidney Lawrence. Leffler, Lincoln, McClelland, McIlvaine, Marsh, Marvin, Morris, Mullin, Nelson, Nes, Newell, Palfrey, Peaslee, Peck, Pollock, Putnam, Reynold, Julius, John A. Rockwell, Root, Rumsey, St. John, Schenck, Sherrill, Silvester, Slingerland, Caleb B. Smith, Truman Smith, Starkweather, Andrew Stewart, Charles E. Stuart, Strohm, Tallmadge, Taylor, Richard W. Thompson, William Thompson, Thurston, Van Dyke, Vinton, Warren, Wentworth, White, Wilmot, Wilson—92,

So the resolution was laid on the table.

Mr. Lincoln voted with the nays.

THE TEN REGIMENT BILL.

On April 3d Mr. Lincoln voted to suspend the rules that the Ten Regiment Bill might be taken up, and again did the same on the 18th of the same month.

THE TARIFF.

June 19, 1848, Mr. Lincoln put himself on record in favor of a protective tariff. Mr. Stewart of Penn., on that day moved a suspension of the rules to enable him to offer the following resolution :

" *Resolved,* That the Committee of Ways and Means be instructed to inquire into the expediency of reporting a bill increasing the duties on foreign luxuries of all kinds and on such foreign manufactures as are now coming into ruinous competition with American labor."

Mr. Lincoln voted in the affirmative.

SLAVERY IN THE TERRITORIES.

On the 28th of July, the famous bill to establish territorial governments for Oregon, California, and New-Mexico, was taken from the Speaker's table as it came from the Senate. The peculiar feature of the bill was a provision in reference to California and New-Mexico, prohibiting the territorial legislatures from passing laws in favor or against slavery, but also providing that all the laws of the territorial legislatures shall be subject to the sanction of Congress. It will be remembered that it was this bill which Mr. Webster, who was then in the Senate, opposed in a great speech ; using the following language :

" We stand here now—at least I do, for one—to say,
that considering that there have been already five
new slaveholding States formed out of newly-acquired
territory, and one only, at most, non-slaveholding
State, I do not feel that I am called on to go farther ;
I do not feel the obligation to yield more. But our
friends of the South say, ' You deprive us of all our
rights ; we have fought for this territory, and you
deny us participation in it.' Let us consider this
question as it really is ; and since the honorable gentleman from Georgia proposes to leave the case to the
enlightened and impartial judgment of mankind, and
as I agree with him that it is a case proper to be
considered by the enlightened part of mankind, let us
consider how the matter in truth stands. What is
the consequence ? Gentlemen who advocate the case
which my honorable friend from Georgia, with so much
ability, sustains, declare that we invade their rights—
that we deprive them of a participation in the enjoyment
of territories acquired by the common services and common exertions of all. Is this true ? How deprived ?
Of what do we deprive them ? Why, they say that we
deprive them of the privilege of carrying their slaves,
as slaves, into the new territories. Well, sir, what is
the amount of that ? They say that in this way we
deprive them of the opportunity of going into this
acquired territory with their property. Their ' property !'—what do they mean by that ? We certainly
do not deprive them of the privilege of going into
these newly-acquired territories with all that, in the
general estimate of human society, in the general, and
common, and universal understanding of mankind, is
esteemed property. Not at all. The truth is just
this : they have in their own States peculiar laws,
which create property in persons. They have a system of local legislation, on which slavery rests, while
everybody agrees that it is against natural law, or at
least against the common understanding which pre-

vails as to what is natural law. I am not going into metaphysics, for therein I should encounter the honorable member from South Carolina, and we should wander, in ' endless mazes lost,' until after the time for the adjournment of Congress. The Southern States have peculiar laws, and by those laws there is property in slaves. This is purely local. The real meaning, then, of Southern gentlemen, in making this complaint, is, that they cannot go into the territories of the United States, carrying with them their own peculiar local law—a law which creates property in persons. This, according to their own statement, is all the ground of complaint they have. Now, here, I think, gentlemen are unjust toward us. How unjust they are, others will judge—generations that will come after us will judge.

" It will not be contended that this sort of personal slavery exists by general law. It exists only by local law. I do not mean to deny the validity of that local law where it is established ; but I say it is, after all, nothing but local law. It is nothing more. And wherever that local law does not extend, property in persons does not exist. Well, sir, what is now the demand on the part of our Southern friends ? They say, ' We will carry our local laws with us wherever we go. We insist that Congress does us injustice unless it establishes in the territory into which we wish to go, our own local law.' This demand I, for one, resist, and shall resist.   *   *   *   *   *

" Let me conclude, therefore, by remarking, that while I am willing to present this as presenting my own judgment and position, in regard to this case—and I beg it to be understood that I am speaking for no other than myself—and while I am willing to present this to the whole world as my own justification, I rest on these propositions : 1st. That when this Constitution was adopted, nobody looked for any new acquisition of territory to be formed into slaveholding States.

2d. That the principles of the Constitution prohibited, and were intended to prohibit, and should be construed to prohibit, all interference of the general government with slavery as it existed and still exists in the States. And then, that, looking to the effect of these new acquisitions which have in this great degree inured to strengthen that interest in the South by the addition of these five States, there is nothing unjust, nothing of which an honest man can complain, if he is intelligent —and I feel there is nothing which the civilized world, if they take notice of so humble a person as myself, will reproach me with, when I say, as I said the other day, that I had made up my mind, for one, that, under no circumstances, would I consent to the further extension of the area of slavery in the United States, or to the further increase of slave representation in the House of Representatives."

Mr. Corwin, too, arguing in the Senate against this bill, said :

" Now, if we can make any law whatever, not contrary to the express prohibitions of the Constitution, we can enact that a man with $60,000 worth of bank notes of Maryland shall forfeit the whole amount if he attempts to pass one of them in the territory of California. We may say, if a man carry a menagerie of wild beasts there, worth $500,000, and undertakes to exhibit them there, he shall forfeit them. The man comes back with his menagerie, and says that the law forbade him to exhibit his animals there ; it was thought that, as an economical arrangement, such things should not be tolerated there. That you may do. He of the lions and tigers goes back, having lost his whole concern. But now you take a slave to California, and instantly your power fails ; all the power of the sovereignty of this country is impotent to stop him. That is a strange sort of argument to me. It has always been considered that when a State forms its constitution it

can exclude slavery. Why so? Becauses it chances
to consider it an evil. If it be a proper subject of legislation in a State, and we have absolute legislative
power, transferred to us by virtue of this bloody power
of conquest, as some say, or by purchase, as others
maintain, I ask—Why may we not act? Again—
considering this an abstract question—are there not duties devolving upon us, for the performance of which
we may not be responsible to any earthly tribunal, but
for which. God, who has created us all, will hold us ac-
countable? What is your duty, above all others, to a
conquered people? You say it is your duty to give
them a government—may you not, then, do everything
for them which you are not forbidden to do by some
fundamental axiomatic truth at the foundation of your
constitution? Show me, then, how your action is
precluded, and I submit. Though I believe it ought
to be otherwise, yet, if the constitution of my country
forbids me, I yield. The constitutions of many States
declare slavery to be an evil. Southern gentlemen
have said, that they would have done away with it if
possible, and they have apologized to the world and to
themselves for the existence of it in their States.
These honest old men of another day never could have
failed to strike off the chains from every negro in the
colonies, if it had been possible for them to do so without upturning the foundations of society.

        *   *   *   *   *   *

"My objection is a radical one to the institution
everywhere. I do believe, if there is any place upon
the globe which we inhabit, where a white man
cannot work, he has no business there. If that place
is fit only for black men to work, let black men
alone work there. I do not know any better law
for man's good than that old one, which was announced to man after the first transgression, that by
the sweat of his brow he should earn his bread. I
don't know what business men have in the world, un-

less it is to work. If any man has no work of head or
hand to do in this world, let him get out of it soon.
The hog is the only gentleman who has nothing to do
but eat and sleep. *Him* we dispose of as soon as he
is fat. Difficult as the settlement of this question
seems to some, it is, in my judgment, only so because
we will not look at it and treat it as an original proposition, to be decided by the influence its determination
may have on the territories themselves. We are ever
running away from this, and inquiring how it will affect the " slave States," or the " free States." The
only question mainly to be considered is, How will this
policy affect the territories for which *this* law is intended ? Is slavery a good thing, or is it a bad thing,
for *them ?* With my views of the subject, I must consider it bad policy to plant slavery in any soil where I
do not find it already growing. I look upon it as an
exotic, that blights with its shade the soil in which you
plant it ; therefore, as I am satisfied of our constitutional power to prohibit it, so I am equally certain it
is our duty to do so."

For these reasons, so admirably expressed by Webster and Corwin, standing by them, and agreeing with
them, Mr. Lincoln voted to lay the territorial bills
upon the table, when they came up there for consideration. This was on the 28th of July, and after a scene
of great confusion and excitement. The motion to lay
on the table was agreed to—ayes, 114 ; nays, 96.
Among the ayes was Stephens, of Georgia, who made
the motion. Afterward, on the 2d day of August,
when the House bill for the organization of the Territory of Oregon was before the House, a motion was
made to strike out that part of the bill which extended
the ordinance of 1787 over Oregon Territory, and Mr.
Lincoln voted, with 113 others, to retain the ordinance.

During the second session of the Thirtieth Congress, December 12, Mr. Lincoln voted for the following resolution, submitted in the House by Mr. Eckert :

"*Resolved,* That the Committee of Ways and Means be instructed to inquire into the expediency of reporting a Tariff Bill, based upon the principles of the tariff of 1842.".

On the 13th, Mr. Palfrey, of Mass., asked leave to introduce a bill for the repeal of all the acts of Congress establishing slavery in the District of Columbia. Mr. Lincoln, not believing in the expediency of intervention against slavery in the District, without compensation to the slave-owner, separated himself from several of his political friends, and voted *against* the proposition of Mr. Palfrey.

THE TERRITORIES.

Later in the day Mr. Root offered the subjoined resolution :

"*Resolved,* That the Committee on Territories be instructed to report to this House, with as little delay as practicable, a bill, or bills, providing a territorial government for each of the territories of New-Mexico and California, *and excluding slavery therefrom.*"

Of the action of the House this day on the slavery question, Dr. Bailey, of the *Era,* who was warmly opposed to General Taylor's election, remarks :

" Mr. Palfrey asked leave to introduce a bill for the repeal of all acts of Congress, or parts of acts, establishing or maintaining slavery or the slave-trade in the District of Columbia. Mr. Holmes, of South Carolina, objected, and the question being taken by yeas and

nays, the vote stood, for granting leave, 70 ; against it,
81. It will be observed that only 151 members out of
228 voted. The House was not full, and some in their
seats refused to vote. Had all the members voted, it is
doubtful what would have been the result. It will be
observed in our report, that very few Democrats of the
North and West opposed the motion for leave. A few
Northern and Western Whigs are recorded in the negative......... Mr. Root brought forward a resolution, that the Committee on the Territories be instructed to report to this House, with as little delay as
practicable, a bill or bills, providing a territorial government for each of the territories of New-Mexico and
California, and excluding slavery therefrom. Root
moved the previous question. Hall, of Missouri, moved
to lay on the table ; Giddings, that there be a call of
the House. The Clerk called the roll—187 members
answered to their names, and further proceedings in the
call were dispensed with. The motion to lay on the
table was lost—yeas 80, nays 107. The previous
question was seconded, the members passing through
the tellers."

The motion was agreed to—ayes 106, nays 80—Mr.
Lincoln, as usual, standing by the slavery-restriction
clause.

THE GOTT RESOLUTION.

On the 21st of December, Mr. Gott offered in the
House the following resolution :

" *Whereas*, The traffic now prosecuted in this metropolis of the Republic, in human beings, as chattels,
is contrary to natural justice and the fundamental
principles of our political system, and is notoriously a

reproach to our country throughout Christendom, and a serious hinderance to the progress of republican liberty among the nations of the earth : Therefore,

"*Resolved*, That the Committee for the District of Columbia be instructed to report a bill, as soon as practicable; prohibiting the slave trade in said District."

The resolution having been read—

Mr. Haralson moved that it be laid on the table.

Mr. Wentworth and Mr. Gott demanded the yeas and nays; which were ordered.

And the resolution having been again read—

The question on the motion of Mr. Haralson was taken, and resulted—yeas 82, nays 85.

Mr. Lincoln, true to his own convictions of what was best under the circumstances, voted *for* the Haralson motion to table the resolution, wishing to accompany such a bill with provisions which he considered necessary to its success.

The question then recurring on the demand for the previous question—

Mr. Vinton rose to inquire of the Chair whether the resolution was open to amendment.

The Speaker said it would be open to amendment if the previous question should not be seconded.

The question being then taken, the demand for the previous question was seconded—yeas 85, nays 49.

Upon the question, "Shall the main question [upon the adoption of the resolution] be now put ?" the yeas and nays were demanded and ordered ; and being taken, the yeas were 112, nays 64.

Mr. Houston, of Alabama, and Mr. Venable, called for the yeas and nays ; which were ordered.

Mr. Donnell inquired of the Chair, if it would not be in order to move that there be a call of the House. The Speaker answered in the negative.

And the main question, " Shall the resolution be adopted ?" was then taken, and decided in the affirmative—yeas 98, nays 87—as follows :

YEAS—Messrs. Abbott, Ashmun, Belcher, Bingham, Blackmar, Blanchard, Butler, Canby, Cathcart, Collamer, Conger, Cranston, Crowell, Cummins, Darling, Dickey, Dickinson, Dixon, Daniel Duncan, Edwards, Embree, Nathan Evans, Faran, Farrelly, Fisher, Freedley, Fries, Giddings, Gott, Greeley, Gregory, Grinnell, Hale, Nathan K. Hall, James G. Hampton, Moses Hampton, Henley, Henry, Elias B. Holmes, Hubbard, Hudson, Hunt, Joseph R. Ingersoll, Irvin, James H. Johnson, Kellogg, Daniel P. King, Lahm, William T. Lawrence, Sidney Lawrence, Leffler, Lord, Lynde, McClelland, McIlvaine, Job Mann, Horace Mann, Marsh, Marvin, Morris, Mullin, Newell, Nicoll, Palfrey, Peaslee, Peck, Pettit, Pollock, Putnam, Reynolds, Richey, Robinson, Rockhill, Julius Rockwell, J. A. Rockwell, Rose, Root, Rumsey, St. John, Sherrill, Silvester, Slingerland, Robert Smith, Starkweather, C. E. Stuart, Strohm, Tallmadge, James Thompson, William Thompson, Thurston, Tuck, Turner, Van Dyke, Vinton, Warren, Wentworth, White and Wilson—98.

NAYS—Messrs. Adams, Barringer, Beale, Bedinger, Bocock, Botts, Bowlin, Boyd, Boydon, Bridges, William G. Brown, Charles Brown, Albert G. Brown, Buckner, Burt, Chapman, Chase, Franklin Clarke, Beverly L. Clarke, Howell Cobb, Williamson R. W. Cobb, Coke, Crisfield, Crozier, Daniel, Donnell, Dunn, Alexander Evans, Featherston, Ficklin, Flournoy, French, Fulton, Gaines, Gentry, Goggin, Green, Willard P. Hall, Hammons, Haralson, Harmanson, Harris, Hill, George S. Houston, John W. Houston, Inge, Charles J. Ingersoll, Iverson, Jameson, Andrew Johnson, G. W. Jones, J. W. Jones, Kennon, Thomas Butler King, La Sere, Ligon, Lincoln, Lumpkin, McClernand, McDowell, McLane, Meade, Miller, Morehead, Morse, Outlaw, Pendleton, Peyton, Pilsbury, Preston, Sawyer, Shepperd, Simpson, Smart, Stanton, Stephens, Strong, Thibodeaux, Thomas, R. W. Thompson, Tompkins, Toombs, Venable, Wallace, Wiley, Williams, and Woodward—88.

So the resolution was adopted.

The *National Era*, which was not inclined to show much mercy toward the supporters of Mr. Taylor's

Administration, gave the following explanation of certain votes cast against the resolution :

"Men will wonder, twenty-five years hence, how eighty-seven men, in an American Congress, could stand up before God, and virtually vote for the continuance of the trade in human beings in the capital of the foremost Republic in the world.

"We would be just, however. A few members from the free States voting *nay* feared any movement which might tend, in their opinion, to embarrass the question of slavery extension. These voted in the negative on the resolution, not because they were opposed to its object, but because they believed this object could be better attained, after the settlement of the question of slavery in the territories. While dissenting from the policy of these gentlemen, this statement from us is a simple act of justice to them."

PUBLIC LANDS.

On the 21st of December, Mr. McClelland in the House of Representatives offered the subjoined resolution :

"*Resolved*, That the present traffic in the public lands should cease, and that they should be disposed of to occupants and cultivators, on proper conditions, at such a price as will nearly indemnify the cost of their purchase, management, and sale."

The previous question was called, and a motion was made to lay the resolution on the table, which prevailed. Mr. Lincoln voted *against* tabling it, because he was ready to do anything which should give the public lands *to the people*, and not to the speculators.

A SLAVE CASE.

On the 6th of January the slave case—that of Antonio Pacheco—was reported to the House, and was taken up. It was a claim for the value of a slave who was hired by a United States officer ; betook himself to the everglades ; fought with the Indians against the whites ; was taken in arms as an enemy, and as an enemy sent out of the Territory, for the purpose of securing the lives of the inhabitants.

Mr. Giddings, speaking of the case, recommended that—

" The Committee on Military Affairs were unable to unite in a report upon the case. Five *slaveholders*, representing slave property on this floor, and constituting a majority of the committee, have reported a bill for the payment of this amount to the claimant. Four Northern members, representing *freemen only*, have made a minority report against the bill. This report, as I think, is sustained by irrefutable arguments.

" The majority of the committee assume the position that slaves are regarded by the Federal Constitution as *property*, and that this government and the people of the free States are bound to regard them as property, and to pay for them as we would for so many mules or oxen taken into the public service. The minority deny this doctrine. They insist that the Federal Constitution treats them as *persons* only, and that this government cannot constitutionally involve the people of the free States in the guilt of sustaining slavery ; that we have no constitutional powers to legislate upon the relation of master and slave.

   ✻   ✻

" In 1772, Lord Mansfield boldly assailed the doctrine laid down in this Hall to-day, and exhibited its absurdity in one of the ablest opinions to be found on record. From that period this doctrine of property in man has found no supporters under the government of England. . With all our refinement as a nation ; with all our boasted adherence to liberty, on this subject we are three quarters of a century behind our mother-country.

"When Sir Warren Hastings was on trial in the House of Peers, in 1787, Mr. Sheridan, speaking on this subject, in his own peculiar and fervid eloquence, declared that 'allegiance to that Power which gives us the *forms* of men, commands us to maintain the *rights* of men ; and never yet was this truth dismissed from the human heart—never, in any time, in any age—never in any clime where rude man ever had any social feelings—never was this unextinguishable truth destroyed from the heart of man, placed as it is in the core and centre of it by his Maker, *that man was not made the property of man.*' This was the language of British statesmen sixty-two years since. To-day we have before this branch of the American Congress the report of a committee avowing that, under this federal government, in the middle of the nineteenth century, '*man is the property of his fellow-mortal.*'

"These sentiments of the British statesmen and jurists inspired the hearts of our Americans patriots in 1776, when they declared it to be a 'SELF-EVIDENT TRUTH THAT ALL MEN ARE CREATED EQUAL.' When they framed our Constitution, they declared their object was '*to establish justice, and to secure to themselves and their posterity the blessings of liberty.*' This subject of holding property in *men* did not escape their attention, nor have they left us ignorant of their views in regard to it. Mr. Madison, the father of the Constitution, has left to us a clear and explicit account of their intentions. He informs us, that on

" ' Wednesday, August 22, the Convention proceeded to consider the report of the Committee of Detail, in relation to duties on exports, a capitation tax, and a navigation act. The fourth section reported was as follows :

" ' No tax or duty shall be laid by the Legislature on articles exported from any State, nor on the migration nor importation of such persons as the several States shall think proper to admit ; nor shall such migration nor importation be prohibited.'

" ' Mr. Gerry thought we had nothing to do with the conduct of the States as to slavery, *but we ought to be careful not to give any sanction.*'

" Our people think with Mr. Gerry, that ' *we have nothing to do with slavery in the States.*' We are determined that we will not be involved in its guilt. With Mr. Gerry, we intend ' *to be careful to give it no sanction.*' No, sir ; we will not sanction your slavery by paying our money for the bodies of slaves. This is the doctrine which we hold, and which we expect to maintain ; yet the members of this body are now engaged in legislating upon the price of human flesh. If we pass this bill, we shall give our most solemn sanction to that institution which Gerry and his compatriots detested. Will the members from Pennsylvania, the successors of Franklin and Wilson, lend their sanction to slavery, by voting the moneys of the People to pay for slaves ?

" But Mr. Madison tells us that ' Mr. Sherman (of Connecticut) was opposed to any tax on slaves, as making the matter worse, *because it implied they were property.*'

" I understand that *some* gentlemen from the North admit that slaves are *property*. Mr. Sherman and the framers of the Constitution would do no act by which it could be *implied* that they were property.

" Mr. Madison also participated in the discussion himself ; and, as he informs us, ' DECLARED THAT HE THOUGHT IT WRONG TO ADMIT THAT THERE COULD BE

3

PROPERTY IN MEN.' And the report of the Committee
was so amended as to exclude that idea.

" In that assemblage of illustrious statesmen, no
man expressed his dissent from these doctrines of
Gerry, of Sherman, and of Madison. These doctrines
are : 1. That we ' *should have nothing to do with
slavery, but ought to be careful not to give it any sanction.*' 2. That ' *we should do no act by which it can
be implied that there can be property in men.*' 3.
That ' it would be WRONG FOR US TO ADMIT THAT
THERE CAN BE PROPERTY IN MEN.' Such were the
views of those who framed the Constitution. They
intended to express their views in such language as to
be understood. Will this House stand by them ?"

      *   *   *   *   *

" With great propriety the gentleman from New-
Hampshire inquired, at what *time* the liability of government to pay for this slave commenced ? The question has not been answered, nor do I think it can be
answered. The undertaking was hazardous in the
highest degree. The troops were all killed but two or
three, by the enemy, and those were supposed to be
dead. This man alone escaped unhurt. This danger
was foreseen, and the master put a price upon the services to compare with the risk. Did this contract bind
the government to pay for the master's loss, admitting
the slave to have been *property ?* Was it any part of
the compact that the government should insure the
property ? It strikes me that no lawyer would answer in the affirmative. The law of bailment is surely
understood by every tyro in the profession. The bailee
for hire is bound to exercise the same degree of care
over the property that careful men ordinarily take of
their own property. If, then, the property be lost, the
owner sustains such loss. Now, conceding this man to
be property, the government would not have been liable, had he ran away, or been killed by accident, or
died of sickness. Yet, sir, when property is lost or

destroyed by the act of God or the common enemies of the country, no bailee is ever holden responsible—not even common carriers, and that is the highest species of bailment. Had this officer, acting on his own responsibility, agreed to take this negro through the country for hire (admitting the man to have been property, and governed by the same rules of law as though he had been a mule or an ass), and he had been captured by the enemy, no law would have held such bailee liable. But, sir, an entirely different rule of law prevails where the owner of a chattel lets it to a bailee for wages. Had this man been a mule or an ass, and the officer had hired him of the owner for wages, to ride through that country, or to work in a team, or in any other manner, and he had been captured by the enemy, the bailee would not have been liable, upon any rule of law or of justice ; nor would he have been liable if lost in any other manner, except by neglect of the bailee.

"The gentleman from South Carolina [Mr. Burt] said he would place this case upon *strictly legal principles*. Sir, I meet the gentleman on that proposition. I, too, for the sake of the argument, am willing to submit it on principles of law ; and I believe that no jurist, or even justice of the peace, would hesitate to reject the case on those grounds. All must admit that the liability of the government concerning this man ceased when he was captured by the enemy ; up to this point the government was not liable. I understood the author of this bill [Mr. Burt] to argue, however, that we became liable under the contract of bailment. That contract was ended when the man was captured. The claimant then failed to perform his part of it. The stipulation on the part of the master was, that the negro should pilot the troops from Fort Brooke to Fort King, the place of their destination, at the rate of twenty-five dollars per month. He was captured when only half the distance was accomplished. Here the master ceased to perform his compact ; it was beyond his power to do so. The contract then ceased to exist ; and from that time forth the claimant had no demand on us, either in equity or in law."

This is the Antonio Pacheco case, stated at some length, for it involved important principles. And here we call attention to the fact that Mr. Lincoln was never found, while in Congress, violating any principle to which he gave his adhesion, no matter how great the temptation or the emergency. He *did* at times waive the assertion of a principle when he thought it would only result in irritation, but he never voted *against* one of those principles.

The case above mentioned, came up in the House Nov. 6, 1849 :

"The first business in order being the pending motion made by Mr. Giddings for a reconsideration of the vote upon the engrossment of the bill to pay the heirs of Antonio Pacheco $1,000, as the value of a slave transported to the West with the Seminole Indians—

"Mr. Giddings proceeded to address the House, having first declined to give way for a motion by Mr. Rockwell, of Connecticut, that the House should consider the bill to establish a Board for the settlement of private claims.

"The previous question, having been moved upon the motion to reconsider, was then seconded, and the main question ordered to be now put.

"Mr. Giddings, with a view to save the time of the House, withdrew his motion, and the question accordingly recurred upon the passage of the bill.

"Upon this question, Mr. Dickey demanded the

yeas and nays, which were ordered ; and the question
being taken—

" The Speaker announced the vote—yeas 90, nays 89.

" The twelfth rule of the House provided, ' that in all
cases of election by the House, the Speaker shall vote ;
in other cases he shall not vote, unless the House be
equally divided, or unless his vote, if given to the minority, will make the division equal ; and in case of
such equal division, the question shall be lost.'

" The Speaker, proceeding to discharge the duty thus
imposed upon him, said :

" ' A case has occurred in which, under the rule of
the House, it is the duty of the Speaker to vote. The
Speaker regrets that in this, as in many other cases, he
has been deprived of the opportunity of listening to the
full discussion of the question, having heard no speech
except that which has been made this morning, the debate having taken place mainly in Committee of the
Whole on the private calendar.

" ' The Speaker also has had little opportunity, if
any, to turn his attention to the principles or the facts
involved in this case. He cannot shrink, however,
from giving his vote. But it is a well-admitted par-
liamentary principle, laid down in the books, that
where the Speaker has any doubt in relation to a
question, his vote shall be given in such a way as not
finally to conclude it. It shall be given in such a way
that the consideration of the question may be again
open to the House, if the House, under any circumstances, shall choose to reconsider it.

" ' The Speaker takes the opportunity to say, that
he does not concur in full with either of the principles

which have been maintained on both sides of the House. So far as the circumstances of the case have come to his knowledge, he doubts exceedingly whether the question of property in slaves is involved. And it has been to him a matter of great doubt, from such part of the arguments as he has heard——'

" At this point of his remarks, the Speaker was interrupted by the Clerk, who showed him a paper containing the state of the vote.

" The Speaker said the Clerk was mistaken in the vote. The vote stands—ninety-one in the affirmative, eighty-nine in the negative.

" So the bill was declared to be passed, Mr. Lincoln voting against the passage.

" Mr. Burt moved a reconsideration of the vote just taken, and that the motion be laid upon the table ; and also moved, that before the vote be taken, there should be a call of the House.

" Mr. Palfrey appealed to the gentleman from South Carolina to allow him the floor a moment, but Mr. Burt peremptorily declined.

" Mr. Wentworth demanded the yeas and nays upon the motion for a call of the House, and being ordered and taken, the result was, yeas 78, nays 105. So the call was refused.

" Mr. Burt, with a view, as he said, to save the time of the House, withdrew his motion for reconsideration.

" Mr. Cocke renewed the motion, and moved that it be laid on the table.

" Mr. Palfrey moved a call of the House, when

" Mr. Cocke withdrew his motion for reconsideration ; and, after some conversation upon points of order, the whole subject was dropped, and the bill was considered *passed*.

" Mr. Wentworth rose (he said) to a privileged question, and said that a mistake had been discovered at the Clerk's desk, in the vote upon the passage of the bill for the relief of the legal representatives of Antonio Pacheco. He asked that the journal might be corrected.

" The Speaker stated that corrections of the journal would be in order on Monday morning, after the reading of the journal.

" Mr. Wentworth asked if it would not be in order now to make a correction in the vote.

" The Speaker replied that it would.

" On motion of Mr. Stephens, the House adjourned."

On the following Monday, immediately after the reading of the journal, the Speaker said :

" The House will remember that the vote on the passage of the bill for the relief of the heirs of Antonio Pacheco, was originally made up by the Clerk, yeas 90, nays 89; and this record having been handed to the Speaker, and by him announced to the House, the Speaker proceeded to make some remarks upon the bill, preparatory to giving the vote contemplated in such cases by the rules of the House. While in the act of explanation, the Speaker was interrupted by the Clerk, who stated that, on a more careful count, the vote was found to be yeas 91, nays 89. The intervention of the Speaker was therefore no longer allowable, and the bill was declared to have passed the House.

" The Chair takes the earliest opportunity to state to the House, this morning, that, upon a re-examination of the yeas and nays, the Clerk has ascertained that an error was still made in the announcement of the vote on Saturday. The vote actually stood, yeas 89, nays 89. The correction will now, accordingly, be made in the journal; and a case is immediately presented, agreeably to the 12th rule of the House, for the interposition of the Speaker's vote.

" At this stage of the proceedings, the Speaker was interrupted by

" Mr. Farrelly, who rose and called for a further correction of the journal, stating that he voted in the negative on Saturday last, and his vote appeared not to have been recorded.

" The Speaker decided that it was the right of the gentleman from Pennsylvania to have his vote recorded, if he voted on Saturday last.

" And the correction was accordingly made.

" The vote was then finally announced—yeas 89, nays 90.

" The Speaker stated that he came into the House this morning with the full expectation of giving his vote upon this bill, and prepared to give his reasons for the vote. But, as the question now stood, although it might be in his power to vote agreeably to the letter of the 12th rule, it was, in his opinion, not within the contemplation or intention of the rule that he should vote. The rule contemplated that the Speaker should be allowed to vote whenever he could make a difference in the result—wherever his vote would either pass or prevent the passage of the proposition before the House. Under present circumstances, the Speaker's vote could not in any way affect the decision of the

House. The bill was already lost by the vote as it stood. A vote against the bill would only increase the majority by which it was defeated ; while a vote in favor of the bill would only make a tie, and the bill would still be lost. The Speaker, therefore, did not consider himself called upon to give any vote on the subject."

Subsequently the case came up again, on a motion *to reconsider*, and the bill was passed, ayes 98, nays 92—Mr. Lincoln voting *no*.

LINCOLN'S AMENDMENT TO LOTT'S RESOLUTION.

On the 16th of January, the celebrated Lott resolution against the slave-trade in the District of Columbia, was again before the House, a motion to reconsider having been entertained previously, and the consideration of the motion having been postponed to this day. It will be remembered that Mr. Lincoln voted to table the original resolution, not liking its terms. He now, by the courtesy of his colleague, Mr. Wentworth, who had the floor, offered the subjoined resolution as a substitute for the Lott resolution :

" *Resolved,* That the Committee on the District of Columbia be instructed to report a bill in substance as follows :

" SEC. 1. *Be it enacted by the Senate and House of Representatives of the United States in Congress assembled,* That no person not now within the District of . Columbia, nor now owned by any person or persons now resident within it, nor hereafter born within it, shall ever be held in slavery within said District.

" SEC. 2. That no person now within said District or

3.

now owned by any person or persons now resident within the same, or hereafter born within it, shall ever be
held in slavery without the limits of said District.
Provided, That officers of the government of the
United States, being citizens of the slaveholding States,
coming into said District on public business, and remaining only so long as may be reasonably necessary
for that object, may be attended into and out of said
District, and while there, by the necessary servants of
themselves and their families, without their right to
hold such servants in service being thereby impaired.

" SEC. 3. That all children born of slave mothers
within said District, on or after the first day of January,
in the year of our Lord 1850, shall be free ; but shall
be reasonably supported and educated by the respective
owners of their mothers or by their heirs and representatives until they respectively arrive at the age of ——
years, when they shall be entirely free. And the municipal authorities of Washington and Georgetown, within
their respective jurisdictional limits, are hereby empowered and required to make all suitable and necessary provisions for enforcing obedience to this section,
on the part of both masters and apprentices.

" SEC. 4. That all persons now within said District,
lawfully held as slaves, or now owned by any person or
persons now resident within said District, shall remain
such at the will of their respective owners, their heirs
and legal representatives. *Provided,* That any such
owner, or his legal representatives, may at any time receive from the treasury of the United States the full
value of his or her slave of the class in this section
mentioned ; upon which such slave shall be forthwith

and for ever free. *And provided further,* That the
President of the United States, the Secretary of State,
and the Secretary of the Treasury, shall be a board,
for determining the value of such slaves as their owners may desire to emancipate under this section, and
whose duty it shall be to hold a session for the purpose, on the first Monday of each calendar month ; to
receive all applications and on satisfactory evidence in
each case, that the person presented for valuation is a
slave, and of the class in this section mentioned, and is
owned by the applicant, shall value such slave at his or
her full cash value and give to the applicant an order
on the treasury for the amount and also to such slave
a certificate of freedom.

" Sec. 5. That the municipal authorities of Washington and Georgetown within their respective jurisdictional limits, are hereby empowered and required to
provide active and efficient means to assert and deliver
up to their owners all fugitive slaves escaping into said
District.

" Sec. 6. That the election officers within said District
of Columbia are hereby empowered and required to
open polls at all the usual places of holding elections
on the first Monday of April next and receive the vote
of every free white male citizen above the age of twenty-one years, having resided within said district for the
period of one year or more next preceding the time of
such voting for or against this act, to proceed in taking
said votes in all respects herein not specified, as at elections under the municipal laws, and with as little delay
as possible to transmit correct statements of the votes
so cast to the President of the United States ; and it

shall be the duty of the President to canvass said votes immediately and if a majority of them be found to be for this act to forthwith issue his proclamation, giving notice of the fact, and this act shall only be in full force and effect on and after the day of such proclamation.

"SEC. 7. That involuntary servitude for the punishment of crime, whereof the party shall have been duly convicted, shall in nowise be prohibited by this act.

"SEC. 8. That for all the purposes of this act the jurisdictional limits of Washington are extended to all parts of the District of Columbia not now included within the present limits of Georgetown."

This bill shows us the real position of Mr. Lincoln on the slavery question, in 1849. He was opposed to the institution, to its extension into the territories, and was in favor of its abolition in the District of Columbia, but with compensation to the owner. He was for reform, but was a cautious, conservative reformer.

On the 31st of January, Mr. Edwards, of the Committee on the District of Columbia, reported a bill to prohibit the introduction of slaves into the District of Columbia as merchandise, or for sale or hire. After it was read twice a motion was made to lay it on the table, which motion was lost, Mr. Lincoln again voting no.

On the 21st of February, a test vote was taken in the House on a bill to abolish the franking privilege. The motion was made to lay the bill on the table. Mr. Lincoln voted with the friends of the bill, who saved it from immediate defeat.

The reader will easily discover Mr. Lincoln's position

in Congress upon the more important subjects before it in this record. On the slavery question he was always true to his principles, ever voting against the extension of slavery, and on the Mexican war occupying the ground of the Whigs of that day ; refusing to justify the war itself, but voting the supplies for it, that the war debt might be liquidated.

He steadily and earnestly opposed the annexation of Texas, and labored with all his powers in behalf of the Wilmot Proviso.

TEN YEARS AT HOME.

In the National Convention of 1848, of which he was a member, he advocated the nomination of General Taylor, and sustained the nomination by an active canvass in Illinois and Indiana.

From 1849 to 1854 Mr. Lincoln was engaged assiduously in the practice of his profession, and being deeply immersed in business, was beginning to lose his interest in politics, when the scheming ambition and grovelling selfishness of an unscrupulous aspirant to the Presidency brought about the repeal of the Missouri Compromise. That act of baseness and perfidy aroused him, and he prepared for new efforts. He threw himself at once into the contest that followed, and fought the battle of freedom on the ground of his former conflicts in Illinois with more than his accustomed energy and zeal. Those who recollect the tremendous battle fought in Illinois that year, will award to Abraham Lincoln fully three fourths of the ability and unwearying labor which resulted in the mighty victory which gave Illinois her first Republican Legislature, and placed Lyman Trumbull in the Senate of the United States.

The Chicago *Tribune,* the editor of which is a personal friend of Mr. Lincoln, and from whom we gather many of the facts of the early life of the subject of this volume, gives the following graphic sketches of the Illinois Campaign of 1854 :

" The first and greatest debate of that year came off between Lincoln and Douglas at Springfield, during the progress of the State Fair, in October. We remember the event as vividly as though it transpired yesterday, and in view of the prominence now given to the chief actor in that exciting event, it cannot fail to be interesting to all.

" The affair came off on the fourth day of October, 1854. The State Fair had been in progress two days, and the capital was full of all manner of men. The Nebraska bill had been passed on the previous twenty-second of May. Mr. Douglas had returned to Illinois to meet an outraged constituency. He had made a fragmentary speech in Chicago, the people filling up each hiatus in a peculiar and good-humored way. He called the people a mob—they called him a rowdy. The ' mob ' had the best of it, both then and at the election which succeeded. The notoriety of all these events had stirred up the politics of the State from bottom to top. Hundreds of politicians had met at Springfield, expecting a tournament of an unusual character—Douglas, Breese, Kœrner, Lincoln, Trumbull, Matteson, Yates, Codding, John Calhoun (of the order of the candle-box); John M. Palmer, the whole house of the McConnells, Singleton (known to fame

in the Mormon war), Thomas L. Harris, and a host of
others. Several speeches were made before, and several
after, the passage between Lincoln and Douglas, but
that was justly held to be *the* event of the season.

"We do not remember whether a challenge to debate passed between the friends of the speakers or not,
but there was a perfectly amicable understanding between Lincoln and Douglas, that the former should
speak two or three hours, and the latter reply in just
as little or as much time as he chose. Mr. Lincoln
took the stand at two o'clock—a large crowd in atten-
dance, and Mr. Douglas seated on a small platform in
front of the desk. The first half-hour of Mr. Lincoln's
speech was taken up with compliments to his distinguished friend Judge Douglas, and dry allusions to the
political events of the past few years. His distinguished friend, Judge Douglas, had taken his seat, as
solemn as the Cock-Lane ghost, evidently with the design of not moving a muscle till it came his turn to
speak. The laughter provoked by Lincoln's exordium,
however, soon began to make him uneasy ; and when
Mr. L. arrived at his (Douglas') speech, pronouncing
the Missouri Compromise 'a sacred thing, which no
ruthless hand would ever be reckless enough to disturb,'
he opened his lips far enough to remark, 'A first-rate
speech!' This was the beginning of an amusing col-
loquy.

"'Yes,' continued Mr. Lincoln, ' so affectionate was
my friend's regard for this compromise line, that when
Texas was admitted into the Union, and it was found
that a strip extended north of 36° 30' he actually in-

troduced a bill extending the line and prohibiting slavery in the northern edge of the new State.'

" ' And you voted against the bill,' said Douglas.

" ' Precisely so,' replied Lincoln; ' I was in favor of
running the line *a great deal farther South.*'

" ' About this time,' the speaker continued, ' my
distinguished friend introduced me to a particular
friend of his, one David Wilmot of Pennsylvania,'
(Laughter.)

" ' I thought,' said Douglas, ' you would find him
congenial company.'

" ' So I did,' replied Lincoln. ' I had the pleasure of
voting for his Proviso, in one way and another about
forty times. It was a *Democratic* measure then, I believe. At any rate, General Cass scolded Honest
John Davis, of Massachusetts, soundly, for taking
away the last hours of the session so that he (Cass)
couldn't crowd it through. Apropos of General Cass :
if I am not greatly mistaken, he has a prior claim to
my distinguished friend, to the authorship of Popular
Sovereignty. The old general has an infirmity for
writing letters. Shortly after the scolding he gave
John Davis, he wrote his Nicholson letter—'

" Douglas (solemnly)—' God Almighty placed man
on the earth, and told him to choose between good and
evil. That was the origin of the Nebraska bill !'

" Lincoln—' Well, the priority of invention being
settled, let us award all credit to Judge Douglas for
being the first to discover it.'

" It would be impossible, in these limits, to give an
idea of the strength of Mr. Lincoln's argument. We
deemed it by far the ablest effort of the campaign—from

whatever source. The occasion was a great one, and the speaker was every way equal to it. The effect produced on the listeners was magnetic. No one who was present will ever forget•the power and vehemence of the following passage :

"'My distinguished friend says it is an insult to the emigrants to Kansas and Nebraska to suppose they are not able to govern themselves. We must not slur over an argument of this kind because it happens to tickle the ear. It must be met and answered. I admit that the emigrant to Kansas and Nebraska is competent to govern *himself*, but,' the speaker rising to his full height, '*I deny his right to govern any other person* WITHOUT THAT PERSON'S CONSENT.' The applause which followed this triumphant refutation of a cunning falsehood, was but an earnest of the victory at the polls which followed just one month from that day.

"When Mr. Lincoln had concluded, Mr. Douglas strode hastily to the stand. As usual, he employed ten minutes in telling how grossly he had been abused. Recollecting himself, he added, ' though in a perfectly courteous manner '—abused in a perfectly courteous manner! He then devoted half an hour to showing that it was indispensably necessary to California emigrants, Sante Fe traders and others, to have organic acts provided for the territories of Kansas and Nebraska—that being precisely the point which nobody disputed. Having established this premiss to his satisfaction, Mr. Douglas launched forth into an argument wholly apart from the positions taken by Mr. Lincoln. He had about half finished at six o'clock, when an adjournment to tea was effected. The speaker insisted strenuously upon his right to resume in the evening, but we believe the second part of that speech has not been delivered to this day. After the Springfield passage, the two speakers went to Peoria, and tried it again, with identically the same results. A friend, who listened to the Peoria debate, informed us that after Lincoln had finished, Douglas 'hadn't much to say '—which we presume to have been Mr. Douglas' view of the case also, for the reason that he ran away from his antagonist and kept out of the way during the remainder of the campaign.

" During this exciting campaign Mr. Lincoln pressed the slavery issue upon the people of Central and Southern Illinois, who were largely made up of the emigration from Kentucky, Tennessee, Virginia, and North Carolina, with all the powers of his mind. He felt the force of the moral causes that must influence the question, and he never failed to appeal to the moral sentiment of the people in aid of the argument drawn from political sources, and to illuminate his theme with the lofty inspirations of an eloquence, pleading for the rights of humanity. A revolution swept the State. For the first time a majority of the Legislature of Illinois was opposed to the Democratic administration of the federal government. A United States Senator was to be elected in place of General Shields who had yielded to the influence of his less scrupulous colleague, and, against his own better judgment, had voted for the Kansas-Nebraska act. The election came on, and a number of ballots were taken, the almost united opposition voting steadily for Lincoln, but the anti-Nebraska Democrats for Trumbull. Mr. Lincoln became ap-

prehensive that those men who had been elected as
Democrats, though opposed to Judge Douglas, would
turn upon some third candidate, of less decided convictions than Judge Trumbull, and possibly elect a Senator who had little or nothing in common with the then
inchoate Republican party. To prevent such a consummation, he went personally to his friends, and by
strong persuasion, induced them to vote for Trumbull.

" He thus secured, by an act of generous self-sacri-
fice, a triumph for the cause of right, and an advocate
of it on the floor of the Senate, not inferior, in earnest
zeal for the principles of Republicanism, to any member of that body.

" Some of his friends on the floor of the Legislature
wept like children when constrained by Mr. Lincoln's
personal appeals to desert him and unite on Trumbull.
It is proper to say in this connection, that between
Trumbull and Lincoln the most cordial relations have
always existed, and that the feeling of envy or rivalry
is not to be found in the breast of either."

At the Peoria debate alluded to above, the arrangement was that Douglas should speak as long as he
pleased, then that Lincoln should do the same, and that
Douglas should have an hour to close. Douglas commenced at 2 o'clock and spoke till six, wearing away
the time in a tedious speech, hoping that the farmers,
who had come in from the country, would not stay to
hear Mr. Lincoln's reply. As soon as Douglas had
concluded his speech, the vast crowd who had patiently
listened to him divided, the Democrats at once leaving
in great numbers for the country, while the Whigs and
Free-Soilers remained and loudly called for Lincoln.

Mr. L., nothing vexed by the consumption by Douglas of the whole afternoon, when no one expected that he would occupy more than an hour and a half or two hours, proposed that the crowd adjourn for tea, which they very reluctantly did. After half an hour the crowd again assembled, and Mr. Lincoln took the stand, and for three hours continued to entrance his hearers by irresistible logic and strains of eloquence never before excelled in any of his public efforts. The whole territorial history of the country was reviewed, and the Kansas-Nebraska bill, then recently passed, was dissected in a manner such as has never been surpassed in the halls of Congress. Never since, in all the discussions, innumerable and interminable, of that subject in the intervening six years, have the inconsistencies of Judge Douglas been shown up as they were then, but all in the utmost good nature. Since then Douglas has invented new subterfuges, but before that audience, all his political tricks and dodges in connection with that bill were thoroughly exposed.

About half-past nine, Douglas rose to take his hour. It was evident he had no heart for the undertaking. He beat a most handsome retreat. He complained of his voice, which he said would not permit of his occupying his hour ; he complimented the city of Peoria —the intelligence of its citizens, and the natural beaut of its location, which, of course, brought down cheers for him ; he complimented Lincoln ; he spoke of the fact that in the cemetery adjacent to the city rested the remains of the lamented Governor Ford—in short, he devoted a quarter of an hour to putting the audience in good humor with him, and then, without attempting a reply to his antagonist's crushing arguments, bid his audience good night.

Mr. Lincoln expected to meet Mr. Douglas next at Lacon, or Henry, north of Peoria, on the Illinois river ; but the " Little Giant" had had enough of " Old Abe" that year, and did not give the latter another opportunity of meeting him during the season.

Mr. Lincoln was offered the nomination for Governor by the Anti-Nebraska (the future Republican) party in 1854 ; but he told his friends, " No—I am not the man ; Bissell will make a better Governor than I, and you can elect him on account of his Democratic antecedents." So, giving to Bissell the flag it was universally desired that he should bear, he himself took the sword, and hewed a way for the triumph of that year.

PART THIRD.

THE GREAT SENATORIAL CONTEST.

In the summer of 1858, the great Senatorial contest of Illinois took place between Mr. Douglas on the one hand, and Mr. Lincoln on the other. The rebellion of Mr. Douglas in the U. S. Senate against the administration—his refusal to assist in the perpetration of the Lecompton fraud, insured him the enmity of the administration ; but in spite of this, his position gave him immense strength both in and outside of Illinois. Prominent Republicans in other States were disposed to. see him returned to the Senate as a rebuke to the administration, vainly hoping that Mr. D. would abandon the Democratic party. Mr. Crittenden wrote a letter advising the Americans or old Whigs of Illinois to vote for Douglas, and in consequence of this outside pressure there can be no doubt that Mr. Douglas was stronger by ten thousand votes *as a rebel*, than he would have been as an administration favorite.

All who know anything at all of Mr. Douglas are aware that as a political debater, either on the stump or on the Senate floor, he has no superior, if he has an equal, in the country. It was, then, no light matter to contest the State of Illinois with such a man as Mr. Douglas, and especially under the circumstances, when the masses of the people sympathized with Mr. D. in his quarrel with the administration.

A Republican State Convention met at Springfield, Illinois, June 2, 1858, and put Mr. Lincoln in nomination as the Republican candidate for United States Senator. The Convention also adopted the subjoined platform :

THE ILLINOIS PLATFORM.

" We, the Republicans of Illinois, in Convention assembled, in addition to our previous affirmations, make the following declaration of our principles :

" 1. We reaffirm our devotion to the Constitution of the country, and to the union of the States, and will steadily resist all attempts for the perversion of the one and the disruption of the other. We recognize the equal rights of all the States, and avow our readiness and willingness to maintain them ; and disclaim all intention of attempting, either directly or indirectly, to assail or abridge the rights of any of the members of the confederacy guaranteed by the Constitution, or in any manner to interfere with the institution of slavery in the States where it exists. Nevertheless, we hold that the government was instituted for freemen, and that it can be perpetuated, and made to fulfil the purposes of its organization only by devoting itself to the promotion of virtue and intelligence among its citizens, and the advancement of their prosperity and happiness ; and to these ends, we hold it to be the duty of the government so to reform the system of disposing of the public lands as to secure the soil to actual settlers, and wrest it from the grasp of men who speculate in the homes of the people, and from corporations that lock it up in dead hands for enhanced profits.

" 2. Free labor being the only true support of republican institutions, our government should maintain its rights ; and we therefore demand the improvement of our harbors and rivers which freight the commerce of the West to a market, and the construction of a central highway, to connect our trade with the Pacific States, as rightful encouragement to home industry ; and, inasmuch as we now compete in the markets of the whole country against the products of unpaid labor, at depreciating prices; it is therefore eminently unjust that the National Administration should attempt, by coercion, to extend a servile system in the territories, or, by patronage, to perpetuate slavery in the States.

" 3. The present administration has proved recreant to the trusts committed to its hands, and by its extraordinary, corrupt, unjust, and undignified, exertions, to give effect to the original intention and purpose of the Kansas-Nebraska bill, by forcing upon the people of Kansas, against their will, and in defiance of their known and earnestly-expressed wishes, a constitution recognizing slavery as one of their domestic institutions, it has forfeited all claim to the support of the friends of free men, free labor, and equal rights.

" 4. It is the duty of the government faithfully and diligently to execute all our treaty stipulations, and to enforce all our laws for the suppression of the slave-trade.

" 5. While we deprecate all interference on the part of political organizations with the action of the Judiciary, if such action is limited to its appropriate sphere, yet we cannot refrain from expressing our condemnation of the principles and tendencies of the extra judicial opinions of a majority of the Judges of the Supreme Court of the United States, in the matter of Dred Scott, wherein the political heresy is put forth, that the Federal Constitution extends slavery into all the territories of the Republic, and so maintains it that neither Congress nor people, through their territorial legislature, can by law abolish it. We hold that Congress possesses sovereign power over the territories while they remain in a territorial condition ; and that it is the duty of the general government to protect the territories from the curse of slavery, and to preserve the public domain for the occupation of free men and free labor. And we declare that no power on earth can carry and maintain slavery in the States against the will of the people and the provisions of their constitutions and laws ; and we fully endorse the recent decision of the Supreme Court of our own State, which declares, " that property in persons is repugnant to the constitution and laws of Illinois, and that all persons within its jurisdiction are supposed to be free ; and that slavery, where it exists, is a municipal regulation, without any extra-territorial operation.

" 6. The policy of this government should be, to live on terms of peace and amity with all the nations of the earth, so far as it can be done consistently with our national honor and interest, and to enter into entangling alliances with none.. Our intercourse with other nations should be conducted upon principles of exact and exalted justice ; and while firmly maintaining our own rights, we should carefully avoid any invasion of the rights of others, and especially those of weaker nations. Our commerce ought to be protected from wanton interruption, and our commercial marine from invasion and search ; and while we would deplore the necessity of war with any of the nations of the earth, we will still firmly, zealously, and patriotically, sustain the government in any just measures which it may so adopt, to obtain redress for indignities which may heretofore have been inflicted upon our citizens navigating the seas, or which may be necessary to secure them against a repetition of like injuries in the future.

" 7. We view, with regret and alarm, the rapidly-increasing expenditures of the general government, which now, in a state of profound peace, threaten the country with national bankruptcy ; and we pledge ourselves, so far as we speak for the Republicans of Illinois, to a thorough and radical reform in the administration of the government finances, in the event that the Republicans are intrusted with the care of national affairs."

4

Mr. Lincoln delivered an able speech to the Convention, which might be said to open the campaign.

On the 24th of July, Mr. Lincoln initiated the correspondence which follows, by sending the letter which is the first of the series :

DOUGLAS AND LINCOLN CORRESPONDENCE.

Mr. Lincoln to Mr. Douglas.

CHICAGO, ILL., *July* 24, 1858.

Hon. S. A. DOUGLAS:

My Dear Sir—Will it be agreeable to you to make an arrangement for you and myself to divide time, and address the same audiences the present canvass ?   Mr. Judd, who will hand you this, is authorized to receive your answer ; and, if agreeable to you, to enter into the terms of such arrangement.

Your obedient servant,

A. LINCOLN.

Mr. Douglas to Mr. Lincoln.

CHICAGO, *July* 24, 1858.

Hon. A. LINCOLN :

Dear Sir—Your note of this date, in which you inquire if it would be agreeable to me to make an arrangement to divide the time and address the same audiences during the present canvass, was handed me by Mr. Judd.   Recent events have interposed difficulties in the way of such an arrangement.

I went to Springfield last week for the purpose of conferring with the Democratic State Central Committee upon the mode of conducting the canvass, and with them, and under their advice, made a list of appointments covering the entire period until late in October.   The people of the several localities have been notified of the times and places of the meetings.   These

appointments have all been made for Democratic meetings, and arrangements have been made by which the
Democratic candidates for Congress, for the Legislature, and other offices, will be present and address the
people. It is evident, therefore, that these various
candidates, in connection with myself, will occupy the
whole time of the day and evening, and leave no opportunity for other speeches.

Besides, there is another consideration which should
be kept in mind. It has been suggested, recently, that
an arrangement had been made to bring out a third
candidate for the United States Senate, who, with
yourself, should canvass the State in opposition to me,
with no other purpose than to insure my defeat, by dividing the Democratic party for your benefit. If I
should make this arrangement with you, it is more
than probable that this other candidate, who has a
common object with you, would desire to become a
party to it, and claim the right to speak from the same
stand ; so that he and you, in concert, might be able
to take the opening and closing speech in every case.

I cannot refrain from expressing my surprise, if it
was your original intention to invite such an arrangement, that you should have waited until after I had
made my appointments, inasmuch as we were both here
in Chicago together for several days after my arrival,
and again at Bloomington, Atlanta, Lincoln, and
Springfield, where it was well known I went for the
purpose of consulting with the State Central Committee, and agreeing upon the plan of the campaign.

While, under these circumstances, I do not feel at
liberty to make any arrangements which would deprive
the Democratic candidates for Congress, State officers,
and the Legislature, from participating in the discussion at the various meetings designated by the Democratic State Central Committee, I will, in order to ac-
commodate you, as far as it is in my power to do so,
take the responsibility of making an arrangement with

you for a discussion between us at one prominent point
in each Congressional District in the State, except the
second and sixth districts, where we have both spoken,
and in each of which cases you had the concluding
speech. If agreeable to you, I will indicate the following places as those most suitable in the several Congressional Districts, at which we should speak, to wit :
Freeport, Ottawa, Galesburgh, Quincy, Alton, Jonesboro', and Charleston. I will confer with you at the
earliest convenient opportunity in regard to the mode
of conducting the debate, the times of meeting at the
several places, subject to the condition, that where appointments have already been made by the Democratic
State Central Committee at any of those places, I must
insist upon your meeting me at the time specified.
Very respectfully,
Your most obedient servant
S. A. DOUGLAS.

Mr. Lincoln to Mr. Douglas.

SPRINGFIELD, *July* 29, 1858.
Hon. S. A. DOUGLAS:
Dear Sir—Yours of the 24th, in relation to an
arrangement to divide time, and address the same audiences, is received ; and, in apology for not sooner replying, allow me to say, that when I sat by you at
dinner yesterday, I was not aware that you had answered my note, nor, certainly, that my own note had
been presented to you. An hour after, I saw a copy of
your answer in the Chicago *Times*, and, reaching home,
I found the original awaiting me. Protesting that
your insinuations of attempted unfairness on my part
are unjust, and with the hope that you did not very
considerately make them, I proceed to reply. To your
statement that " It has been suggested, recently, that an
arrangement had been made to bring out a third candidate for the U. S. Senate, who, with yourself, should

canvass the State in opposition to me," etc., I can only say, that such suggestion must have been made by yourself, for certainly none such has been made by or to me, or otherwise, to my knowledge. Surely you did not *deliberately* conclude, as you insinuate, that I was expecting to draw you into an arrangement of terms, to be agreed on by yourself, by which a third candidate and myself, " in concert, might be able to take the opening and closing speech in every case."

As to your surprise that I did not sooner make the proposal to divide time with you, I can only say, I made it as soon as I resolved to make it. I did not know but that such proposal would come from you ; I waited, respectfully, to see. It may have been well known to you that you went to Springfield for the purpose of agreeing on the plan of campaign ; but it was not so known to me. When your appointments were announced in the papers, extending only to the 21st of August, I, for the first time, considered it certain that you would make no proposal to me, and then resolved that, if my friends concurred, I would make one to you. As soon thereafter as I could see and consult with friends satisfactorily, I did make the proposal. It did not occur to me that the proposed arrangement could derange your plans after the latest of your appointments already made. After that, there was, before the election, largely over two months of clear time.

For you to say that we have already spoken at Chicago and Springfield, and that on both occasions I had the concluding speech, is hardly a fair statement. The truth rather is this : At Chicago, July 9th, you made a carefully-prepared conclusion on my speech of June 16th. Twenty-four hours after, I made a hasty conclusion on yours of the 9th. You had six days to prepare, and concluded on me again at Bloomington on the 16th. Twenty-four hours after I concluded again on you at Springfield. In the meantime, you had made another conclusion on me at Springfield, which I did not hear, and of the contents of which I knew nothing when I spoke ; so that your speech made in daylight, and mine at night, on the 17th, at Springfield, were both made in perfect independence of each other. The dates of making all these speeches will show, I think, that in the matter of time for preparation, the advantage has been all on your side ; and that none of the external circumstances has stood to my advantage.

I agree to an arrangement for us to speak at the seven places you have named, and at your own times, provided you name the times at once, so that I, as well as you, can have to myself the time not covered by the arrangement. As to the other details, I wish perfect reciprocity, and no more. I wish as much time as you, and that conclusions shall alternate. That is all.

Your obedient servant,
A. LINCOLN.

P. S. As matters now stand, I shall be at no more of your exclusive meetings ; and for about a week from to-day a letter from you will reach me at Springfield.
A. L.

Mr. Douglas to Mr. Lincoln.

BEMENT, PIATT CO., ILL., *July* 30, 1858.

Dear Sir—Your letter, dated yesterday, accepting ny proposition for a joint discussion at one prominent point in each Congressional District, as stated in my previous letter, was received this morning.

The times and places designated are as follows:

Ottawa, La Salle county	August	21st, 1858.
Freeport, Stephenson county	"	27th, "
Jonesboro, Union county	September	15th, "
Charleston, Coles county	"	18th, "
Galesburgh, Knox county	October	7th, "
Quincy, Adams county	"	13th, "
Alton, Madison county	"	15th, "

. I agree to your suggestion that we shall alternately open and close the discussion. I will speak at Ottawa one hour, you can reply, occnpying an hour and a half, and I will then follow for half an hour. At Freeport, you shall open the discussion and speak one hour, I will follow for an hour and a half, and you can then reply for half an hour. We will alternate in like manner at each successive place.

Very respectfully, your obedient servant,

S. A. DOUGLAS.

Hon. A. LINCOLN, Springfield, Ill.

[*Mr. Lincoln to Mr. Douglas.*]

SPRINGFIELD, *July* 31, 1858.

Hon. S. A. DOUGLAS : *Dear Sir*—Yours of yesterday, naming places, times, and terms, for joint discussions between us, was received this morning. Although, by the terms, as you propose, you take *four* openings and closes, to my *three*, I accede, and thus close the arrangement. I direct this to you at Hillsboro, and shall try to have both your letter and this appear in the *Journal* and *Register* of Mónday morning.

Your obedient servant,

A. LINCOLN.

Of the joint debates which followed this correspondence the press of the entire country has spoken, and it is the highest praise of Mr. Lincoln to say, as the press everywhere said, that he held his ground in every encounter with Mr. Douglas, as a debater and as an orator. He had truth on his side to be sure, which is always a great advantage, but neither in repartee nor in argument did Mr. Douglas for once confuse or confute his opponent. An Illinois correspondent of a Boston journal, said to be the President of an Illinois College, wrote, after witnessing the joint debate at Galesburgh, as follows :

" The men are entirely dissimilar. Mr. Douglas is a thick-set, finely-built, courageous man, and has an air of self-confidence that does not a little to inspire his supporters with hope. Mr. Lincoln is a tall, lank man, awkward, apparently diffident, and when not speaking has neither firmness in his countenance nor fire in his eye.   *   *   *   *

" Mr. Lincoln has a rich, silvery voice, enunciates with great distinctness, and has a fine command of language. He commenced by a review of the points Mr. Douglas had made. In this he showed great tact, and his retorts, though gentlemanly, were sharp, and reached to the core the subject in dispute. While he gave but little time to the work of review, we did not feel that anything was omitted which deserved attention.

" He then proceeded to defend the Republican party. Here he charged Mr. Douglas with doing nothing for freedom ; with disregarding the rights and interests of the colored man ; and for about forty minutes he spoke with a power that we have seldom heard equalled. There was a grandeur in his thoughts, a comprehensiveness in his arguments, and a binding force in his conclusions, which were perfectly irresistible. The vast throng were silent as death ; every eye was fixed upon the speaker, and all gave him serious attention. He was the tall man eloquent ; his countenance glowed with animation, and his eye glistened with an intelligence that made it lustrous. He was no longer awkward and ungainly ; but graceful, bold, commanding.

" Mr. Douglas had been quietly smoking up to this time ; but here he forgot his cigar and listened with anxious attention. When he rose to reply he appeared excited, disturbed, and his second effort seemed to us vastly inferior to his first. Mr. Lincoln had given him a great task, and Mr. Douglas had not time to answer him, even if he had the ability."

THE DEBATES.

Mr. Lincoln, on the evening before the Freeport debate, upon informing a few of his friends of the queries he was going to put to Mr. Douglas (including that, in reference to the power of the territorial legislature, notwithstanding the Dred Scott decision, to exclude slavery), was told by his friends that if he cornered Douglas on that question, the latter would surely " take the bull by the horns," and, making a virtue of necessity, assert his Squatter Sovereignty in defiance of the Dred Scott decision ; " and that," remarked Mr. L.'s friends, "will make him Senator." " That may be," said Lincoln, and his large gray eye twinkled ; " but if he takes that shoot, HE never can be President." All that has transpired since has but justified Mr. L.'s prediction. The Republicans, after the Supreme Court had made their decision, and Douglas had unreservedly endorsed it, saw the advantage they had over the Democrats in the canvass, for they could quote Dred Scott as a knock-down argument against Popular Sovereignty. Mr. Douglas, too, saw this, and said very little in his first speeches about popular sovereignty, but assumed the offensive, and attacked the Republican party, charging it with negro equality, &c. If he could have got through with that canvass without expressing his opinion as to the power of a territorial legislature over the subject of slavery—which opinion he had sedulously avoided expressing during all the Lecompton controversy in the Senate—he un-

4*

doubtedly could now have been able to reconcile all
other differences of opinion between himself and the
Southern Democracy. But Mr. Lincoln's logical mind
was more eager to probe this gigantic sophistry, with
which the American public were being cheated, than to
be Senator. So, while Douglas was making *ad captan-
dum* appeals to the prejudices of the people, Lincoln
was weaving around him, slowly but surely, the web in
which, at Freeport, he became entangled, and from
which he has ever since been vainly endeavoring to ex-
tricate himself.

Of this great contest the Philadelphia *North American*, always conservative and cautious, remarks :

"Stephen A. Douglas had ten times his education.
Mr. Lincoln was mostly engaged in his profession, mastered amidst great discouragements, but practised with
ominent success. He had some experience, however,
as a general politician, besides serving for a while in
the Illinois Legislature, and for two years in Congress.
Mr. Douglas, on the other hand, a man of great native
force, and possessing ten times the scholastic training
of his rival, had been for full fifteen years in the very
heart of national politics. Indeed, he is the strongest
among the representatives of democracy under its
northern phase, and we doubt if Toombs, Stephens,
Benjamin, or Davis, bright luminaries of its southern
hemisphere, can rank at all before him.

"With all these differences in political and other
education, in a State that has been democratic ever
since its admission into the 'happy family,' and in opposition to a popular dogma, Lincoln stumped Illinois
against Douglas, *and carried it*. The speeches on both
sides were many and able.

"Lincoln was, on several occasions, partly foiled or,
at least, badly bothered. In most cases it seemed to

be, so far as regarded strength and skill, a drawn battle. In more than one instance he floored the 'little giant' flatly and fairly. We consider it, on the whole, an equal fight. Lincoln showed as much knowledge, and as much logic, with more wit, good humor, and courtesy. Douglas, while more rough and overbearing, was also much superior in a certain force, directness and determination. But it was about an equal match in ability. As for the result, Douglas carried the legislature, and Lincoln took the popular vote, as he can do again. Such is the man whom democracy will now endeavor to decry—the man who matched, and fully matched, their foremost champion. Both of them are self-made men; both of them are very able; both sprang from obscurity to distinction; both belong to the common people; and both will be found to be strong with the masses. We would advise democracy, not for its own sake, but for ours, to go on ridiculing Abraham Lincoln for having once mauled logs, and describing him as a third-rate man. These little popguns will soon be silenced by the roar of the popular Paixhans."

Mr. Greeley says:

"I tell you, the man who stumps a State with Stephen A. Douglas, and meets him, day after day, before the people, has got to be no fool. Many a man will make a better first speech than Douglas, but, giving and taking, back and forward, he is very sharp. Now, the man who went through the State, speaking against Stephen A. Douglas, and was not beaten, as no man says he was, is not a common man; for no common man will answer for that work; and at the end of that cumpaign Mr. Lincoln came out with 4,000 majority on the popular vote, although Mr. Buchanan had beaten Fremont 9,000, and the general feeling outside of the State was that Douglas had better be elected. Mr. Crittenden wrote a letter which elected Douglas; he

said that it was better that Douglas should be elected,
and there were 30,000 Americans there ; I don't believe we have got another man living who would have
fought through that campaign so effectively and at the
same time so good-naturedly as he did. Mr. Trumbull
would have begun a little ranker, but one or the other
would soon have been knocked off the platform. Mr.
Lincoln went through with perfect good nature and entire suavity, and beat Stephen A. Douglas, it being
the first time any man on our side ever carried that
State."

In a recent debate in the Senate of the United
States, Senator Benjamin, one of the ablest men in the
Senate and the finest orator, took up the debates between Mr. Douglas and Mr. Lincoln for examination,
and though the vehement enemy of Republicans and
Republicanism, he complimented Mr. Lincoln very
highly. Said Mr. Benjamin :

"Here, Mr. President, let me come back to an explanation of that fact which I spoke of before, and to
which I asked the attention of the Senate and the
country. There stands the explanation of the sudden
change that has been wrought in the relations of the
Senator from Illinois with the rest of the Democratic
party. It was when, in the year 1858, the year following this decision, pressed by a canvass at home, eager
to return to the Senate, he joined in canvassing the
State of Illinois with the gentleman who is now the
candidate of the Black Republican party for the Presidency. Pressed in different portions of the State
with this very argument, that he had agreed to leave
the question to the court, that the court had decided it
in favor of the South, and that, therefore, under the
Kansas-Nebraska bill, slavery was fixed in all the territories of the United States—finding himself going
down in Illinois, in that canvass, he backed out from

his promise, and directly told the people of his State that, whether it had been decided or not, and no matter what the court might decide, the Kansas-Nebraska bill had fixed the power in the people of the North to make every territory in the Union free.

" In that contest the two candidates for the Senate of the United States, in the State of Illinois, went before their people. They agreed to discuss the issues ; they put questions to each other for answer ; and I must say here, for I must be just to all, that I have been surprised in the examination that I made again within the last few days of this discussion between Mr. Lincoln and Mr. Douglas, to find that Mr. Lincoln is a far more conservative man, unless he has since changed his opinions, than I had supposed him to be. There was no dodging on his part. Mr. Douglas started with his questions. Here they are, with Mr. Lincoln's answers :

" *Question* 1. ' I desire to know whether Lincoln to-day stands, as he did in 1854, in favor of the unconditional repeal of the fugitive slave law ?'

" *Answer.* ' I do not now, nor ever did, stand in favor of the unconditional repeal of the fugitive slave law.'

" *Question* 2. ' I desire him to answer whether he stands pledged to-day, as he did in 1854, against the admission of any more slave States into the Union, even if the people want them ?'

" *Answer.* ' I do not now, nor ever did, stand pledged against the admission of any more slave States into the Union.'

" *Question* 3. ' I want to know whether he stands pledged against the admission of a new State into the Union with such a constitution as the people of that State may see fit to make ?'

" *Answer.* ' I do not stand pledged against the admission of a new State into the Union with such a constitution as the people of that State may see fit to make ?'

"*Question* 4. 'I want to know whether he stands to-day pledged to the abolition of slavery in the District of Columbia ?'

"*Answer.* 'I do not stand to-day pledged to the abolition of slavery in the District of Columbia.'

"*Question* 5. 'I desire him to answer whether he stands pledged to the prohibition of the slave trade between the different States ?'

"*Answer.* 'I do not stand pledged to the prohibition of the slave trade between the different States.'

"*Question* 6. 'I desire to know whether he stands pledged to prohibit slavery in all the territories of the United States, north as well as south of the Missouri Compromise line ?'

"*Answer.* 'I am impliedly, if not expressly, pledged to a belief in the *right* and *duty* of Congress to prohibit slavery in all the United States territories.'

"*Question* 7. 'I desire him to answer whether he is opposed to the acquisition of any new territory unless slavery is first prohibited therein ?'

"*Answer.* 'I am not generally opposed to honest acquisition of territory ; and, in any given case, I would or would not oppose such acquisition, accordingly as I might think such acquisition would or would not aggravate the slavery question among ourselves.'

"It is impossible, Mr. President, however we may differ in opinion with the man, not to admire the perfect candor and frankness with which these answers were given ; no equivocation—no evasion. The Senator from Illinois had his questions put to him in his turn. All I propose to do now is to read his answer to the second question :

" ' The next question propounded to me by Mr. Lincoln is, ' Can the people of a territory, in any lawful way, against the wishes of any citizen of the United States, exclude slavery from their limits prior to the formation of a State constitution ?' I answer emphatically, as

Mr. Lincoln has heard me answer a hundred times from every stump in Illinois, that, in my opinion, the people of a territory can, by lawful means, exclude slavery from their limits prior to the formation of a State constitution. Mr. Lincoln knew that I had answered that question over and over again. He heard me argue the Nebraska bill on that principle all over the State in 1854, in 1855, and in 1856, and he has no excuse for pretending to be in doubt as to my position on that question.'

" All that was true ; but see the art ; the decision had not come yet ; now the decision has come ; now what ?

" ' It matters not what way the Supreme Court may hereafter decide as to the abstract question, whether slavery may or may not go into a territory under the Constitution, the people have the lawful means to introduce or exclude it as they please, for the reason that slavery cannot exist a day or an hour anywhere unless it is supported by local police regulations. Those police regulations can only be established by the local legislature ; and if the people are opposed to slavery, they will elect representatives to that body who will, by unfriendly legislation, effectually prevent the introduction of it into their midst. If, on the contrary, they are for it, their legislation will favor its extension. Hence, no matter what the decision of the Supreme Court may be on that abstract question, still the right of the people to make a slave territory or a free territory is perfect and complete under the Nebraska bill. I hope Mr. Lincoln deems my answer satisfactory on that point.'   *   *   *   *   *

" Well, sir, what occurred further in that controversy ? His competitor was shocked at the profligacy of the Senator. His competitor said to him— and here is the argument—' Everybody knows that the Dred Scott decision has determined the principle that a citizen of the South has a right to go into the terri-

tory, and there, under the Constitution, his property
is protected, and yet you are telling the people here
that their legislators, when they swear to support the
Constitution, can violate that constitutional provision.'
Mr. Lincoln held up his hands in horror at the proposition. He was bold in the assertion of his own principles ; but he told the Senator from Illinois in that
discussion, that what he was saying was a gross outrage on propriety, and was breaking the bargain he
had made. But again, sir, he told the Senator from
Illinois that he did not believe in the Dred Scott decision, because, said he, if the Dred Scott decision be
true, and slavery exists in the territories under the
Constitution of the United States, then it also exists
in the States—it exists in Pennsylvania as well as in
Kansas.

"The contest ended. On the popular vote, the
Senator from Illinois was beaten ; but according to
the division of the representative and senatorial districts of the State, he was re-elected. The popular
vote upon the election of members of the Senate and
Legislature was one hundred and twenty-one thousand
in his favor, one hundred and twenty-five thousand in
favor of the Republican candidate, and five thousand
votes in favor of what he called the Danites. All the
State Republican officers were elected ; but there was
a majority of the Legislature of Illinois elected in favor
the Senator from Illinois, and he came back here in
triumph.

" Last spring I was forced to leave my country from
an attack of a disease in the eyes, which required attention abroad. I went to get the attention of eminent oculists abroad. For six or eight months I was
debarred from reading or writing. I came back just
before the opening of this Congress ; and I found that
during my absence the honorable Senator from Illinois
had been engaged in a controversy in the public journals and magazines of the country in relation to the

principles that governed the territories of the United States, and that he had copied into those articles the very arguments that his Republican opponent in Illinois had used against him, and was then using against the Democratic party. [Laughter.] I have got them here. First, that it may not be said that I originated this charge, after these magazine articles were printed, and after the Senator's opponent, Mr. Lincoln, had taxed him with want of good faith under the Constitution for alleging the power of the local legislature to go through with this unfriendly legislation, in a subsequent speech, delivered at Columbus, Ohio, in September, 1859, Mr. Lincoln said to the people :

"Judge Douglas says, if the Constitution carries slavery into the territories, beyond the power of the people of the territories to control it as other property, then it follows logically that every one who swears to support the Constitution of the United States must give that support to that property which it needs. And if the Constitution carries slavery into the territories, beyond the power of the people to control it as other property, then it also carries it into the States, because the Constitution is the supreme law of the land. Now, gentlemen, if it were not for my excessive modesty, I would say that I told that very thing to Judge Douglas quite a year ago. This argument is here in print, and if it were not for my modesty, as I said, I might call your attention to it. If you read it, you will find that I not only made that argument, but made it better than he has made it since." (Laughter.)

The first debate took place at Ottawa, and Mr. Douglas made the opening speech, in the course of which he made a singular charge against Mr. Lincoln, which was as follows :

"In 1854, Mr. Abraham Lincoln and Mr. Trumbull entered into an arrangement, one with the other, and each with his respective friends, to dissolve the old Whig party on the one hand, and to dissolve the old Democratic party on the other, and to connect the members of both into an Abolition party, under the name and disguise of a Republican party. The terms of that arrangement between Mr. Lincoln and Mr. Trumbull have been published to the world by Mr. Lincoln's special friend, James H. Matheny, Esq., and they were, that Lincoln should have Shields' place in the U. S. Senate, which was then about to become vacant, and that Trumbull should have my seat when my term expired. Lincoln went to work to abolitionize the old Whig party all over the State, pretending that he was then as good a Whig as ever ; and Trumbull went to work in his part of the State preaching abolitionism in its milder and lighter form, and trying to abolitionize the Democratic party, and bring old Democrats, handcuffed and bound hand and foot, into the Abolition camp. In pursuance of the arrangement, the parties met in Springfield in October, 1854, and proclaimed their new platform. Lincoln was to bring into the Abolition camp the old line Whigs, and transfer them over to Giddings, Chase, Fred. Douglas, and Parson Lovejoy, who were ready to receive them, and christen them in their new faith. They laid down, on that occasion, a platform for their new Republican party, which was to be thus constructed."

To this charge, Mr. Lincoln replied :

" When a man hears himself somewhat misrepresented, it provokes him—at least, I find it so with myself ; but when misrepresentation becomes very gross and palpable, it is more apt to amuse him. The first thing I see fit to notice, is the fact that Judge Douglas alleges, after running through the history of the old Democratic and the old Whig parties, that Judge Trumbull and myself made an arrangement in 1854, by which I was to have the place of General Shields in the United States Senate, and Judge Trumbull was to have the place of Judge Douglas. Now, all I have to say upon that subject is, that I think no man—not even Judge Douglas—can prove it, *because it is not true.* I have no doubt he is '*conscientious*' in saying it. As to those resolutions that he took such a length of time to read, as being the platform of the Republican party in 1854, I say that I never had anything to do with them, and I think Trumbull never had. Judge Douglas cannot show that either of us ever did have anything to do with them. I believe *this* is true about those resolutions : There was a call for a convention to form a Republican party at Springfield, and I think that my friend, Mr. Lovejoy, who is here upon this stand, had a hand in it. I think this is true, and I think if he will remember accurately, he will be able to recollect that he tried to get me into it, and I would not go in. I believe it is also true that I went away from Springfield when the convention was in session, to attend court in Tazewell county. It is true they did place my name, though without authority, upon the committee, and afterward wrote me to attend the meeting of the committee, but I refused to do so, and I never had anything to do with that organization. This is the plain truth about all that matter of the resolutions.''

In the reply, Mr. Lincoln uttered the subjoined forcible and eloquent paragraph, upon negro equality :

"Now, gentlemen, I don't want to read at any greater length, but this is the true complexion of all I have ever said in regard to the institution of slavery and the black race. This is the whole of it, and any-thing that argues me into his idea of perfect social and political equality with the negro, is but a specious and fantastic arrangement of words, by which a man can prove a horse-chestnut to be a chestnut-horse. I will say here, while upon this subject, that I have no purpose, directly or indirectly, to interfere with the institution of slavery in the States where it now exists. I believe I have no lawful right to do so, and I have no inclination to do so. I have no·purpose to introduce political and social equality between the white and the black races. There is a physical difference between the two, which, in my judgment, will probably forever forbid their living together upon the footing of perfect equality, and inasmuch as it becomes a necessity that there must be a difference, I, as well as Judge Douglas, am in favor of the race to which I belong having the superior position. I have never said anything to the contrary, but I hold that, notwithstanding all this, there is no reason in the world why the negro is not entitled to all the natural rights enumerated in the Declaration of Independence—the right to life, liberty, and the pursuit of happiness. I hold that he is as much entitled to these as the white man. I agree with Judge Douglas he is not my equal in many respects—certainly not in color, perhaps not in moral or intellectual endowment. But in the right to eat the bread, without the leave of any one else, which his own hand earns, *he is my equal, and the equal of Judge Douglas, and the equal of every living man.*"

Mr. Douglas also undertook to give a little sketch of his opponent's personal history in his speech, and after the following fashion.

" In the remarks I have made on this platform, and the position of Mr. Lincoln upon it, I mean nothing personally disrespectful or unkind to that gentleman. I have known him for nearly twenty-five years. There were many points of sympathy between us when we first got acquainted. We were both comparatively boys, and both struggling with poverty in a strange land. I was a school-teacher in the town of Winchester, and he a flourishing grocery-keeper in the town of Salem. He was more successful in his occupation than

I was in mine, and hence more fortunate in this world's goods. Lincoln is one of those peculiar men who perform with admirable skill everything which they undertake. I made as good a school-teacher as I could, and when a cabinet-maker I made a good bedstead and tables; although my old boss said I succeeded better with bureaus and secretaries than with anything else ; but I believe that Lincoln was always more successful in business than I, for his business enabled him to get into the Legislature. I met him there, however, and had a sympathy with him, because of the up-hill struggle we both had in life. He was then just as good at telling an anecdote as now. He could beat any of the boys wrestling, or running a foot-race, in pitching quoits or tossing a copper ; could ruin more liquor than all the boys of the town together, and the dignity and impartiality with which he presided at a horse-race or fist-fight, excited the admiration and won the praise of everybody that was present and participated. I sympathized with him, because he was struggling with difficulties, and so was I. Mr. Lincoln served with me in the Legislature in 1836, when we both retired, and he subsided, or became submerged, and he was lost sight of as a public man for some years. In 1846, when Wilmot introduced the celebrated proviso, and the Abolition tornado swept over the country, Lincoln again turned up as a member of Congress from the Sangamon district. I was then in the Senate of the United States, and was glad to welcome my old friend and companion. While in Congress, he distinguished himself by his opposition to the Mexican war, taking the side of the common enemy against his own country ; and when he returned home he found that the indignation of the people followed him everywhere, and he was again submerged or obliged to retire into private life, forgotten by his former friends."

To which Mr. Lincoln replied:

" The Judge is wofully at fault about his early friend
Lincoln being a ' grocery-keeper.' I don't know as it
would be a great sin if I had been ; but he is mistaken. Lincoln never kept a grocery anywhere in the
world. It is true that Lincoln did work the latter part
of one winter in a little still-house up at the head of a
hollow. And so I think my friend, the Judge, is
equally at fault when he charges me at the time when
I was in Congress of having opposed our soldiers who
were fighting in the Mexican war. The Judge did not
make his charge very distinctly, but I can tell you
what he can prove by referring to the record. You remember I was an old Whig, and whenever the Democratic party tried to get me to vote that the war had
been righteously begun by the President, I would not
do it. But whenever they asked for any money, or
land-warrants, or anything to pay the soldiers there,
during all that time, I gave the same vote that Judge
Douglas did. You can think as you please as to whether
that was consistent. Such is the truth ; and the Judge
has a right to make all he can out of it. But when he,
by a general charge, conveys the idea that I withheld
supplies from the soldiers who were fighting in the
Mexican war, or did anything else to hinder the soldiers, he is, to say the least, grossly and altogether mistaken, as a consultation of the records will prove to
him."

Mr. Lincoln, before he was through, made the following amusing point on Mr. Douglas, in reply to his continual talk about the Supreme Court and reverence for
its decisions :

" This man sticks to a decision which forbids the people of a territory from excluding slavery, and he does so
not because he says it is right in itself—he does not give
any opinion on that—but because it has been *decided by
the court,* and being decided by the court, he is, and

you are bound to take it in your political action as *law*—not that he judges at all of its merits, but because a decision of the court is to him a *"Thus saith the Lord."* He places it on that ground alone, and you will bear in mind that, thus committing himself unreservedly to this decision, *commits him to the next one* just as firmly as to this. He did not commit himself on account of the merit or demerit of the decision, but it is a *Thus saith the Lord.* The next decision, as much as this, will be a *Thus saith the Lord.* There is nothing that can divert or turn him away from this decision. It is nothing that I point out to him that his great prototype, Gen. Jackson, did not believe in the binding force of decisions. It is nothing to him that Jefferson did not so believe. I have said that I have often heard him approve of Jackson's course in disregarding the decision of the Supreme Court pronouncing a National Bank constitutional. He says, I did not hear him say so. He denies the accuracy of my recollection. I say he ought to know better than I, but I will make no question about this thing, though it still seems to me that I heard him say it twenty times. I will tell him though, that he now claims to stand on the Cincinnati platform, which affirms that Congress *cannot* charter a National Bank, in the teeth of that old standing decision that Congress *can* charter a bank. And I remind him of another piece of history on the question of respect for judicial decisions, and it is a piece of Illinois history, belonging to a time when the large party to which Judge Douglas belonged, were displeased with a decision of the Supreme Court of Illinois, because they had decided that a Governor could not remove a Secretary of State. You will find the whole story in Ford's *History of Illinois*, and I know that Judge Douglas will not deny that he was then in favor of overslaughing that decision by the mode of adding five new Judges, so as to vote down the four old ones. Not only so, but it ended in *the Judge's sitting*

*down on that very bench as one of the five new Judges
to break down the four old ones.* It was in this way
precisely that he got his title of Judge. Now, when
the Judge tells me that men appointed conditionally to
sit as members of a court, will have to be catechised
beforehand on some subject, I say, 'You know, Judge ;
you have tried it." When he says a court of this kind
will lose the confidence of all men, will be prostituted
and disgraced by such a proceeding, I say, ' You know
best, Judge ; you have been through the mill." But
I cannot shake Judge Douglas's teeth loose from the
Dred Scott decision. Like some obstinate animal (I
mean no disrespect), that will hang on when he has
once got his teeth fixed ; you may cut off a leg, or you
may tear away an arm, still he will not relax his hold.
And so I may point out to the Judge, and say that he
is bespattered all over, from the beginning of his political life to the present time, with attacks upon judicial
decisions—*I* may cut off limb after limb of his public
record, and strive to wrench him from a single dictum
of the court—yet I cannot divert him from it. He
hangs, to the last, to the Dred Scott decision. These
things show there is a purpose *strong as death and
eternity* for which he adheres to this decision, and for
which he will adhere to *all other decisions* of the same
court."

We may safely challenge the annals of stump-speak-
ing in the West or at the South for a more overwhelming rejoinder than this.

In the third debate, at Jonesboro, Mr. Lincoln said :

" I find a report of a speech made by Judge Douglas at Joliet, since we last met at Freeport—published,
I believe, in the *Missouri Republican*—on the 9th of
this month, in which Judge Douglas says :

" ' You know at Ottawa, I read this platform, and
asked him if he concurred in each and all of the principles set forth in it. He would not answer these ques-

tions. At last I said frankly, "I wish you to answer them, because when I get them up here where the color of your principles are a little darker than in Egypt, I intend to trot you down to Jonesboro." The very notice that I was going to take him down to Egypt made him tremble in the knees so that he had to be carried from the platform. He laid up seven days, and in the meantime held a consultation with his political physicians ; they had Lovejoy and Farnsworth and all the leaders of the Abolition party, they consulted it · all over, and at last Lincoln came to the conclusion that he would answer, so he came up to Freeport last Friday.'

" Now that statement altogether furnishes a subject for philosophical contemplation. I have been treating it in that way, and I have really come to the conclusion that I can explain it in no other way than by believing the Judge is crazy. If he was in his right mind, I cannot conceive how he would have risked disgusting the four or five thousand of his own friends who stood there, and knew, as to my having been carried from the platform, that there was not a word of truth in it."

JUDGE DOUGLAS—" Didn't they carry you off ?"

MR. LINCOLN—" There ; that question illustrates the character of this man Douglas, exactly. He smiles now and says, ' Didn't they carry you off ?' But he said then, ' *he had to be carried off;*' and he said it to convince the country that he had so completely broken me down by his speech that I had to be carried away. Now he seeks to dodge it, and asks, ' Didn't they carry you off ?' Yes, they did. *But, Judge Douglas, why didn't you tell the truth ?* I would like to know why you didn't tell the truth about it. And then again, ' He laid up seven days.' He puts this in print for the people of the country to read as a serious document. I think if he had been in his sober senses he would not have risked that barefacedness in the presence of thousands of his own friends, who knew that I made

5

speeches within six of the seven days at Henry, Marshall county, Augusta, Hancock county, and Macomb,
McDonough county, including all the necessary travel
to meet him again at Freeport at the end of the six
days.   Now, I say, there is no charitable way to look
at that statement, except to conclude that he is actually crazy.   There is another thing in that statement that alarmed me very greatly as he states
it, that he was going to 'trot me down to Egypt.'
Thereby he would have you to infer that I would not
come to Egypt unless he forced me—that I could not
be got here, unless he, giantlike, had hauled me down
here.   That statement he makes, too, in the teeth of
the knowledge that I had made the stipulation to come
down here, *and that he himself had been very reluc-
tant to enter into the stipulation.*   More than all this,
Judge Douglas, when he made that statement, must
have been crazy, and wholly out of his sober senses,
or else he would have known that when he got me
down here—that promise—that windy promise—of his
powers to annihilate me, wouldn't amount to anything.
Now, how little do I look like being carried away
trembling ?   Let the Judge go on, and after he is done
with his half hour, I want you all, if I can't go home
myself, to let me stay and rot here ; and if anything
happens to the Judge, if I cannot carry him to the
hotel and put him to bed, let me stay here and rot.   I
say, then, there is something *extraordinary* in this
statement.   I ask you if you know any other living
man who would make such a statement ?   I will ask
my friend Casey, over there, if he would do such a
thing ?   Would he send that out and have his men
take it as the truth ?   Did the Judge talk of trotting
me down to Egypt to scare me to death ?   Why, I
know this people better than he does.   I was raised
just a little east of here.   I am a part of this people.
But the Judge was raised further north, and, perhaps,
he has some horrid idea of what this people might be

induced to do. But really I have talked about this matter perhaps longer than I ought, for it is no great thing, and yet the smallest are often the most difficult things to deal with. The Judge has set about seriously trying to make the impression that when we meet at different places I am literally in his clutches—that I am a poor, helpless, decrepit mouse, and that I can do nothing at all. This is one of the ways he has taken to create that impression. I don't know any other way to meet it, except this. I don't wan't to quarrel with him—to call him a liar—but when I come square up to him I don't know what else to call him, if I must tell the truth out. I want to be at peace, and reserve all my fighting powers for necessary occasions. My time, now, is very nearly out, and I give up the trifle that is left to the Judge, to let him set my knees trembling again, if he can."

Mr. Greeley, in the *Tribune*, speaks of this great Senatorial contest, and its result, as follows :

" In 1858, the Republican State Convention *unanimously* designated him as their representative man to stump the State against Stephen A. Douglas. They knew that the struggle would be a desperate one—that they must put their very best foot foremost. If they had had a champion whom they supposed abler and worthier than Mr. Lincoln, they would have chosen that champion for this arduous service. They had nearly all heard Lincoln and their other speakers, and ought to have known by this time who was their best man ; yet they choose Abraham Lincoln. If they don't know who is their best man, should not missionaries be sent out to teach them ?

"Mr. Lincoln went into this canvass under most discouraging auspices. Many leading Republicans out of the State thought the opposition to Mr. Douglas impolitic and mistaken. *We* certainly thought so ; and, though we said little on the point, our very silence was damaging in a State where more people read this paper than any other. It has been a hundred times asserted that *The Tribune* ' defeated Lincoln.' But there were other outside influences, as adverse and at least equally potent. In 1856, the State polled 37,444 American or Whig votes for Fillmore. Many of these were cast by natives of Kentucky ; all by men who love and confide in John J. Crittenden. In the thickest of the fray, a letter from Mr. Crittenden was published, 'advising them to favor Mr. Douglas's reëlection. Undoubtedly, this had an overruling influence with thousands. Yet, after Messrs. Lincoln and Douglas had thoroughly canvassed the State, the people voted with the following result :

	FREMONT.	FILLMORE.	BUCHANAN.
Total vote in 1856..........	96,189	37,444	105,348
	LINCOLN.	LECOMPTON.	DOUGLAS.
Total vote in 1858..........	125,275	5,071	121,190

Linco n's gain on 1856..................................	29,086
Douglas' "	15,742
Lincoln's net gain..................................	14,345

Or, give Douglas the entire Lecompton vote in additior to his own, and Lincoln still gains on him 9,273.

" Bear in mind that this was a contest in which the sympathies of men indifferent to party were almost wholly with Douglas, wherein many Republicans supported him throughout, wherein Crittenden summoned the Americans to his aid, and wherein he stood boldly on the ground of Popular Sovereignty, with the prestige of having just before defeated the infamous Lecompton bill. All things considered, we recall nothing in the history of political campaigning more creditable to a canvasser than this vote is to Lincoln.

" We have thus dwelt throughout on facts of public record or of universal notoriety. The speeches made to the same audiences in that canvass, by Messrs. Lincoln and Douglas, were collected and printed by the Republicans of Ohio, for cheap and general dissemina-

8888

8

tion, long before they dreamed that Mr. Lincoln would be the Republican candidate for President. We had sold hundreds of them at our counter, as we had thousands of Mr. Lincoln's speech in this city, before the meeting of the Chicago Convention ; we expect to sell thousands of the former and tens of thousands of the latter forthwith. Every reader can herein see just what manner of man Mr. Lincoln is, and how he bears himself when confronted with one of the very best and most effective· popular canvassers in the democratic ranks. If Mr. Lincoln is weak, or ill-informed, or anywise deficient, this protracted discussion with Douglas must show it."

The Chicago *Tribune,* shortly after the election took place, made the subjoined statement :

" The majorities for members of Congress are as follows :

First district, E. B. Washburne, Rep.................. 9.414
Second district, J F. Farnsworth, Rep.............. 8,639
Third district, Owen Lovejoy, Rep. 7.443
Fourth district, William Kellogg, Rep............... 2,711
Fifth district, Isaac N. Morris, Dem................. 1,961
Sixth district, Thomas L. Harris, Dem.. 4,447
Seventh district, J. C. Robinson, Dem............... 1,759
Eighth district, Philip B. Foulke, Dem............... 2,939
Ninth district, John A. Logan. Dem................12,847

" The aggregate votes on the Congressional tickets were : Republican, 126,084 ; Douglas Democratic, 121,940 ; Buchanan Democratic, 5,091.

" The vote on State Treasurer stands : James Miller, Republican, 125,828 ; W. B. Fondey, Douglas Democrat, 121,803 ; John Dougherty, Buchanan Democrat, 5,091.

" These returns show, that taking the vote on Congressmen as the test, the Republican majority over both the Buchanan and Douglas parties is 97. The entire Buchanan vote is 5,091. The Republicans retained every county that went for Fremont or Bissell in 1856.

159517

They lost not one which they carried at the Presidential election; and they have redeemed from the Democrats seven counties which .went for Buchanan two
years ago, viz. : De Witt, Logan, Coles, Edgar, Platt,
Edwards, and Bond, all of which went against Governor Bissell, except Edwards. Peoria can almost be
added to the column of the redeemed counties:
    " Despite the unfair apportionment, by which Mr.
Douglas has secured both branches of the Legislature,
the Republicans of Illinois have abundant reason to be
satisfied with the result of the contest through which
they have just passed. Taking Fremont's vote as a
standard of comparison, they have gained nearly 30,000
since 1856. The entire vote of the State is 252,722,
against 238,981 two years ago—a difference of 13,741."

    Mr. Lincoln and his fellow Republicans of Illinois,
far from being discouraged by the result of the campaign, were greatly encouraged, well knowing that
with such gains, such a steady increase, by the Republican party in Illinois, its day of complete triumph
could not be far off.
    During the past autumn and winter Mr. Lincoln
visited various parts of the country, delivering lectures
upon the political condition of the country, and creating unbounded enthusiaism wherever he went. The
Leavenworth *Register* speaks as follows of his visit to
Kansas :

    " Hon. Abraham Lincoln arrived this afternoon,
about two o'clock. Notwithstanding the inclemency of
the weather, he was met on Sixth street by a large concourse of our people, which augmented as it neared
Turner's Hall, and when it reached Delaware street it
contained seven or eight hundred persons. The procession moved down Delaware street and turned up Maine

to Shawnee, and up Shawnee to the Mansion House. Along the sidewalks a dense crowd moved with the procession. All the doors, windows, balconies, and porticoes, were filled with men and women, all anxious to get a sight of 'Honest Old Abe.' On arriving at the Mansion House the concourse halted, and three long and loud cheers were given for Lincoln.

"The crowd by this time had swelled to an immense audience, filled with admiration for the man of the people and the veteran warrior of freedom. The marshals of the day, Capt. Dickison and Capt. Hays of the Turner Association, assisted by Mr. Ketner and others, deserve credit for the manner in which the reception was conducted.

" Never did man receive such honors at the hands of our people, and never did our people pay honors to a better man, or one who has been a truer friend to Kansas. The name of ' Abe Lincoln' is a household word in Illinois, Indiana, and Ohio. Let it be so in Kansas, for we owe much to him for his early efforts in behalf of freedom in Kansas."

The subjoined paragraph is from his speech at Leavenworth, and is upon the subject of the dissolution of the Union. Said he :

" But you, Democrats, are for the Union ; and you greatly fear the success of the Republicans would destroy the Union. Why ? Do the Republicans declare against the Union ? Nothing like it. Your own statement of it is, that if the Black Republicans elect a President, you *won't stand it!"* You will break up the Union. That will be your act, not ours. To justify it, you must show that our policy gives you just cause for such desperate action. Can you do that ? When you attempt it, you will find that our policy is exactly the policy of the men who made the Union. Nothing more and nothing less. Do you really think you are justified to break the government rather than have it administered as it was by Washington, and other great and good men who made it, and first administered it ? If you do, you are very unreasonable, and more reasonable men cannot and will not submit to you. While you elect Presidents we submit, neither breaking nor attempting to break up the Union. If we shall constitutionally elect a President, it will be our duty to see that you also submit. Old John Brown has been executed for treason against a State. We cannot object, even though he agreed with us in thinking slavery wrong. That cannot excuse violence, bloodshed, and treason. It could avail him nothing that he might think himself right. So, if constitutionally we elect a President, and, therefore, you undertake to destroy the Union, it will be our duty to deal with you as old John Brown has been dealt with. We shall try to do our duty. We hope and believe that in no section will a majority so act as to render such extreme measures necessary."

Mr. Lincoln is described by one who is familiar with his appearance and manners, as follows :

" Mr. Lincoln stands six feet and four inches high in his stockings. His frame is not muscular, but gaunt and wiry ; his arms are long, but not unreasonably so for a person of his height ; his lower limbs are not disproportioned to his body. In walking, his gait, though firm, is never brisk. He steps slowly and deliberately, almost always with his head inclined forward, and his hands clasped behind his back. In matters of dress he is by no means precise. Always clean, he is never fashionable ; he is careless, but not slovenly. In manner he is remarkably cordial, and, at the same time, simple. His politeness is always sincere, but never elaborate and oppressive. A warm shake of the hand, and a warmer smile of recognition, are his methods of greeting his friends. At rest, his features, though

those of a man of mark, are not such as belong to a
handsome man ; but when his fine dark gray eyes are
lighted up by any emotion, and his features begin their
play, he would be chosen from among a crowd as one
who had in him not only the kindly sentiments which
women love, but the heavier metal of which full-grown
men and Presidents are made. His hair is black, and
though thin is wiry. His head sits well on his shoulders,
but beyond that it defies description. It nearer resem-
bles that of Clay than that of Webster ; but it is
unlike either. It is very large, and, phrenologically,
well proportioned, betokening power in all its developments. A slightly Roman nose, a wide-cut mouth,
and a dark complexion, with the appearance of having
been weather-beaten, complete the description.

"In his personal habits, Mr. Lincoln is as simple as
a child. He loves a good dinner, and eats with the appetite which goes with a great brain ; but his food is
plain and nutritious. He never drinks intoxicating
liquors of any sort, not even a glass of wine. He is
not addicted to tobacco in any of its shapes. He never
was accused of a licentious act in all his life. He
never uses profane language.

"A friend says that once, when in a towering rage,
in consequence of the efforts of certain parties to per-
petrate a fraud on the State, he was heard to say :
' They sha'n't do it, d—n 'em !' but beyond an expression of that kind, his bitterest feelings never carry him.
He never gambles ; we doubt if he ever indulges in
any games of chance. He is particularly cautious
about incurring pecuniary obligations for any purpose
whatever, and in debt, he is never content until the
score is discharged. We presume he owes no man a
dollar. He never speculates. The rage for the sudden
acquisition of wealth never took hold of him. His
gains from his profession have been moderate, but sufficient for his purposes. While others have dreamed of
gold, he has been in pursuit of knowledge. In all his

dealings he has the reputation of being generous but
exact, and, above all, religiously honest. He would be
a bold man who would say that Abraham Lincoln ever
wronged any one out of a cent, or ever spent a dollar
that he had not honestly earned. His struggles in early
life have made him careful of money ; but his gener-
osity with his own is proverbial. He is a regular
attendant upon religious worship, and though not a
communicant, is a pew-hòlder and liberal supporter of
the Presbyterian Church, in Springfield, to which Mrs.
Lincoln belongs. He is a scrupulous teller of the
truth—too exact in his notions to suit the atmosphere
of Washington, as it now is. His enemies may say
that he tells Black Republican lies ; but no man ever
charged that, in a professional capacity, or as a citizen
dealing with his neighbors, he would depart from the
Scriptural command. At home, he lives like a gentleman of modest means and simple tastes. A good-sized
house of wood, simply but tastefully furnished, surrounded by trees and flowers, is his own, and there he
lives, at peace with himself, the idol of his family, and
for his honesty, ability, and patriotism, the admiration
of his countrymen."

Another person gives the subjoined sketch of him : ·

" In personal appearance, Mr. Lincoln, or, as he is
more familiarly termed among those who know him
best, ' Old Uncle Abe,' is long, lean, and wiry. In
motion he has a great deal of the elasticity and awkwardness which indicate the rough training of his early
life, and his conversation savors strongly of Western
idioms and pronunciation. His height is six feet four
inches. His complexion is about that of an octoroon ;
his face, without being by any means beautiful, is genial looking, and good humor seems to lurk in every
corner of its innumerable angles. He has dark hair
tinged with gray, a good forehead, small eyes, a long
penetrating nose, with nostrils such as Napoleon al-

ways liked to find in his best generals, because they indicated a long head and clear thoughts ; and a mouth, which, aside from being of magnificent proportions, is probably the most expressive feature of his face.

"As a speaker he is ready, precise, and fluent. His manner before a popular assembly is as he pleases to make it, being either superlatively ludicrous, or very impressive. He employs but little gesticulation, but when he desires to make a point, produces a shrug of his shoulders, an elevation of his eyebrows, a depression of his mouth, and a general malformation of countenance so comically awkward that it never fails to 'bring down the house.' His enunciation is slow and emphatic, and his voice, though sharp and powerful, at times has a frequent tendency to dwindle into a shrill and unpleasant sound ; but as before stated, the peculiar characteristic of his delivery is the remarkable mobility of his features, the frequent contortions of which excite a merriment his words could not produce."

A good story is told of Mr. Lincoln in connection with the Harper's Ferry affair—and by the way it is but one of a thousand which might be told of him, for he is a rare story-teller—it is said that when he first heard of the Harper's Ferry invasion, he remarked, that it was " a shocking and lamentable occurrence ;" but foreseeing the capital which the democracy would make out of it, he added, " I do not think the democracy can cross the river of their difficulties at Harper's Ferry."

We subjoin another amusing one from a Chicago journal :

" A great deal of fun was had by the jokers in Springfield, about an affair in which, long time ago, our good friend Lincoln, *the* candidate for the Presidency, was engaged.   A young lady of that city, now the wife of a distinguished statesman, wrote a paragraph in a burlesque vein, for the *Sangamon Journal*, in which Gen. Shields was good humoredly ridiculed for his connection with some public measure.   The General was greatly incensed, and demanded of the editor the name of the offending party.   'Old Sim' put him off with a request for twenty-four hours to consider the matter, and, shortly afterward meeting Lincoln, told him his perplexity.   'Tell him I wrote it,' said Lincoln ; and tell him he did.   After a deal of diplomacy to get a retraction of the offensive parts of the paragraph in question, Shields sent a challenge, which Lincoln accepted, named broadswords as the weapons, and an unfrequented, well-wooded island in the Mississippi, just below Alton, as the place.   'Old Abe' was first on the ground, and when Shields arrived he found his antagonist, his sword in one hand and a hatchet in the other, with his coat off, clearing away the underbrush !   Before the preliminary arrangements were completed, John J. Hardin, who, somehow, had got wind of what was afloat, appeared on the scene, called them both d—d fools, and by his arguments, addressed to their common sense, and by his ridicule of the figure that they, two well-grown, bearded men, were making there, each with a frog-sticker in his hand, broke up the fight.   We do not know how Gen. Shields feels, but we have heard of Lincoln's saying, that the acceptance of the challenge was the meanest thing he ever did in his life.   Hardin—than whom a braver man never stood—never came out of that terrible charge at Buena Vista, to which he led the Second Regiment of Illinois Volunteers.   If the events of his life passed in quick review before his mind, as he lay wounded and dying in that fatal ravine, we doubt not this act of his, by which he prevented two really brave men from engaging in fatal strife, was not the least of the consolations of that bitter hour."

" While the late Illinois State Republican Convention was in session, the Hon. Abraham Lincoln stepped in to witness the proceedings. His appearance was greeted with the utmost enthusiasm. He had hardly taken his seat when Mr. Oglesby of Decatur announced to the delegates that an old Democrat of Macon county, who had grown gray in the service of that party desired to make a contribution to the Convention, and the offer being accepted, forthwith two old-time fence rails, decorated with flags and streamers, were borne through the crowd into the Convention, bearing the inscription :

ABRAHAM LINCOLN,

The Rail Candidate

FOR PRESIDENT IN 1860.

Two rails from a lot of 3,000 made in 1830, by Thos. Hanks and Abe Lincoln —whose father was the first pioneer of Macon County.

" The effect was electrical. One spontaneous burst of applause went up from all parts of the ' wigwam,' which grew more and more deafening as it was prolonged, and which did not wholly subside for ten or fifteen minutes after. The cheers upon cheers which rent the air could have been heard all over the adjacent country. Of course ' Old Abe' was called out, and made an explanation of the matter. He stated that, some thirty years ago, then just emigrating to the State, he stopped with his mother's family, for one season, in what is now Macon county ; that he built a cabin, *split rails,* and cultivated a small farm down on the Sangamon river, some six or eight miles from

Decatur. These, he was informed, were taken from
that fence ; but, whether they were or not, he had
mauled many and many better ones since he had grown
to manhood. ·The cheers were renewed 'with the same
vigor when he concluded his remarks."

A Western Republican relates the following thrilling
episode in the life of Mr. Lincoln : " Mr. Lincoln, or
' Old Abe,' as his friends familiarly call him, is a self-
made man. A Kentuckian by birth, he emigrated to
Illinois in his boyhood, where he earned his living at
the anvil, devoting his leisure hours to study. Having
chosen the law as his future calling, he devoted himself
assiduously to its mastery, contending at every step
with adverse fortune. During this period of study, he
for some time found a home under the hospitable roof
of one Armstrong, a farmer, who lived in a log-house
some eight miles from the village of Petersburg, Menard county. Here, clad in homespun, with elbows
out, and knees covered with patches, young Lincoln
would master his lessons by the firelight of the cabin,
and then walk to town for the purpose of recitation.
This man Armstrong was himself poor, but he saw the
genius struggling in the young student, and opened to
him his rude home, and bid him welcome to his coarse
fare. How Lincoln graduated with promise, how he
has more than fulfilled that promise, how honorably he
acquitted himself alike on the battle-field, in defending·
our border settlements against the ravages of the savage
foes, and in the halls of our national legislature, are
matters of history, and need no repetition here. But
one little incident of a more private nature, standing
as it does as a sort of sequel to some things already

alluded to, I deem worthy of record. Some few years
since the oldest son of Mr. Lincoln's old friend Armstrong, the chief support of his widowed mother—the
good old man having some time previously passed from
earth—was arrested on the charge of murder. A young
man had been killed during a riotous melee, in the
night-time, at a camp-meeting, and one of his associates stated that the death-wound was inflicted by
young Armstrong. A preliminary examination was
gone into, at which the accuser testified so positively
that there seemed no doubt of the guilt of the prisoner,
and, therefore, he was held for trial. As is too often
the case, the bloody act caused an undue degree of excitement in the public mind. Every improper incident
in the life of the prisoner—each act which bore the
least semblance to rowdyism—each school-boy quarrel
—was suddenly remembered and magnified, until they
pictured him as a fiend of the most horrid hue. As
these rumors spread abroad, they were received as
gospel truth, and a feverish desire for vengeance seized
upon the infatuated populace, while only prison-bars
prevented a horrible death at the hands of a mob.
The events were heralded in the county papers, painted
in the highest colors, accompanied by rejoicings over
the certainty of punishment being meted out to the
guilty party. The prisoner, overwhelmed by the
circumstances under which he found himself placed,
fell into a melancholy condition, bordering upon de-
spair ; and the widowed mother, looking through her
tears, saw no cause for hope from earthly aid.

    " At this juncture, the widow received a letter from
Mr. Lincoln, volunteering his services in an effort to

save the youth from the impending stroke. Gladly was
his aid accepted, although it seemed impossible for
even his sagacity to prevail in such a desperate case ;
but the heart of the attorney was in his work, and he
set about it with a will that knew no such word as fail.
Feeling that the poisoned condition of the public mind
was such as to preclude the possibility of impanelling
an impartial jury in the court having jurisdiction, he
procured a change of venue, and a postponement of the
trial. He then went studiously to work unravelling the
history of the case, and satisfied himself that his client
was the victim of malice, and that the statement of
the accuser was a tissue of falsehoods.

" When the trial was called on, the prisoner, pale and
emaciated, with hopelessness written on every feature,
and accompanied by his half-hoping, half-despairing
mother—whose only hope was a mother's belief of her
son's innocence, in the justice of the God she worship-
ped, and in the noble counsel, who, without hope of fee
or reward upon earth, had undertaken the cause—took
his seat in the prisoner's box, and with a ' stony firmness' listened to the reading of the indictment. Lincoln sat quietly by, while the large auditory looked on
him as though wondering what he could say in defence
of one whose guilt they regarded as certain. The examination of witnesses for the State was begun, and a
well-arranged mass of evidence, circumstantial and positive, was introduced, which seemed to impale the prisoner beyond the possibility of extrication. The counsel for the defence propounded but few questions, and
those of a character which excited no uneasiness on the
part of the prosecutor—merely, in most cases, requir-

ing the main witness to be definite as to time and place.
When the evidence of the prosecution was ended, Lincoln introduced a few witnesses to remove some erroneous impressions in regard to the previous character of
his client, who, though somewhat rowdyish, had never
been known to commit a vicious act ; and to show that
a greater degree of ill-feeling existed between the accuser and accused than the accused and the deceased.
The prosecutor felt that the case was a clear one, and
his opening speech was brief and formal.   Lincoln
arose, while a deathly silence pervaded the vast audience, and in a clear but moderate tone began his argument.   Slowly and carefully he reviewed the testimony,
pointing out the hitherto unobserved decrepancies in
the statements of the principal witness.   That which
had seemed plain and plausible, he made to appear
crooked as a serpent's path.   The witness had stated
that the affair took place at a certain hour in the evening, and that, by the aid of the brightly shining moon,
he saw the prisoner inflict the death blow with a slung-
shot.   Mr. Lincoln showed that at the hour referred to,
the moon had not yet appeared above the horizon, and
consequently the whole tale was a fabrication.   An almost instantaneous change seemed to have been wrought
in the minds of his auditors, and the verdict of ' not
guilty' was at the end of every tongue.   But the advocate was not content with this intellectual achievement.
His whole being had for months been bound up in this
work of gratitude and mercy, and, as the lava of the
overcharged crater bursts from its imprisonment, so
great thoughts and burning words leaped forth from
the soul of the eloquent Lincoln.   He drew a picture

of the perjurer so horrid and ghastly that the accuser
could sit under it no longer, but reeled and staggered
from the court-room, while the audience fancied they
could see the brand upon his brow. Then in words of
thrilling pathos, Lincoln appealed to the jurors as fathers of sons who might become fatherless, and as husbands of wives who might be widowed, to yield to no
previous impressions, no ill-founded prejudice, but to
do his client justice ; and as he alluded to the debt of
gratitude which he owed to the boy's sire, tears were
seen to fall from many eyes unused to weep. It was
near night when he concluded by saying that, if justice
were done—as he believed it would be—before the sun
should set, it would shine upon his client a free man.
The jury retired, and the court adjourned for the day.
Half an hour had not elapsed, when, as the officers of
the court and the volunteer attorney sat at the tea-ta-
ble of their hotel, a messenger announced that the jury
had returned to their seats. All repaired immediately
to the court-house, and while the prisoner was being
brought from the jail, the court-room was filled to
overflowing with citizens of the town. When the prisoner and his mother entered, silence reigned as completely as though the house was empty. The foreman
of the jury, in answer to the usual inquiry of the
court, delivered the verdict of ' Not Guilty !' The
widow dropped into the arms of her son, who lifted her
up, and told her to look upon him as before—free and
innocent. Then, with the words, ' Where is Mr. Lincoln ?' he rushed across the room and grasped the hand
of his deliverer, while his heart was too full for utterance. Lincoln turned his eyes toward the West, where

the sun still lingered in view, and then, turning to the youth, said, 'It is not yet sundown, and you are free.' I confess that my cheeks were not wholly unwet by tears, and I turned from the affecting scene. As I cast a glance behind, I saw Abraham Lincoln obeying the divine injunction by comforting the widowed and the fatherless."

In May, 1859, Mr. Lincoln wrote the subjoined letter to a German citizen of Illinois. The letter speaks for itself, and needs no comment :

"SPRINGFIELD, *May* 17, 1859.

" *Dear Sir*—Your letter, in which you inquire, on your own account and in behalf of certain other German citizens, whether I approve or oppose the constitutional provision in relation to naturalized citizens which was lately enacted in Massachusetts, and whether I favor or oppose a fusion of the Republicans with the other Opposition elements in the campaign of 1860, has been received.

" Massachusetts is a sovereign and independent State, and I have no right to advise her in her policy. Yet, if any one is desirous to draw a conclusion as to what I would do from what she has done, I may speak without impropriety. I say, then, that so far as I understand the Massachusetts provision, I am against its adoption, not only in Illinois, but in every other place in which I have the right to oppose it. As I understand the spirit of our institutions, it is designed to promote the *elevation* of men. I am, therefore, hostile to anything that tends to their debasement. It is well known that I deplore the oppressed condition of the blacks, and it would, therefore, be very inconsistent for me to look with approval upon any measure that infringes upon the inalienable rights of white men, whether or not they are born in another land or speak a different language from our own.

" In respect to a fusion, I am in favor of it whenever it can be effected on Republican principles, but upon *no other condition.* A fusion upon any other platform would be as insane as unprincipled. It would thereby lose the whole North, while the common enemy would still have the support of the entire South. The question in relation to men is different. There are good and patriotic men and able statesmen in the South whom I would willingly support if they would place themselves on Republican ground ; but I shall oppose the lowering of the Republican standard even by a *hair's-breadth.*

" I have written in haste, but I believe I have answered your questions substantially.

" Respectfully, yours,
" ABRAHAM LINCOLN.

"DR. THEODOR CANISIUS."

" We have heard," says the *The Evansville* (Ind.) *Journal,* " the following anecdote related of the people's candidate for the Presidency, which shows the love of knowledge, the industry, the conscientiousness. and the integrity of the subject of this sketch :

"It is well known that he lived in Spencer county, above here in Indiana, in his young days. He was a hard-working lad, and very eager in his thirst for knowledge. A man, named Crawford, owned a copy of *Weems's Life of Washington*—the only one in the whole neighborhood. Young Lincoln borrowed that interesting book (not having money to spare to buy one), and while reading it, by a slight negligence, left it in a window, when a rain-storm came up and wet the book so as to ruin it. Young Lincoln felt badly, but, like an honest boy, he went to Mr. Crawford with the ruined book, acknowledged his accountability for its destruction, and his willingness to make due compensation. He said he had no money, but would work out the value of the book.

" The owner of the book said to him, 'Well, Abe, being as it's you, I won't be hard on you. If you will come over and pull fodder for two days, I'll let you off.'

" Abe went over accordingly, and pulled fodder the requisite time ; and so tall and handy a lad was he, that Crawford required him to pull the fodder off of the tallest stalks, while he took the shortest ones himself."

PART FOURTH.

THE CONVENTION AND ITS NOMINATIONS.

ON the sixteenth day of May the Republican National Convention met at Chicago in a large building put up for the purpose and called the " Wigwam." The doors were opened at 11 o'clock.

Long before that hour the concourse of people assembled around the doors numbered many thousands more than could gain admittance to the building. As soon as the doors were opened the entire body of the Wigwam was solidly packed with men. The seats in the galleries were equally closely packed with ladies. The interior of the hall was handsomely decorated with evergreen, statuary, and flowers, and presented a striking appearance. There were not less than ten thousand persons in the building, while the open doors displayed to view crowds in the streets unable to obtain more than a glimpse inside of the hall.

At 12 o'clock the Convention was called to order by Gov. Morgan of New-York, Chairman of the National Committee, who named the honorable DAVID WILMOT of Pennsylvania for temporary President.

The Chair named Judge Marshall of Md., and Gov. Cleveland of Conn., to conduct Mr. Wilmot to his seat. Judge Marshall introduced Mr. Wilmot as the man who dared to do right regardless of consequences. With such a man, he said, there is no such word as fail.

Mr. WILMOT addressed the Convention briefly, returning thanks for the high and undeserved honor. He would carry the remembrance of it with him to the day of his death. It was unnecessary for him to remind the Convention of the high duty devolved upon them. A great sectional interest had for years dominated with a high hand over the affairs of the country. It had bent all its energy to the extension and naturalization of slavery. It is the mission of the Republican party to oppose this policy, and restore to the government the policy of the Revolutionary fathers ; to resist the dogma that slavery exists wherever the Constitution extends ; to read the Constitution as our fathers read it. That Constitution was not ordained to embrace slavery within all the limits of the country. They lived and died in the faith that slavery was a blot, and would soon be washed out. Had they deemed that the Revolution was to establish a great slave empire, not one would have drawn the sword in such a cause. The battle was fought to establish freedom. Slavery is sectional—freedom is national. [Applause.] He deemed it unnecessary to remind the delegates of the outrages and usurpations of the Democratic party.

Those outrages will not be confined to the limits of the slave States if the South have the power, and the safety of the free States requires the Republicans should take the government, and administer it as it has been administered by Washington, Jefferson, and Jackson—even down to Van Buren and Polk—before these new dogmas were engrafted in the Democratic policy. He assumed his duties, exhorting a spirit of harmony to control the action of the delegates.

Committees on business and credentials were appointed. In the afternoon session, the Committee on Organization reported the name of George Ashmun, of Massachusetts, for President, and Vice-Presidents and Secretaries from every State represented in the Convention. The subjoined Committee on Resolutions was appointed :

Maine...........George Talbot.	Iowa...........·John A. Kasson.
New-Hampshire....Amos Tuck.	Minnesota.......Stephen Miller.
Vermont..........E. M. Briggs.	Delaware.......N. D. Smithers.
Massachusetts...G. S. Boutwell.	Maryland...........F. P. Blair.
Rhode Island......B. T. Earner.	Virginia........Alfred Caldwell.
Connecticut......S. W. Kellogg.	Kentucky.....George T. Blakely.
New-York.....Henry K. Selden.	Michigan..........Austin Blair.
New-Jersey..Thomas S. Dudley.	Missouri.....Charles M. Bernais.
Pennsylvania....William Jessup.	California.........·...F. P. Tracy.
Ohio..............J. H. Barrett.	Texas...............J. Strauss.
Indiana........William T. Otto.	District of Columbia..G. A. Hall.
Illinois........Gustavus Koeler.	Nebraska........A. S. Bradlock.
Wisconsin..........Carl Schurz.	Kansas.....J. F. Hatterscheidt

On Thursday morning the Convention met at ten o'clock. The greatest enthusiasm was manifested, both inside and outside of the " Wigwam." The entire day was consumed in the consideration of the proper rules to be adopted for the government of the Convention, and in discussing the resolutions reported from the Committee. It was agreed that *a majority* should nominate the candidates. The following resolutions were adopted by the Convention as

THE PLATFORM OF THE REPUBLICAN PARTY.

" *Resolved*, That we, the delegated representatives of the Republican electors of the United States, in Convention assembled, in the discharge of the duty we owe to our constituents and our country, unite in the following declarations :

"*First :* That the history of the nation during the last four years has fully established the propriety and necessity of the organization and perpetuation of the Repablican party, and that the causes which called it into existence are permanent in their nature, and now, more than ever before, demand its peaceful and constitutional triumph.

"*Second :* That the maintenance of the principles promulgated in the Declaration of Independence, and embodied in the Federal Constitution, is essential to the preservation of our republican institutions ; that the Federal Constitution, the rights of the States, and the Union of the States, must and shall be preserved ; and that we reassert ' these truths to be self-evident, that all men are created equal ; that they are endowed by their Creator with certain inalienable rights ; that among these are life, liberty, and the pursuit of happiness. That to secure these rights, governments are instituted among men, deriving their just powers from the consent of the governed.'

"*Third :* That to the Union of the States this nation owes its unprecedented increase in population ; its surprising development of material resources ; its rapid augmentation of wealth ; its happiness at home, and its honor abroad ; and we hold in abhorrence all schemes for disunion, come from whatever source they may ; and we congratulate the country that no Republican member of Congress has uttered or countenanced a threat of disunion, so often made by Democratic members of Congress without rebuke, and with applause from their political associates ; and we denounce those threats of disunion, in case of a popular overthrow of their ascendency, as denying the vital principles of a free government, and as an avowal of contemplated treason, which it is the imperative duty of an indignant people strongly to rebuke and forever silence.

6

Fourth : That the maintenance inviolate of the rights of the States, and especially the right of each State to order and control its own domestic institutions, according to its own judgment exclusively, is essential to that balance of power on which the perfection and endurance of our political faith depends, and we denounce the lawless invasion by armed force of any State or Territory, no matter under what pretext, as among the gravest of crimes.

" *Fifth :* That the present Democratic administration has far exceeded our worst apprehensions in its measureless subserviency to the exactions of a sectional interest, as is especially evident in its desperate exertions to force the infamous Lecompton Constitution upon the protesting people of Kansas—in construing the personal relation between master and servant to involve an unqualified property in persons—in its attempted enforcement everywhere, on land and sea, through the intervention of Congress and the Federal Courts, of the extreme pretensions of a purely local interest, and in its general and unvarying abuse of the power intrusted to it by a confiding people.

" *Sixth :* That the people justly view with alarm the reckless extravagance which pervades every department of the federal government; that a return to rigid economy and accountability is indispensable to arrest the system of plunder of the public treasury by favored partisans ; while the recent startling developments of fraud and corruption at the federal metropolis, show that an entire change of administration is imperatively demanded.

" *Seventh :* That the new dogma that the Constitution, of its own force, carries slavery into any or all the territories of the United States, is a dangerous political heresy, at variance with the explicit provisions of that instrument itself, with cotemporaneous expositions, and with legislative and judicial precedent, is revolutionary in its tendency, and subversive of the peace and harmony of the country.

"*Eighth :* That the normal condition of all the territory of the United States is that of freedom ; that as our republican fathers, when they had abolished slavery in all our national territory, ordained that no person should be deprived of life, liberty, or property, without the process of law, it becomes our duty, by legislation, whenever such legislation is necessary, to maintain this provision of the Constitution against all attempts to violate it ; and we deny the authority of Congress, of a territorial legislature, or of any individuals, to give legal existence to slavery in any territory of the United States.

"*Ninth :* That we brand the recent re-opening of the African slave-trade, under the cover of our national flag, aided by perversions of judicial power, as a crime against humanity, a burning shame to our country and age ; and we call upon Congress to take prompt and efficient measures for the total and final suppression of that execrable traffic.

"*Tenth :* That in the recent vetoes by their federal governors, of the acts of the legislatures of Kansas and Nebraska, prohibiting slavery in those territories, we find a practical illustration of the boasted democratic principle of non-intervention and Popular Sovereignty, embodied in the Kansas and Nebraska bill, and a denunciation of the deception and fraud involved therein.

"*Eleventh :* That Kansas should of right be immediately admitted as a State, under the constitution recently formed and adopted by her people, and accepted by the House of Representatives.

"*Twelfth :* That while providing revenue for the support of the general government by duties upon imposts, sound policy requires such an adjustment of these imposts as to encourage the development of the industrial interest of the whole country, and we commend that policy of national exchanges which secures to the working man liberal wages, to agriculture remunerating prices, to mechanics and manufacturers an adequate reward for their skill, labor, and enterprise, and to the nation commercial prosperity and independence.

"*Thirteenth :* That we protest against any sale or alienation to others of the public lands held by actual settlers, and against any view of the free homestead policy which regards the settlers as paupers or supplicants for public bounty ; and we demand the passage by Congress of the complete and satisfactory homestead measure which has already passed the House.

"*Fourteenth :* That the Republican party is opposed to any change in our naturalization laws, or any State legislation by which the rights of citizenship hitherto accorded to immigrants from foreign lands shall be abridged or impaired ; and in favor of giving a full and efficient protection to the rights of all classes of citizens, whether native or naturalized, both at home and abroad.

"*Fifteenth :* That appropriations by Congress for river and harbor improvements, of a national character, required for the accommodation and security of an existing commerce, are authorized by the Constitution and justified by an obligation of the government to protect the lives and property of its citizens.

" *Sixteenth :* That a railroad to the Pacific Ocean is imperatively demanded by the interests of the whole country ; that the federal government ought to render immediate and efficient aid in its construction, and that, as preliminary thereto, a daily overland mail should be promptly established.

" *Seventeenth :* Finally, having thus set forth our distinctive principles and views, we invite the co-operation of all citizens, however differing on other questions, who substantially agree with us in their affirmance and support."

A scene of the wildest excitement followed the adoption of the platform, the immense multitude rising and giving round after round of applause ; ten thousand voices swelled into a roar so deafening that, for several minutes, every attompt to restore order was hopelessly vain. The multitude outside took up and re-echoed the cheers, making the scene of enthusiasm and excitement unparalleled in any similar gathering.

On Friday morning the wigwam was closely packed for a full hour before the Convention assembled. The interest in the proceedings appeared on the increase as the time for balloting approached. A crowd, numbered by thousands, had been outside the building since nine o'clock, anxiously awaiting intelligence from the inside. Arrangements had been made for passing the result of the ballots up from the platform to the roof of the building, and through the skylight, men being stationed above to convey speedily the intelligence to the multitude in the streets.

A large procession was formed by the various delegations, to march to the hall, preceded by bands of music.

As the delegates entered on the platform the several distinguished men were greeted with rounds of applause by the audience.

The Convention then voted to proceed to ballot for a candidate for President of the United States.

Wm. M. Evarts, of New-York, did not rise for the purpose of making a speech, but only to ask if at this time it is in order to put candidates in nomination.

The President : The Chair considers it in order to name candidates without debate.

Wm. M. Evarts rose and said—I beg leave to offer the name of Wm. H. Seward as a candidate before this Convention, for the nomination of President of the United States.

This nomination was received with loud and long-continued applause.

Mr. Judd, of Illinois, rose and said : Mr. President, I beg leave to offer, as a candidate before this Convention for President of the United States, the name of Abraham Lincoln, of Illinois.

The crowded audience greeted this nomination with perfectly deafening applause, the shouts swelling into a perfect roar, and being continued for several minutes, the wildest excitement and enthusiasm prevailing.

Mr. Dudley, of New-Jersey, presented the name of Wm. L. Dayton.

Gov. Reeder, of Pennsylvania : The State of Pennsylvania desires to present, as her candidate, the name of Simon Cameron.

Mr. Carter, of Ohio, put forward the name of Salmon P. Chase, of Ohio.

Mr. Smith of Maryland—I am instructed by the State of Indiana to second the nomination of Abraham Lincoln. [Another outburst of enthusiastic applause from the body of the Hall, mingled with some hisses.]

Francis P. Blair of Missouri nominated Edward Bates of Missouri.

Mr. Blair of Michigan said, on the part of Michigan, I desire to say that the Republicans of that State second the nomination of William H. Seward for the Presidency.

Tremendous applause followed this speech, thousands of those present rising and waving their hats and handkerchiefs, and swelling the applause to a thundering roar through several minutes.

Tom Corwin of Ohio nominated John McLean of Ohio for the Presidency. [Loud applause.]

Carl Schurz of Wisconsin, on the part of his State, here rose and seconded the nomination of William H. Seward.

Upon this another scene of the greatest enthusiasm and tumultuous excitement ensued.

Mr. North of Minnesota also seconded, on the part of Minnesota, the nomination of Mr. Seward. [Tremendous applause.]

Mr. Wilson of Kansas—The delegates and people of Kansas second the nomination. [Renewed cheers.]

Mr. Delano of Ohio, on the part of a large number of people of Ohio—I desire to second the nomination of the man who can split rails and maul Democrats, Abraham Lincoln. [Rounds of applause by Lincoln men.]

A delegate from Iowa also seconded the nomination of Mr. Lincoln, on the part of that State, amidst renewed applause and excitement.

A Voice—Abe Lincoln has it by the sound now. Let us ballot.

Judge Logan of Illinois—Mr. President, in order or out of order, I propose this Convention and audience give three cheers for the man who is evidently their nominee.

The President—If the Convention will get over this irrepressible excitement, the roll will be called.

After some further excitement the calling of the roll commenced, the applause at the different announcements being with difficulty checked.

When Maryland was called, the Chairman of the

delegation cast the vote of the State for Bates, two delegates claiming their right to individual votes.

After some discussion the Convention rejected the votes as cast by the Chairman, and received the votes of the delegates separately.

On the first ballot Mr. Seward received 173½ votes ; Mr. Lincoln, 102 ; and Mr. Bates, 48. The balance were divided between Messrs. Cameron, Chase, McLean, Wade, etc., etc. The States voting for Mr. Lincoln, were Illinois, Indiana, and, *in part*, Maine, New-Hampshire, Massachusetts, Connecticut, Pennsylvania, Virginia, Kentucky, Ohio, and Iowa.

The second ballot was then taken.

Mr. Cameron's name was withdrawn.

For Mr. Lincoln.

New-Hampshire	9	Delaware	6
Vermont	10	Kentucky	9
Rhode Island	3	Ohio	14
Pennsylvania	48	Iowa	5

The whole vote for Lincoln was 181.

For Mr. Seward.

Massachusetts	22	Kentucky	7
New-Jersey	4	Texas	6
Pennsylvania	2½	Nebraska	8

The whole vote for Mr. Seward was 184½.

Bates	35	Cameron	2
McLean	8	Dayton	10
Chase	42½	C. M. Clay	2

The third ballot was taken amid excitement, and cries for " the ballot." Intense feeling existed during the ballot, each vote being awarded in breathless silence and expectancy.

For Mr. Lincoln.

Massachusetts............ 8	Maryland.............. 9
Rhode Island. 5	Kentucky............... 13
New-Jersey............. 8	Ohio (applause) 29
Pennsylvania 52	Oregon................14

This gave Lincoln 230½ votes, or within 1½ of a nomination.

Mr. Andrew of Massachusetts then rose and corrected the vote of Massachusetts, by changing four votes, and giving them to Lincoln, thus nominating him by 2½ majority.

The Convention immediately became wildly excited.

A large portion of the delegates, who had kept tally, at once said the struggle was decided, and half the Convention rose, cheering, shouting, and waving hats.

The audience took up the cheers, and the confusion became deafening.

State after State rose, striving to change their votes to the winning candidate, but the noise and enthusiasm rendered it impossible for the delegates to make themselves heard.

Mr. McCrillis of Maine, making himself heard, said that the young giant of the West is now of age. Maine now casts for him her 16 votes.

Mr. Andrew of Massachusetts changed the vote of that State, giving 18 to Mr. Lincoln and 8 to Mr. Seward.

Intelligence of the nomination was now conveyed to the men on the roof of the building, who immediately made the outside multitude aware of the result. The first roar of the cannon soon mingled itself with the cheers of the people, and the same moment a man

6*

appeared in the hall bringing a large painting of Mr. Lincoln. The scene at the time beggars description ; 11,000 people inside, and 20,000 or 25,000 outside, were yelling and shouting at once. Two cannon sent forth roar after roar in quick succession. Delegates bore up the sticks and boards bearing the names of the several States, and waved them aloft over their heads, and the vast multitude before the platform were waving hats and handkerchiefs. The whole scene was one of the wildest enthusiasm.

Mr. Brown, of Mo., desired to change 18 votes of Missouri for the gallant son of the West, Abraham Lincoln ; Iowa, Connecticut, Kentucky, and Minnesota, also changed their votes. The result of the third ballot was announced :

Whole number of votes cast.......................... 466
Necessary to a choice............. 234

Mr. Abraham Lincoln received 354, and was declared duly nominated.

The States still voting for Seward were Massachusetts, 8 ; New-York, 70 ; New-Jersey, 5 ; Pennsylvania, ½ ; Maryland, 2 ; Michigan, 12 ; Wisconsin, 10 ; California, 3—total, 110½.

Mr. Dayton received one vote from New-Jersey, and Mr. McLean half a vote from Pennsylvania.

The result was received with renewed applause.

When silence was restored, Wm. M. Evarts came forward on the Secretary's table, and spoke as follows:

"*Mr. Chairman, Gentlemen of the National Convention :*—The State of New-York, by a full delegation, with complete unanimity in purpose at home, came to the Convention and presented its choice, one of its citizens, who had served the State from boyhood up, and labored for and loved it. We came here, a great State, with, as 'we thought, a great statesman (applause), and our love of the great Republic, from which we are all delegates. The great Republic of the American Union, and our love for the great Republican party of the Union, and our love for our statesman and candidate, made us think we did our duty to the country, and the whole country, in expressing our preference and love for him. (Applause.) But, gentlemen, it was from Governor Seward that most of us learned to love Republican principles and the Republican party. (Cheers.) His fidelity to the country, the Constitution, and the laws—his fidelity to the party and the principle that majorities govern—his interest in the advancement of our party to its victory, that our country may rise to its true glory, induces me to declare that I speak his sentiments, as I do the united opinion of our delegation, when I move, sir, as I do now, that the nomination of Abraham Lincoln, of Illinois, as the Republican candidate for the suffrages of the whole country for the office of Chief Magistrate of the American Union, be made unanimous." (Applause, and three cheers for New-York.)

The life-size portrait of Abraham Lincoln was here exhibited from the platform, amid renewed cheers.

Mr. Andrews, of Massachusetts, on the part of the united delegation of that State, seconded the motion of the gentleman of New-York, that the nomination be made unanimous.

Eloquent speeches, endorsing the nominee, were also made by Carl Schurz, F. P. Blair, of Missouri, and

Mr. Browning, of Illinois, all of which breathed a spirit of confidence and enthusiasm.

At the close, three hearty cheers 'were given for New-York, and the nomination of Mr. Lincoln made unanimous.

With loud cheers for Lincoln, the Convention adjourned till five o'clock.

On the first ballot, in the evening session, Mr. Hamlin, of Maine, received 194 votes for the Vice-Presidency, and was nominated with enthusiasm.

THE RATIFICATION BY THE PEOPLE.

Everywhere, throughout the land, in New-York as well as Illinois, in Pennsylvania as well as Indiana, *everywhere*, the voice of the people has gone up in shouts of joy over the nomination of Lincoln and Hamlin. Even from Albany, where the friends of Mr. Seward were so strong, comes a despatch like the following, dated the night of the day on which the nominations were made :

" *Nine o'clock, p. m.*—The Republicans of this city are now fairly waked up, and the wildest excitement prevails in regard to the nomination of Lincoln. State street is a perfect sea of fire from burning tar barrels. The whole heavens are illuminated with a red glare, cannon is firing, music is playing, and the people are shouting on State street and Broadway. Both streets are literally jammed with men of all parties, who are earnestly discussing the action of the Convention.

" The Republicans of the city are now more reconciled to the nomination, and unite in hearty approval of it. They consider that while Lincoln may not be as strong in the State as Seward, he will be less objectionable throughout the Union.

" Since the reception of the successful laying of the Atlantic cable, no more animated scene has ever been witnessed in this city than has been seen this evening.

" In New-York two six-pounders were brought to the Park, and fired each a hundred times—one of them by order of the Republican General Committee, and the other under the patronage of private citizens. Besides these the Central Committee ordered one hundred guns to be fired in Madison and Hamilton squares respectively. In Mount Morris square, also, the big gun was brought out, and a hundred rounds announced to the citizens the nomination of Lincoln and Hamlin. Great numbers of enthusiastic Republicans gathered in the square, and the excitement was intense."

In Philadelphia : " The Republicans opened their campaign by an immense mass meeting in Independence Square. JOHN B. MYERS, Esq. presided at the main stand, and three other meetings were organized—two at opposite angles of the square and one within the State-House. The meeting having been called to ratify the nominations made by the Chicago Convention, this was done in a series of resolutions highly eulogistic of the candidates and approving and adopting the platform on which they have been placed. Speeches were delivered by Mr. Senator TRUMBULL, of Illinois ; CHARLES R. TRAIN, of Massachusetts ; Wm. M. DUNN, of Indiana ; ORRIS S. FERRY, of Connecticut ; JAMES H. CAMPBELL, of Pennsylvania ; JOHN SHERMAN, of Ohio ; G. A. GROW, of Pennsylvania ; JUSTIN S. MORRIL, of Vermont ; M. S. WILKINSON, of Minnesota ; and other distinguished gentlemen. The assemblage, in the display of numbers and enthusiasm, has rarely if ever been surpassed. Ward processions marched to the square with bands of music, fireworks, transparencies, rails, etc. ; and when the series of meetings concluded, at about half-past ten o'clock, the multitude then proceeded to the Continental hotel in compliment to the distinguished speakers.

In a speech at a Republican ratification meeting at Harrisburg, Senator Cameron, while declaring that he had hoped for the nomination of Mr. Seward, described Mr. Lincoln as "a candidate less known in public life, perhaps, but who, on all occasions, when demands have been made upon his zeal and patriotism, has borne himself bravely and honorably. In regard to the great interests of Pennsylvania, the subject of protection to labor, his record is clear, emphatic, and beyond suspicion. He will require no endorsement to convince the people of Pennsylvania that their interests will be perfectly secure in his hands. Himself a laborer in early life, he has struggled with adversity until he has reached the proud position he now occupies, by the single aid of a strong purpose, seconded by an unyielding will ; and it is not in the hearts of Pennsylvanians to doubt such a man. The laboring men of this State ever control the ballot-box when they arise in the majesty of their strength. Let them go to the election next autumn, and, while they are securing their own interests, let them elevate to the highest place in their election gift, Abraham Lincoln, a workingman like themselves."

At Washington, D. C., an enthusiastic ratification meeting was held—the first time such a meeting has been held in that city.

The public press was never before so unanimous in its commendation of a candidate.

The N. Y. *Tribune* says :

" While Mr. Lincoln's position as a Republican renders him satisfactory to the most zealous member of the party, the moderation of his character, and the conservative tendencies of his mind, long improved and well known of all men in public life, commend him to every section of the opposition. There is no good reason why Americans and Whigs, and in short all who are inspired rather by patriotism than by party feeling, should not rally to his support. Republicans and conservatives, those who dread the extension of Slavery, and those who dread the progress of administrative and legislative corruption, may be assured that in him both these evils will find a stern and immovable antagonist and an impassable barrier. At the same time, as a man of the people, raised by his own genius and integrity from the humblest to the highest position, having made for himself an honored name as a lawyer, an advocate, a popular orator, a statesman, and a man, the industrious and intelligent masses of the country may well hail his nomination with a swelling tide of enthusiasm, of which the wild and prolonged outbursts at Chicago yesterday are the fitting prelude and beginning.

We need hardly say that the election of Mr. Lincoln, though it cannot be accomplished without arduous and persistent efforts, is eminently a *thing that can be done.* The disruption of the Democratic Party, now perhaps less likely to be repaired than before his nomination, the fact that he was put forward by one of the doubtful States, Illinois, and nominated in great measure by votes from two others, namely Pennsylvania and New-Jersey, the universal desire of the country to settle the vexatious Slavery question in accordance with the views of the fathers—all these are powerful in behalf of the Chicago ticket."

The Springfield, Mass., *Republican* :

"In ways, which it is useless to mention now, we are, of course, disappointed ; in ways, which we shall have frequent occasion to mention between this date and November, we are glad and grateful. The nominee is a positive man—a live man—and in these respects matches well with the platform, which is bold, manly, and comprehensive. The many friends of Mr. Seward, particularly, will féel aggrieved by this result, but it could not have been otherwise. The States which must be carried to secure a Republican triumph did not dare to assume Mr. Seward, and the forcing upon them of a name that would weaken them, and develop opposition—organized and consolidated—would have been neither wise nor fair. We predict for the ticket a popularity that will grow, as the campaign advances, into a furor of enthusiasm. We predict, furthermore, that it will be elected."

The Boston *Atlas :*

" As in 1840 and 1848, the Whig party passed by the prominent names before the Conventions at the outset, and as in 1844 and in 1852 the Democratic party did the same thing, and elected men who were not the most prominently before the people, the Republicans have in this instance taken up men fresh from the people, of broad and statesmanlike qualities, of unquestioned abilities, and of tried patriotism, in what is to be to them a great, and, as we confidently believe, a triumphantly successful campaign. In a nomination of this nature, there must have been necessarily many preferences from people of different sections, some of which were to be set aside. Mr. Seward, Mr. Chase, Mr. Cameron, Mr. Banks, Mr. Bates, and Mr. McLean, all have friends presented their names for the first or second place on the ticket. For ourselves, we might have had personal preferences equally strong with others. But at a time like this, personal preferences are to be subordinated to the will of the majority, as expressed

in the Convention, as to the success of the ticket as indicated by the judgment of that body."

The N. Y. *Evening Post :*

" Our country is not, however, distinguished alone for
its stupendous physical progress, for those grand triumphs over nature which have sprinkled the whole continent with cities, and connected its remotest parts by
railroads and telegraphs. It has also worked out for itself a peculiar social and political constitution. Placing, for the first time in the history of mankind, the
controlling power of government in the hands of the
whole people, it has constructed a vast fabric of society on that new basis. It has said to all ranks and or-
ders of men, here you are free ; here you are equal in
rights to each other ; here the careers of life are open
to every comer ; men are thrown upon their own
intrinsic manhood for their reliance, and it belongs to
each one to become the architect of his own fortunes.
This unlimited freedom of action, though it has produced some social evils, has produced much greater
good, and we do not believe that there is a nation on
the globe in which the masses of the people are so
prosperous, so intelligent, and so contented as they are
in this nation. What more striking illustration of its
effects could we have, than the rise of Mr. Lincoln to
his present importance in the eyes of the world ? Is
he not pre-eminently the child of our free institutions ?
A poor orphan, without education or friends, by the
labor of his hands, by the energy of his will, by the
manliness and probity of his character, he raises himself to fortune and fame ; a powerful party, which
contains, to say the least, as much virtue and intelligence as any other, assigns him, without intrigues or
efforts of his own, the first place in its regards, making
him the bearer of its standard in a momentous political conflict ; and in a few months more we may see the
once friendless boy the occupant of the Presidential

chair. Thus the spirit of our institutions is strikingly
embodied in his career, which is itself an admirable
commentary on their excellence."

And the conservative Philadelphia *North American :*

" The people of Pennsylvania are eminently practical in all their views and actions. We are not hasty
nor inconsiderate. We take time to reflect and generally act intelligently. It has been so in this case.
Our State entered into the canvass at Chicago with
a spirit, a determination, and an indomitable energy
which completely surprised the gentlemen from the extreme North, and served us a rallying point for all the
moderates. The Pennsylvania delegation was generally accredited with the selfish purpose of going to Chicago to secure the nomination of one of our own sons.
Such was far from the truth. When the ground was
surveyed, it was found that from the Atlantic seacoast
of Jersey to the Mississippi river, in the whole belt of
States south of New-York and Michigan, there was a
settled determination not to take Mr. Seward, nor, indeed, any extreme man. Yet ths councils of these
States were divided, and no chance of concentration
seemed to present itself. At length Pennsylvania, by
the force of her numbers and courage, solved the problem. She sacrificed her own canditate, and rushed
over to the side of the Illinois favorite, Lincoln.

" This nomination was made by Pennsylvania, and it
could not have been accomplished without her. She
brought together, for the first time, this noble phalanx
of central free States, and gave them a community of
feeling and purpose. From the first moment that this
movement was begun victory was no longer doubtful.
Pennsylvania demanded a protectionist, and so did all
the States of this combination. Her demand could
not be refused, and in Mr. Lincoln we have one whose
devotion to American interests has been lifelong.

Sprung, too, from good old Pennsylvania stock, he was peculiarly entitled to her support.

" Under these circumstances it is clear that our gallant State has gained a signal triumph at Chicago, and one, too, the effects of which are likely to prove lasting. In the demonstration of joy with which the nomination has been hailed at Easton, Westchester, and other points throughout the interior, we read the indications of the popular feeling. The belief is general that this is a Pennsylvania ticket, and must receive the vote of the State. In fact, the people of this commonwealth are determined not to permit the election of another Democratic President, no matter with how much clamor any particular section of the country may demand it. The interests of the whole country must be attended to first, and those of sections afterward. We must purge the government of the corruptions which befoul every department at Washington. We must substitute honest, and patriotic, and sensible men for reckless, and intriguing, and plunder-seeking factionists, to whom the interests of humanity, the progress of civilization and enlightenment, and the rights and privileges of citizenship, are too small for serious consideration."

And so we might go on, quoting hundreds of pages of similar remarks from the American Press.

MR. LINCOLN AT HOME.

The Committee appointed by the National Convention to wait upon Mr. Lincoln, and inform him of his nomination, immediately performed their duty. A correspondent of the Chicago *Journal* gives the subjoined graphic account of the visit of the Committee :

" The excursion train bearing the Committee appointed by the National Convention at Chicago to wait on

Mr. Lincoln and notify him of his nomination, consisting of the President of the Convention, the Hon. Geo.
Ashmun of Mass., and the chairmen of the different
State delegations, arrived at Springfield, Friday evening at seven o'clock.

"A great crowd was awaiting them at the depot, and
greeted their coming with enthusiastic shouts. From
the depot they marched to the hotel, accompanied by
the crowd, and two or three bands discoursing stirring
music. The appearance and names of the more distinguished delegates were received with vociferous applause, especially the venerable and famous Francis P.
Blair of Maryland, the Hon. E. D. Morgan, Governor
of New-York, and Governor Boutwell of Massachusetts.

"When they arrived at the hotel the crowd, still
increasing, deployed off to the State-House square, to
give vent to their enthusiasm in almost continual
cheers, and listen to fervent speeches.

"Having partaken of a bountiful supper, the delegates
proceeded quietly, by such streets as would escape the
crowd, to the residence of Mr. Lincoln. Quite a number of outsiders were along, among whom were half a
dozen editors, including the Hon. Henry J. Raymond of
The New-York Times.

"Among the delegates composing the Committee, were
many of the most distinguished men in that great Convention, such as Mr. Evarts of New-York, the accomplished and eloquent spokesman of the delegation from
the Empire State, and friend of Mr. Seward ; Judge
Kelly of Pennsylvania, whose tall form and sonorous
eloquence excited so much attention ; Mr. Andrew of
Massachusetts, the round-faced, handsome man, who
made such a beautiful and telling speech on behalf of
the old Bay State, in seconding the motion to make
Lincoln's nomination unanimous ; Mr. Simmons, the
gray-headed United States Senator from Rhode Island;
Mr. Ashmun, the President of the Convention, so long

the bosom friend and ardent admirer of Daniel Webster, and the leader of the Massachusetts Whigs ; the veteran Blair, and his gallant sons, Frank P. and Montgomery ; brave old Blakie of Kentucky ; Gallagher, the literary man of Ohio ; burly, loud-voiced Cartter of Ohio, who announced the four votes that gave Lincoln the nomination, and others that I have not time to mention.

" In a few minutes (it now being about 8 P. M.), they were at Lincoln's house—an elegant two-story dwelling, fronting west, of pleasing exterior, with a neat and roomy appearance, situated in the quiet part of the town, surrounded with shrubbery. As they were passing in at the gate and up the steps, two handsome lads of eight or ten years met them with a courteous ' Good evening, gentlemen.'

" 'Are you Mr. Lincoln's son ? ' said Mr. Evarts of New-York. ' Yes, sir,' said the boy. ' Then let's shake hands ;' and they began greeting him so warmly as to excite the younger one's attention, who had stood silently by the opposite gatepost, and he sang out, ' I'm a Lincoln, too ;' whereupon several delegates, amid much laughter, saluted the young Lincoln.

Having all collected in the large north parlor, Mr. Ashmun addressed Mr. Lincoln, who stood at the east end of the room, as follows :

" ' I have, sir, the honor, in behalf of the gentlemen who are present, a Committee appointed by the Republican Convention, recently assembled at Chicago, to discharge a most pleasant duty. We have come, sir, under a vote of instructions to that Committee, to notify you that you have been selected by the Convention of the Republicans at Chicago, for President of the United States. They instruct us, sir, to notify you of that selection, and that Committee deem it not only respectful to yourself, but appropriate to the important matter which they have in hand, that they should come in person, and present to you the authentic evidence-of the action of that Convention ; and, sir, without any phrase which shall either be considered personally plauditory to yourself; or which shall have any reference to the principles involved in the questions which are connected with your nomination, I desire to present to you the letter which has been prepared, and which informs you of the nomination, and with it the platform, resolutions, and sentiments, which the Convention adopted.   Sir, at your convenience, we shall be glad to receive from you such a response as it may be your pleasure to give us.'

" Mr. Lincoln listened with a countenance grave and earnest, almost to sternness, regarding Mr. Ashmun with the profoundest attention, and at the conclusion of that gentleman's remarks, after an impressive pause, he replied in a clear but subdued voice, with that perfect enunciation, which always marks his utterance, and a dignified sincerity of manner suited to the man and the occasion, in the following words :

"'MR. CHAIRMAN, AND GENTLEMEN OF THE COMMITTEE : I tender to you, and through you to the Republican National Convention, and all the people represented in it, my profoundest thanks for the high honor done me, which you now formally announce. Deeply, and even painfully sensible of the great responsibility which is inseparable from this high honor—a responsibility which I could almost wish had fallen upon some one of the far more eminent men and experienced statesmen whose distinguished names wer before the Convention, I shall, by your leave, consider more fully the resolutions of the Convention, denominated the platform, and without unnecessary or unreasonable delay, respond to you, Mr. Chairman, in writing, not doubting that the platform will be found satisfactory, and the nomination gratefully accepted.

" ' And now I will not longer defer the pleasure of taking you, and each of you, by the hand.'

" Mr. Ashmun then introduced the delegates-person-
ally to Mr. Lincoln, who shook them heartily by the
hand. Gov. Morgan, Mr. Blair, Senator Simmons, Mr.
Welles, and Mr. Fogg, of Connecticut, were first introduced ; then came hearty old Mr. Blakie, of Kentucky, Lincoln's native State, and, of course, they had
to compare notes, inquire up old neighbors, and, if the
time had allowed, they would soon have started to
tracing out the old pioneer families. Major Ben.
Eggleston, of Cincinnati, was next, and his greeting
and reception were equally hearty. Tall Judge Kelly,
of Pennsylvania, was then presented by Mr. Ashmun
to Mr. Lincoln. As they shook hands, each eyed the
other's ample proportions, with genuine admiration—
Lincoln, for once, standing erect as an Indian during
this evening, and showing his tall form in its full
dignity.

" ' What's your height ?' inquired Lincoln.

" ' Six feet three ; what is yours, Mr. Lincoln !'
said Judge Kelly, in his round, deliberate tone.

" ' Six feet four,' replied Lincoln.

" ' Then,' said Judge Kelly, ' Pennsylvania bows
to Illinois. My dear man, for years my heart has been
aching for a President that I could *look up to*, and I've
found him at last in the land where we thought there
were none but *little* giants.'

" Mr. Evarts, of New-York, expressed very gracefully
his gratification at meeting Mr. Lincoln, whom he had
heard at Cooper Institute, but where, on account of
the pressure and crowd, he had to go away without an
introduction.

" Mr. Andrews, of Massachusetts, said, ' We claim
you, Mr. Lincoln, as coming from Massachusetts, because all the old Lincoln name are from Plymouth Col-
ony.'

" ' We'll consider it so this evening,' said Lincoln.

" Various others were presented, when Mr. Ashmun
asked them to come up and introduce themselves.

'Come up, gentlemen,' said Mr. Judd, ' it's nobody but
Old Abe Lincoln.' The greatest good feeling prevailed. As the delegates fell back, each congratulated
the other that they had got just the sort of man. A
neatly-dressed New-Englander remarked to us, ' I was
afraid I should meet a gigantic rail-splitter, with the
manners of a flatboatman, and the ugliest face in
creation ; and he's a complete gentleman.'

"Mrs. Lincoln received the delegates in the south
parlor, where they were severally conducted after their
official duty was performed. It will, no doubt, be a
gratification to those who have not seen this amiable
and accomplished lady to know that she adorns a draw-
ing-room, presides over a table, does the honors on an
occasion like the present, or will do the honors at the
White-House, with appropriate grace. She is a daughter of Dr. Todd, formerly of Kentucky, and long one
of the prominent citizens of Springfield. She is one
of three sisters noted for their beauty and accomplish-
ments. One of them is now the wife of Ninian W.
Edwards, Esq., son of old Gov. Edwards. Mrs. Lincoln is now apparently about 35 years of age, is a very
handsome woman, with a vivacious and graceful manner ; is an interesting and often sparkling talker.
Standing by her almost gigantic husband, she appears
petite, but is really about the average height of ladies.
They have three sons, two of them already mentioned,
and an older one—a young man of 16 or 18 years, now
at Harvard College, Mass.

" Mr. Lincoln bore himself during the evening with
dignity and ease. His kindly and sincere manner, frank
and honest expression, unaffected, pleasant conversation, soon made every one feel at ease, and rendered
the hour and a half which they spent with him one of
great pleasure to the delegates. He was dressed with
perfect neatness, almost elegance—though, as all Illi-
noians know, he usually is as plain in his attire as he
is modest and unassuming in deportment. He stood

erect, displaying to excellent advantage his tall and manly figure.

"Perhaps some reader will be curious to know how 'Honest Old Abe' received the news of his nomination. He had been up in the telegraph office during the first and second ballots on Friday morning. As the vote of each State was announced on the platform at Chicago, it was telegraphed to Springfield, and those who were gathered there figured up the vote, and hung over the result with the same breathless anxiety as the crowd at the Wigwam. As soon as the second ballot was taken, and before it had been counted and announced by the secretaries, Mr. Lincoln walked over to the *State Journal* office. He was sitting there conversing while the third ballot was being taken. When Cartter, of Ohio, announced the change of four votes, giving Lincoln a majority, and before the great tumult of applause in the Wigwam had fairly begun, it was telegraphed to Springfield. Mr. Wilson, telegraph superintendent, who was in the office, instantly wrote on a scrap of paper, 'Mr. Lincoln, you are nominated on the third ballot,' and gave it to a boy, who ran with it to Mr. Lincoln. He took the paper in his hand, and looked at it long and silently, not heeding the noisy exultation of all around, and then rising and putting the note in his vest pocket, he quietly remarked, 'There's a little woman down at our house would like to hear this. I'll go down and tell her.'

"It is needless to say that the people of Springfield were delirious with joy and enthusiasm both that evening and since. As the delegates returned to the hotel —the sky blazing with rockets, cannon roaring at intervals, bonfires blazing at the street corners, long rows of buildings brilliantly illuminated, the State-House overflowing with shouting people, speakers awakening new enthusiasm—one of the New-England delegates remarked that there were more enthusiasm and sky-rockets than he ever saw in a town of that size before.

7

" The Ohio delegates brought back with them a *rail*, one of the original three thousand split by Lincoln in 1830 ; and though it bears the marks of years, is still tough enough for service. It is for Tom Corwin, who intends taking it with him as he stumps the Buckeye State for honest old Abe."

A correspondent of the New-York *Evening Post* describes his visit to Mr. Lincoln in the following manner :

" It had been reported by some of Mr. Lincoln's political enemies, that he was a man who lived in the 'lowest hoosier style,' and I thought I would see for myself. Accordingly, as soon as the business of the Convention was closed, I took the cars for Springfield. I found Mr. Lincoln living in a handsome, but not pretentious, double two-story frame house, having a wide hall running through the centre, with parlors on both sides, neatly, but not ostentatiously, furnished. It was just such a dwelling as a majority of the well-to-do residents of these fine western towns occupy. Everything about it had a look of comfort and independence. The library I remarked in passing, particularly, and I was pleased to see long rows of books, which told of the scholarly tastes and culture of the family.

" Lincoln received us with great, and to me, surprising urbanity. I had seen him before in New-York, and brought with me an impression of his awkward and ungainly manner ; but in his own house, where he doubtless feels himself freer than in the strange New-York circles, he had thrown this off, and appeared easy, if not graceful. He is, as you know, a tall, lank man, with a long neck, and his ordinary movements are unusually angular, even out West. As soon, however, as he gets interested in conversation, his face lights up, and his attitudes and gestures assume a certain dignity and impressiveness. ' His conversation is fluent, agreeable and polite. You see at once from it that he is a man of decided and original character. His views are all his own ; such as he has worked out from a patient and varied scrutiny of life, and not such as he has learned from others. Yet he cannot be called opinion- ated. He listens to others like one eager to learn, and his replies evince at the same time, both modesty and self-reliance. I should say that sound common sense was the principal quality of his mind, although at times a striking phrase or word reveals a peculiar vein of thought. He tells a story well, with a strong idiomatic smack, and seems to relish humor, both in himself and others. Our conversation was mainly political, but of a general nature. One thing Mr. Lincoln remarked, which I will venture to repeat. He said that in the coming presidential canvass he was wholly uncommitted to any cabals or cliques, and that he meant to keep himself free from them, and from all pledges and promises.

"I had the pleasure, also, of a brief interview with Mrs. Lincoln, and, in the circumstances of these per- sons, I trust I am not trespassing on the sanctities of private life, in saying a word in regard to that lady. Whatever of awkwardness may be ascribed to her husband, there is none of it in her. On the contrary, she is quite a pattern of lady-like courtesy and polish. She converses with freedom and grace, and is thoroughly au fait in all the little amenities of society. Mrs. Lincoln belongs, by the mother's side, to the Preston family of Kentucky, has received a liberal and refined education, and should she ever reach it, will adorn the White-House. She is, I am told, a strict and consis- tent member of the Presbyterian Church.

"Not a man of us who saw Mr. Lincoln but was impressed by his ability and character. In illustration of the last let me mention one or two things, which your readers, I think, will be pleased to hear. Mr. Lincoln's early life, as you know, was passed in the roughest kind of experience on the frontier, and among the roughest sort of people. Yet, I have been told that, in the face of all these influences, he is a strictly temperate man, never using wine or strong drink ; and stranger still, he does not ' twist the filthy weed,' nor smoke, nor use profane language of any kind. When we consider how common these vices are all over our country, particularly in the West, it must be admitted that it exhibits no little strength of character to have refrained from them.

" Mr. Lincoln is popular with his friends and neighbors ; the habitual equity of his mind points him out as a peacemaker and composer of difficulties ; his integrity is proverbial ; and his legal abilities are regarded as of the highest order. The *soubriquet* of ' Honest old Abe,' has been won by years of upright conduct, and is the popular homage to his probity. He carries the marks of honesty in his face and entire deportment.

" I am the more convinced by this personal intercourse with Mr. Lincoln, that the action of our Convention was altogether judicious and proper."

The *Tribune* gives the subjoined incident :

" Probably no attribute of our candidate will, after all, endear him so much to the popular heart as the cooviction that he is emphatically ' one of the people.' His manhood has not been compressed into the artificial track of society ; but his great heart and vigorous intellect have been allowed a generous development amid his solitary struggles in the forest and the prairie. With vision unobscured by the mists of sophistry, he distinguishes at the first glance between what is true and what is false, and with will and courage fortified by his life of hardship, he is not the man to shirk any responsibility, or to shrink from any opposition. Moreover, he is peculiarly one to win our confidence and affection. To know ' honest Abe' is to love him ; and his neighbors in the West, although voting for him to a man, will mourn the victory which is to deprive them

of his presence. The following incident will exhibit
Lincoln in one of those unobtrusive acts of goodness
which adorn his life. The circumstance was related by
a teacher from the Five-Points' House of Industry in
this city : ' Our Sunday-school in the Five-Points was
assembled, one Sabbath morning, a few months since,
when I noticed a tall and remarkable looking man enter
the room and take a seat among us. He listened with
fixed attention to our exercises, and his countenance
manifested such genuine interest, that I approached
him and suggested that he might be willing to say
something to the children. He accepted the invitation
with evident pleasure, and coming forward, began a
simple address, which at once fascinated every little
hearer, and hushed the room into silence. His language was strikingly beautiful, and his tones musical
with intensest feeling. The little faces around would
droop into sad conviction, as he uttered sentences of
warning, and would brighten into sunshine as he spoke
cheerful words of promise. Once or twice he attempted
to close his remarks, but the imperative shout of ." Go
on !" "Oh, do go on !" would compel him to resume.
As I looked upon the gaunt and sinewy frame of the
stranger, and marked his powerful head and determined features, now touched into softness by the impressions of the moment, I felt an irrepressible curiosity
to learn something more about him, and when he was
quietly leaving the room, I begged to know his name.
He courteously replied, " It is Abraham Lincoln, from
Illinois !" ' "

That the Convention at Chicago acted wisely and
sagaciously, no man can for a moment doubt who looks
over the field and sees the enthusiasm of *the people*
over the nominations. *That Lincoln and Hamlin can
be, and will be, elected to the places to which they have
been nominated we have no manner of doubt,* and we

cannot do better than to finish our sketch of Mr. Lincoln by quoting the following admirable song of one of America's most gifted sons, William Henry Burleigh, of New-York :

Up, again for the conflict! our banner fling out,
And rally around it with song and with shout !
Stout of heart, firm of hand, should the gallant boys be,
Who bear to the battle the Flag of the Free !
Like our fathers, when Liberty called to the strife,
They should pledge to her cause fortune, honor, and life !
And follow wherever she beckons them on,
Till Freedom exults in a victory won !
    Then fling out the banner, the old starry banner,
    The battle-torn banner that beckons us on !

They come from the hillside, they come from the glen—
From the streets thronged with traffic, and surging with men
From loom and from ledger, from workshop and farm,
The fearless of heart, and the mighty of arm.
As the mountain-born torrents exultingly leap,
When their ice-fetters melt, to the breast of the deep ;
As the winds of the prairie, the waves of the sea,
They are coming—are coming—the Sons of the Free !
    Then fling out the banner, the old starry banner,
    The war-tattered banner, the flag of the Free !

Our Leader is one who, with conquerless will,
Has climbed from the base to the brow of the hill :
Undaunted in peril, unwavering in strife,
He has fought a good fight in the Battle of Life
And we trust him as one who, come woe or come weal,
Is as firm as the rock, and as true as the steel,
Right loyal and brave, with no stain on his crest,
Then, hurrah, boys, for honest " Old Abe of the West !"
    And fling out your banner, the old starry banner,
    The signal of triumph for " Abe of the West !"

The West, whose broad acres, from lake-shore to sea,
Now wait for the harvest and homes of the free !
Shall the dark tide of Slavery roll o'er the sod,
That Freedom makes bloom like the garden of God ?
The bread of our children be torn from their mouth,
To feed the fierce dragon that preys on the South ?
No, never ! the trust which our Washington laid
On us, for the Future, shall ne'er be betrayed !
    Then fling out the banner, the old starry banner,
    And on to the conflict with hearts undismayed !

SPEECHES OF ABRAHAM LINCOLN.

PART FIFTH.

SPEECH OF MR. LINCOLN,

AT SPRINGFIELD, *June* 17, 1858.

[The following speech was delivered at Springfield, Ill., at the close of the Republican State Convention, held at that time and place, and by which Convention Mr. Lincoln had been named as their candidate for United States Senator. Mr. Douglas was not present.]

MR. PRESIDENT, AND GENTLEMEN OF THE CONVENTION: If we could first know where we are, and whither we are tending, we could better judge what to do, and how to do it. We are now far into the fifth year, since a policy was initiated with the avowed object, and confident promise, of putting an end to slavery agitation. Under the operation of that policy, that agitation has not only not ceased, but has constantly augmented. In my opinion, it will not cease, until a crisis shall have been reached and passed. "A house divided against itself cannot stand." I believe this government cannot endure permanently half slave and half free. I do not expect the Union to be dissolved—I do not expect the house to fall—but I do expect it will cease to be divided. It will become all one thing, or all the other. Either the opponents of slavery will arrest the further spread of it, and place it where the public mind shall rest in the belief that it is in the course of ultimate extinction ; or its advocates will push it forward, till it shall become alike lawful in all the States, old as well as new—North as well as South.

Have we no tendency to the latter condition?

Let any one who doubts, carefully contemplate that now

7*

almost complete legal combination—piece of machinery, so to speak—compounded of the Nebraska doctrine, and the Dred Scott decision. Let him consider not only what work the machinery is adapted to do, and how well adapted ; but also, let him study the history of its construction, and trace, if he can, or rather fail, if he can, to trace, the evidences of design, and concert of action, among its chief architects, from the beginning.

The new year of 1854 found slavery excluded from more than half the States by State constitutions, and from most of the national territory by Congressional prohibition. Four days later, commenced the struggle which ended in repealing that Congressional prohibition. This opened all the national territory to slavery, and was the first point gained.

But, so far, Congress only had acted ; and an endorsement by the people, real or apparent, was indispensable, to save the point already gained, and give chance for more.

This necessity had not been overlooked ; but had been provided for, as well as might be, in the notable argument of "squatter sovereignty," otherwise called "sacred right of self-government" which latter phrase, though expressive of the only rightful basis of any government, was so perverted in this attempted use of it as to amount to just this : That if any *one* man choose to enslave *another*, no *third* man shall be allowed to object. That argument was incorporated into the Nebraska bill itself, in the language which follows : "It being the true intent and meaning of this act not to legislate slavery into any territory or State, nor to exclude it therefrom ; but to leave the people thereof perfectly free to form and regulate their domestic institutions in their own way, subject only to the Constitution of the United States." Then opened the roar of loose declamation in favor of "squatter sovereignty," and "sacred rights of self-government." "But," said opposition members, "let us amend the bill so as to expressly declare that the people of the territory may exclude slavery." "Not we," said the friends of the measure; and down they voted the amendment.

While the Nebrask a bill was passing through Congress, a *law case* involving the question of a negro's freedom, by reason of his owner having voluntarily taken him first into a free State and then into a territory covered by the Congressional prohibition, and held him as a slave for a long time in each, was passing through the U. S. Circuit Court for the District of Missouri ; and both Nebraska bill and law suit were brought to a decision in the same month of May, 1854. The negro's name was " Dred Scott," which name now designates the decision finally made in the case. Before the then next Presidential election, the law case came to, and was argued in, the Supreme Court of the United States ; but the decision of it was deferred until after the election. Still, before the election, Senator Trumbull, on the floor of the Senate, re-quested the leading advocate of the Nebraska bill to state *his* *opinion* whether the people of a territory can constitutionally exclude slavery from their limits; and the latter answers : " That is a question for the Supreme Court."

The election came. Mr. Buchanan was elected, and the endorsement, such as it was, secured. That was the second point gained. The endorsement, however, fell short of a clear popular majority by nearly four hundred thousand votes, and so, perhaps, was not overwhelmingly reliable and satisfactory. The outgoing President, in his last annual message, as impres-sively as possible echoed back upon the people the weight and authority of the endorsement. The Supreme Court met again ; did not announce their decision, but ordered a re-argument. The Presidential inauguration came, and still no decision of the court ; but the incoming President, in his inaugural ad-dress, fervently exhorted the people to abide by the forthcom-ing decision, whatever it might be. Then, in a few days, came the decision.

The reputed author of the Nebraska bill finds an early oc-casion to make a speech at this capital endorsing of the Dred Scott decision, and vehemently denouncing all opposition to it. The new President, too, seizes the early occasion of the Silliman letter to endorse and strongly construe that decision, and to express his astonishment that any different view had ever been entertained !

At length a squabble springs up between the President and the author of the Nebraska bill, on the mere question of *fact*, whether the Lecompton Constitution was, or was not, in any just sense, made by the people of Kansas ; and, in that quarrel, the latter declares that all he wants is a fair vote of the people, and that he cares not whether

slavery be voted *down* or voted *up*.   I do not understand his declaration that he cares not whether slavery be
voted down or voted up, to be intended by him other than as
an apt definition of the policy he would impress upon the public mind—the principle for which he declares he has suffered
so much, and is ready to suffer to the end.   And well may he
cling to that principle.   If he has any parental feeling, well
may he cling to it.   That principle is the only shred left of
his original Nebraska doctrine.   Under the Dred Scott decision, "squatter sovereignty" squatted out of existence, tum-
bled down like temporary scaffolding—like the, mould at the
foundry served through one blast and fell back into loose sand
—helped to carry an election, and then was kicked to the
winds.   His late joint struggle with the Republicans, against
the Lecompton Constitution, involves nothing of the original
Nebraska doctrine.   That struggle was made on a point—
the right of a people to make their own constitution—upon
which he and the Republicans have never differed.

The several points of the Dred Scott decision, in connection
with Senator Douglas's "care not" policy, constitute the piece
of machinery, in its present state of advancement.   This was
the third point gained.   The working points of that machinery are :   .

First, That no negro slave, imported as such from Africa,
and no descendant of such slave, can ever be a citizen of any
State, in the sense of that term as used in the Constitution of
the United States.   This point is made in order to deprive
the negro, in every possible event, of the benefit of that provision of the United States Constitution, which declares that
"The citizens of each State shall be entitled to all privileges
and immunities of citizens in the several States."

Secondly, That "subject to the Constitution of the United
States," neither Congress nor a territorial legislature can exclude slavery from any United States territory.   This point is
made in order that individual men may fill up the territories
with slaves, without danger of losing them as property, and
thus to enhance the chances of permanency to the institution
through all the future.

Thirdly, That whether the holding a negro in actual slavery in a free State, makes him free, as against the holder, the
United States courts will not decide, but will leave to be de-

cided by the courts of any slave State the negro may be forced
into by the master. This point is made, not to be pressed immediately ; but, if acquiesced in for a while, and apparently
endorsed by the people at an election, then to sustain the logical conclusion that what Dred Scott's master might lawfully
do with Dred Scott, in the free State of Illinois, every other
master may lawfully do with any other one, or one thousand
slaves, in Illinois, or in any other free State.

Auxiliary to all this, and working hand in hand with it,
the Nebraska doctrine, or what is left of it, is to educate and
mould public opinion, at least Northern public opinion, not
to care whether slavery is voted down or voted up. This
shows exactly where we now are ; and partially, also, whither we are tending.

It will throw additional light on the latter, to go back, and
run the mind over the string of historical facts already stated.
Several things will now appear less dark and mysterious than
they did when they were transpiring. The people were to be
left "perfectly free," "subject only to the Constitution."
What the Constitution had to do with it outsiders could not
then see. Plainly enough now, it was an exactly fitted niche,
for the Dred Scott decision to afterward come in, and declare
the perfect freedom of the people to be just no freedom at all.
Why was the amendment, expressly declaring the right of the
people, voted down ? Plainly enough now : the adoption of
it would have spoiled the niche for the Dred Scott decision.
Why was the court decision held up ? Why even a Senator's
individual opinion withheld, till after the Presidential election ? Plainly enough now : the speaking out then would
have damaged the perfectly free argument upon which the
election was to be carried. Why the outgoing President's fe-
licitation on the endorsement ? Why the delay of a re-argument ? Why the incoming President's advance exhortation
in favor of the decision ? These things look like the cautious
patting and petting of a spirited horse preparatory to mount-
ing him, when it is dreaded that he may give the rider a fall.
And why the hasty after-endorsement of the decision by the
President and others ?

We cannot absolutely know that all these exact adaptations
are the result of pre-concert. But when we see a lot of framed
timbers, different portions of which we know have been gotten

out at different times and places and by different workmen—
Stephen, Franklin, Roger, and James, for instance—and when
we see these timbers joined together, and see they exactly
make the frame of a house or a mill, all the tenons and mor-
tices exactly fitting, all the lengths and proportions of the different pieces exactly adapted to their respective places, and
not a piece too many or too few—not omitting even scaffolding—or, if a single piece be lacking, we see the place in the
frame exactly fitted and prepared yet to bring such piece in—
in such a case, we find it impossible not to believe that Stephen and Franklin, and Roger and James, all understood one
another from the beginning, and all worked upon a common
plan or draft drawn up before the first blow was struck.

It should not be overlooked that, by the Nebraska bill, the
people of a *State* as well as territory, were to be left " perfectly free," " subject only to the Constitution." Why mention a State? They were legislating for territories, and not
for or about States. Certainly the people of a State are and
ought to be subject to the Constitution of the United States ;
but why is mention of this lugged into this merely territorial
law? Why are the people of a territory and the people of a
State therein lumped together, and their relation to the Constitution therein treated as being precisely the same? While
the opinion of the court, by Chief Justice Taney, in the Dred
Scott case, and the separate opinions of all the concurring
Judges, expressly declare that the Constitution of the United
States neither permits Congress nor a territorial legislature to
exclude slavery from any United States territory, they all omit
to declare whether or not the same Constitution permits a
State, or the people of a State, to exclude it. *Possibly*, this is
a mere omission ; but who can be quite sure, if McLean or
Curtis had sought to get into the opinion a declaration of unlimited power in the people of a State to exclude slavery from
their limits, just as Chase and Mace sought to get such declaration, in behalf of the people of a territory, into the Nebraska bill—I ask, who can be quite sure that it would not
have been voted down in the one case as it had been in the
other? The nearest approach to the point of declaring the
power of a State over slavery, is made by Judge Nelson. He
approaches it more than once, using the precise idea, and almost the language, too, of the Nebraska act. On one occa-

sion, his exact language is, "except in cases where the power
is restrained by the Constitution of the United States, the law
of the State is supreme over the subject of slavery within its
jurisdiction." In what cases the power of the State is so restrained by the United States Constitution, is left an open
question, preeisely as the same question, as to the restraint on
the power of the territories, was left open in the Nebraska
act. Put this and that together, and we have another nice
little niche, which we may, ere long, see filled with another
Supreme Court decision, declaring that the Consfitution of the
United States does not permit a *State* to exclude slavery from
its limits. And this may especially be expected if the doctrine of "care not whether slavery be voted down or voted
up," shall gain upon the public mind suffieiently to give
promise that such a decision can be maintained when made.

Such a decision is all that slavery now lacks of being alike
lawful in all the States. Welcome, or unwelcome, such decision is probably coming, and will soon be upon us, unless
the power of the present political dynasty shall be met and
overthrown. We shall lie down pleasantly dreaming that the
people of Missouri are on the verge of making their State free,
and we shall awake to the reality instead, that the Supreme
Court has made Illinois a slave State. To meet and overthrow the power of that dynasty, is the work now before all
those who would prevent that consummation. That is what
we have to do. How can we best do it?

There are those who denounce us openly to their own
friends, and yet whisper us softly, that Senator Douglas is the
aptest instrument there is with which to effect that object.
They wish us to *infer* all, from the fact that he now has a little quarrel with the present head of the dynasty; and that he
has regularly voted with us on a single point, upon which he
and we have never differed. They remind us that he is a great
man, and that the largest of us are very small ones. Let this
be granted. But "a living dog is better than a dead lion."
Judge Douglas, if not a dead lion, for this work, is at least a
caged and toothless one. How can he oppose the advances of
slavery? He don't care anything about it. His avowed
mission is impressing the "public heart" to *care nothing about
it.* A leading Douglas democratic newspaper thinks Douglas's superior talent will be needed to resist the revival of the

African slave trade. Does Douglas believe an effort to revive that trade is approaching? He has not said so. Does
he really think so? But if it is, how can he resist it? For
years he has labored to prove it a sacred right of white men
to take negro slaves into the new territories. Can he possibly show that it is less a sacred right to buy them where they
can be bought cheapest? And unquestionably they can be
bought cheaper in Africa than in Virginia. He has done all
in his power to reduce the whole question of slavery to one of
a mere right of property ; and as such, how can he oppose
the foreign slave trade—how can he refuse that trade in that
" property" shall be " perfectly free"—unless he does it as a
protection to the home production? And as the home pro-
ducers will probably not ask the protection, he will be wholly
without a ground of opposition.

Senator Douglas holds, we know, that a man may rightfully be wiser to-day than he was yesterday—that he may
rightfully change when he finds himself wrong. But can we,
for that reason, run ahead, and infer that he will make any
particular change, of which he, himself, has given no intima-
tion? Can we safely base our action upon any such vague
inference? Now, as ever, I wish not to misrepresent Judge
Douglas's position, question his motives, or do aught that can
be personally offensive to him. Whenever, if ever, he and we
can come together on principle, so that our cause may have
assistance from his great ability, I hope to have interposed no
adventitious obstacle. But clearly, he is not now with us—
he does not pretend to be—he does not promise ever to be.

Our cause, then, must be intrusted to, and conducted by, its
own undoubted friends—those whose hands are free, whose
hearts are in the work—who *do care* for the result. Two
years ago the Republicans of the nation mustered over thirteen
hundred thousand strong. We did this under the single im-
pulse of resistance to a common danger, with every external
circumstance against us. Of strange, discordant, and even
hostile elements, we gathered from the four winds, and formed
and fought the battle through, under the constant hot fire of a
disciplined, proud, and pampered enemy. Did we brave all
then, to falter now?—now, when that same enemy is waver-
ing, dissevered, and belligerent? The result is not doubtful.
We shall not fail—if we stand firm, we *shall not fail.* Wise

counsels may accelerate, or mistakes delay it, but sooner or later, the victory is sure to come.

MR. LINCOLN'S SPEECH IN REPLY TO MR. DOUGLAS,

At Chicago, *July* 10, 1858.

Mr. Lincoln was introduced by C. L. Wilson, Esq., and as he made his appearance he was greeted with a perfect storm of applause. For some moments the enthusiasm continued unabated. At last, when by a wave of his hand partial silence was restored, Mr. Lincoln said :

My Fellow-citizens : On yesterday evening, upon the occasion of the reception given to Senator Douglas, I was furnished with a seat very convenient for hearing him, and was otherwise very courteously treated by him and his friends, and for which I thank him and them. . During the course of his remarks my name was mentioned in such a way as, I suppose, renders it at least not improper that I should make some sort of reply to him. I shall not attempt to follow him in the precise order in which he addressed the assembled multitude upon that occasion, though I shall, perhaps, do so in the main.

There was one question to which he asked the attention of the crowd, which I deem of somewhat less importance—at least of propriety for me to dwell upon—than the others, which he brought in near the close of his speech, and which I think it would not be entirely proper for me to omit attending to ; and yet, if I were not to give some attention to it now, I should probably forget it altogether. While I am upon this subject, allow me to say, that I do not intend to indulge in that inconvenient mode sometimes adopted in public speaking, of reading from documents ; but I shall depart from that rule so far as to read a little scrap from his speech, which notices this first topic of which I shall speak—that is, provided I can find it in the paper.

"I have made up my mind to appeal to the people against the combination that has been made against me!—the Republican leaders having formed an alliance, an unholy and unnatural alliance, with a portion of unscrupulous federal officeholders. I intend to fight that allied army wherever I meet them. I know they deny the alliance, but yet these men who are trying to divide the Democratic party for the purpose of electing a Republican Senator in my place, are just as much the agents and tools of the supporters of Mr. Lincoln. Hence I shall deal with this allied army just as the Russians dealt with the allies at Sebastopol—that is, the Russians did not stop to inquire, when they fired a broadside, whether it hit an Englishman, a Frenchman, or a Turk. Nor will I stop to inquire, nor shall I hesitate, whether my blows shall hit these Republican leaders or their allies, who are holding the federal offices and yet acting in concert with them."

Well, now, gentlemen, is not that very alarming! Just to think of it! right at the outset of the canvass, I, a poor, kind, amiable, intelligent gentleman, I am to be slain in this way! Why, my friend, the Judge, is not only, as it turns out, not a dead lion, nor even a living one—he is the rugged Russian bear!

But if they will have it—for he says that we deny it—that there is any such alliance, as he says there is—and I don't propose hanging very much upon this question of veracity—but if he will have it that there is such an alliance—that the administration men and we are allied, and we stand in the attitude of English, French, and Turk, he occupying the position of the Russian, in that case, I beg that he will indulge us while we barely suggest to him that these allies took Sebastopol.

Gentlemen, only a few more words as to this alliance. For my part, I have to say, that whether there be such an alliance, depends, so far as I know, upon what may be a right definition of the term *alliance*. If for the Republican party to see the other great party to which they are opposed divided among themselves, and not try to stop the division, and rather be glad of it—if that is an alliance, I confess I am in; but if it is meant to be said that the Republicans have formed an alliance going beyond that, by which there is contribution of money or sacrifice of principle, on the one side or the other, so far as the Republican party is concerned, if there be any such thing, I protest that I neither know anything of it, nor do I believe it. I will, however, say—as I think this branch of the argument is lugged in—I would before I leave it, state, for the benefit of those concerned, that one of those same Buchanan men did once tell me of an argument that he made for his opposition to Judge Douglas. He said that a friend of our Senator Douglas had been talking to him, and had, among other things, said to him: "Why, you don't want to beat Douglas?" "Yes," said he, "I do want to beat him, and I will tell you why. I believe his original Nebraska bill was right in the abstract, but it was wrong in the time that it was brought forward. It was wrong in the application to a territory in regard to which the question had been settled ; it was brought forward at a time when nobody asked him ; it was tendered to the South when the South had not asked for it, but when they could not well refuse it ; and for this same reason he forced that question upon our party ; it has sunk the best men all over the nation, everywhere ; and now, when our President, struggling with the difficulties of this man's getting up, has reached the very hardest point to turn in the case, he deserts him, and I am for putting him where he will trouble us no more."

Now, gentlemen, that is not my argument—that is not my argument at all. I have only been stating to you the argument of a Buchanan man. You will judge if there is any force in it.

Popular sovereignty! everlasting popular sovereignty! Let us for a moment inquire into this vast matter of popular sovereignty. What is popular sovereignty? We recollect that at an early period in the history of this struggle, there was another name for the same thing—*squatter sovereignty.* It was not exactly popular sovereignty, but squatter sovereignty. What do those terms mean? What do those terms mean when used now? And vast credit is taken by our friend, the Judge, in regard to his support of it, when he declares the last years of his life have been, and all the future years of his life shall be, devoted to this matter of popular sovereignty. What is it? Why, it is the sovereignty of the people! What was squatter sovereignty? I suppose, if it had any significance at all, it was the right of the people to govern themselves, to be sovereign in their own affairs while they were squatted down in a territory not their own, while they had squatted on a territory that did not belong to them, in the sense that a State belongs to the people who inhabit it—when it belonged to the nation—such right to govern themselves was called " squatter sovereignty."

Now, I wish you to mark. What has become of that squatter sovereignty? What has become of it? Can you get anybody to tell you now that the people of a territory have any authority to govern themselves, in regard to this mooted question of slavery, before they form a State constitution? No such thing at all, although there is a general running fire, and although there has been a hurrah made in every speech on that side, assuming that policy had given the people of a territory the right to govern themselves upon this question ; yet the point is dodged. To-day it has been decided— no more than a year ago it was decided by the Supreme Court of the United States, and is insisted upon to-day, that the people of a territory have no right to exclude slavery from a territory ; that if any one man chooses to take slaves into a territory, all the rest of the people have no right to keep them out. This being so, and this decision being made one of the points that the Judge approved, and one in the approval of which he says he means to keep me down—put me down, I should not say, for I have never been up. He says he is in favor of it, and sticks to it, and expects to win his battle on that decision, which says that there is no such thing as squatter sovereignty ; but that any one may take slaves into a territory, and all the other men in a territory may be opposed to it, and yet, by reason of the Constitution, they cannot prohibit it. When that is so, how much is left of this vast matter of squatter sovereignty, I should like to know?

When we get back, we get to the point of the right of the people to make a constitution. Kansas was settled, for example, in 1854. It was a territory yet, without having formed a constitution, in a very regular way, for three years. All this time negro slavery could be taken in by any few individuals, and by that decision of the Supreme Court, which the Judge approves, all the rest of the people canot keep it out ; but when they come to make a constitution, they may say they will not have slavery. But it is there ; they are

obliged to tolerate it some way, and all experience shows it
will be so—for they will not take the negro slaves and absolutely deprive the owners of them. All experience shows
this to be so. All that space of time that runs from the beginning of the settlement of the territory, until there is sufficiency
of people to make a State constitution—all that portion of
time—popular sovereignty is given up. The seal is absolutely
put down upon it by the court decision, and Judge Douglas
puts his own upon the top of that, yet he is appealing to the
people to give him vast credit for his devotion to popular sovereignty.

Again, when we get to the question of the right of the
people to form a State constitution as they please, to form it
with slavery or without slavery—if that is anything new, I
confess I don't know it. Has there ever been a time when
anybody said that any other than the people of a territory
itself should form a constitution? What is now in it that
Judge Douglas should have fought several years of his life,
and pledge himself to fight all the remaining years of his life,
for? Can Judge Douglas find anybody on earth that said
that anybody else should form a constitution for a people?
[A voice—"Yes."] Well, I should like you to name him; I
should like to know who he was. [Same voice—"John Calhoun."]

Mr. Lincoln—No, sir, I never heard of even John Calhoun
saying such a thing. He insisted on the same principle as
Judge Douglas; but his mode of applying it, in fact, was
wrong. It is enough for my purpose to ask this crowd, whenever a Republican said anything against it? They never said
anything against it, but they have constantly spoken for it;
and whosoever will undertake to examine the platform, and
the speeches of responsible men of the party, and of irre-
sponsible men, too, if you please, will be unable to find one
word from anybody in the Republican ranks, opposed to that
popular sovereignty which Judge Douglas thinks that he has
invented. I suppose that Judge Douglas will claim, in a
little while, that he is the inventor of the idea that the people should govern themselves; that nobody ever thought of
such a thing until he brought it forward. We do not remember, that in that old Declaration of Independence, it is said
that "We hold these truths to be self-evident, that all men

are created equal; that they are endowed by their Creator
with certain inalienable rights; that among these are life,
liberty, and the pursuit of happiness; that to secure these
rights, governments are instituted among men, deriving their
just powers from the consent of the governed." There is the
origin of popular sovereignty. Who then, shall come in at
this day and claim that he invented it?

The Lecompton constitution connects itself with this question, for it is in this matter of the Lecompton constitution
that our friend Judge Douglas claims such vast credit. I
agree that, in opposing the Lecompton constitution, so far as
I can perceive, he was right. I do not deny that at all; and,
gentlemen, you will readily see why I could not deny it, even
if I wanted to. But I do not wish to; for all the Republicans in the nation opposed it, and they would have opposed it
just as much without Judge Douglas' aid as with it. They
had all taken ground against it long before he did. Why, the
reason that he urges against that constitution, I urged against
him a year before. I have the printed speech in my hand.
The argument that he makes, why that constitution should
not be adopted, that the people were not fairly represented
nor allowed to vote, I pointed out in a speech a year ago,
which I hold in my hand now, that no fair chance was to be
given to the people. ["Read it," "Read it."] I shall not
waste your time by trying to read it. ["Read it," "Read it."]
Gentlemen, reading from speeches is a very tedious business,
particularly for an old man that has to put on spectacles, and
more so if the man be so tall that he has to bend over to the
light.

A little more, now, as to this matter of popular sovereignty, and the Lecompton constitution. The Lecompton constitution, as the Judge tells us, was defeated. The defeat of
it was a good thing or it was not. He thinks the defeat of it
was a good thing, and so do I, and we agree in that. Who
defeated it?

A voice—"Judge Douglas."

Mr. Lincoln—Yes, he furnished himself, and if you suppose
he controlled the other Democrats that went with him, he
furnished *three* votes, while the Republicans furnished *twenty*.
That is what he did to defeat it. In the House of Representatives he and his friends furnished some twenty votes, and

the Republicans furnished *ninety odd.* Now who was it that did the work?

A voice—" Douglas."

Mr. Lincoln—Why, yes, Douglas did it! To be sure he did.

Let us, however, put. that proposition another way.- The Republicans could not have done it without Judge Douglas. Could he have done it without them? Which could have come the nearest to doing it without the other?

A voice—" Who killed the bill?"

Another voice—" Douglas."

Mr. Lincoln—Ground was taken against it by the Republicans long before Douglas did it. The proportion of opposition to that measure is about five to one.

A voice—" Why don't they come out on it?"

Mr. Lincoln—You don't know what you are talking about, my friend. I am quite willing to answer any gentleman in the crowd who asks an *intelligent* question.

Now who, in all this country, has ever found any of our friends of Judge Douglas' way of thinking, and who• have acted upon this main question, that has ever thought of uttering a word in behalf of Judge Trumbull?

A voice—" We have."

Mr. Lincoln—I defy you to show a printed resolution passed in a Democratic meeting—I take it upon myself to defy any man to show a printed resolution of a Democratic meeting, large or small, in favor of Judge Trumbull, or any of the five to one Republicans who beat that bill. Everything must be for the Democrats! They did everything, and the five to the one that really did the thing, they snub over, and they do not seem to remember that they have an existence upon the face of the earth.

Gentlemen, I fear that I shall become tedious. I leave this branch of the subject to take hold of another. I take up that part of Judge Douglas' speech in which he respectfully attended to me.

Judge Douglas made two points upon my recent speech at Springfield. He says they are to be the issues of this campaign. The first one of these points he bases upon the language in a speech which I delivered at Springfield, which I believe I can quote correctly from memory. I said there that

" we are now far into the fifth year since a policy was instituted for the avowed object, and with the confident promise,
of putting an end to the slavery agitation ; under the operation of that policy, that agitation had only not ceased, but
had constantly augmented." " I believe it will not cease until
a crisis shall have been reached and passed. 'A house divided against itself cannot stand.' I believe this government
cannot endure permanently half slave and half free." " I do
not expect the Union to be dissolved"—I am quoting from
my speech—" I do not expect the house to fall, but I do expect it will cease to be divided. It will become all one thing
or the other. Either the opponents of slavery will arrest the
spread of it, and place it where the public mind shall rest, in
the belief that it is in the course of ultimate extinction, or its
advocates will push it forward until it shall become alike lawful in all the States, North as well as South."

What is the paragraph? In this paragraph, which I have
quoted in your hearing, and to which I ask the attention of
all, Judge Douglas thinks he discovers great political heresy.
I want your attention particularly to what he has inferred
from it. He says I am in favor of making all the States of
this Union uniform in all their internal regulations ; that in
all their domestic concerns I am in favor of making them entirely uniform. He draws this inference from the language I
have quoted to you. He says that I am in favor of making
war by the North upon the South, for the extinction of slavery ; that I am also in favor of inviting (as he expresses it)
the South to a war upon the North, for the purpose of nationalizing slavery. Now, it is singular enough, if you will
carefully read that passage over, that I did not say that I was
in favor of anything in it. I only said what I expected
would take place. I made a prediction only—it may have
been a foolish one, perhaps. I did not even say that I desired
that slavery should be put in course of ultimate extinction. I
do say so now, however, so there need be no longer any difficulty about that. It may be written down in the great
speech.

Gentlemen, Judge Douglas informed you that this speech
of mine was probably carefully prepared. I admit that it
was. I am not master of language ; I have not a fine education ; I am not capable of entering into a disquisition upon

dialectics, as I believe you call it; but I do not believe the language I employed bears any such construction as Judge. Douglas puts upon it. But I don't care about a quibble in regard to words   I know what I meant, and I will not leave this crowd in doubt, if I can explain it to them, what I really meant in the use of that paragraph.

I am not, in the first place, unaware that this government has endured eighty-two years, half slave and half free. I know that. I am tolerably well acquainted with the history of the country, and I know that it has endured eighty-two years, half slave and half free. I *believe*—and that is what I meant to allude to there—I *believe* it has endured, because during all that time, until the introduction of the Nebraska bill, the public mind did rest all the time in the belief that slavery was in course of ultimate extinction. That was what gave us the rest that we had through that period of eighty-two years; at least, so I believe. I have always hated slavery, I think, as much as any abolitionist—I have been an Old Line Whig—I have always hated it, but I have always been quiet about it until this new era of the introduction of the Nebraska bill began. I always believed that everybody was against it, and that it was in course of ultimate extinction. [Pointing to Mr. Browning, who stood near by.] Browning thought so; the great mass of the nation have rested in the belief that slavery was in course of ultimate extinction. They had reason so to believe.

The adoption of the Constitution and its attendant history led the people to believe so; and that such was the belief of the framers of the Constitution itself, why did those old men, about the time of the adoption of the Constitution, decree that slavery should not go into the new territory, where it had not already gone? Why declare that within twenty years the African slave-trade, by which slaves are supplied, might be cut off by Congress? Why were all these acts? I might enumerate more of these acts—but enough. What were they but a clear indication that the framers of the Constitution intended and expected the ultimate extinction of that institution? And now, when I say, as I said in my speech that Judge Douglas has quoted from, when I say that I think the opponents of slavery will resist the further spread of it, and place it where the public mind shall rest with the belief that

8

it is in course of ultimate extinction, I only mean to say, that
they will place it where the founders of this government originally placed it.

I have said a hundred times, and I have now no inclination to take it back, that I believe there is no right, and ought to
be no inclination in the people of the free States to enter into
the slave States, and interfere with the question of slavery at
all.   I have said that always; Judge Douglas has heard me
say it—if not quite a hundred times, at least as good as a
hundred times; and when it is said that I am in favor of interfering with slavery where it exists, I know it is unwar-
ranted by anything I have ever *intended*, and, as I believe, by
anything I have ever *said*.   If, by any means, I have ever
used language which could fairly be so construed (as, however, I believe I never have), I now correct it.

So much, then, for the inference that Judge Douglas draws,
that I am in favor of setting the sections at war with one
another.   I know that I never meant any such thing, and I
believe that no fair mind can infer any such thing from anything I have ever said.

Now in relation to his inference that I am in favor of a
general consolidation of all the local institutions of the various
States.   I will attend to that for a little while, and try to inquire, if I can, how on earth it could be that any man could
draw such an inference from anything I said.   I have said,
very many times, in Judge Douglas's hearing, that no man
believed more than I in the principal of self-government; that
it lies at the bottom of all my ideas of just government, from
beginning to end.   I have denied that his use of that term
applies properly.   But for the thing itself, I deny that any
man has ever gone ahead of me in his devotion to the principle, whatever he may have done in efficiency in advocating it.
I think that I have said it in your hearing—that I believe
each individual is naturally entitled to do as he pleases with
himself and the fruit of his labor, so far as it in no wise interferes with any other man's rights—that each community,
as a State, has a right to do exactly as it pleases with all the
concerns within that State that interferes with the right of no
other State, and that the general government, upon principle, has no right to interfere with anything other than that
general class of things that does concern the whole.   I have

said that at all times. I have said, as illustrations, that I do not believe in the right of Illinois to interfere with the cranberry laws of Indiana, the oyster laws of Virginia, or the liquor laws of Maine. I have said these things over and over again, and I repeat them here as my sentiments.

How is it, then, that Judge Douglas infers, because I hope to see slavery put where the public mind shall rest in the belief that it is in the course of ultimate extinction, that I am in favor of Illinois going over and interfering with the cranberry laws of Indiana? What can authorize him to draw any such inference? I suppose there might be one thing that at least enabled *him* to draw such an inference that would not be true with me or many others, that is, because he looks upon all this matter of slavery as an exceedingly little thing—this matter of keeping one sixth of the population of the whole nation in a state of oppression and tyranny unequalled in the world. He looks upon it as being an exceedingly little thing—only equal to the question of the cranberry laws of Indiana—as something having no moral question in it—as something on a par with the question of whether a man shall pasture his land with cattle, or plant it with tobacco—so little and so small a thing, that he concludes, if I could desire that if anything should be done to bring about the ultimate extinction of that little thing, I must be in favor of bringing about an amalgamation of all the other little things in the Union. Now, it so happens—and there, I presume, is the foundation of this mistake—that the Judge thinks thus; and it so happens that there is a vast portion of the American people that do *not* look upon that matter as being this very little thing. They look upon it as a vast moral evil; they can prove it as such by the writings of those who gave us the blessings of liberty which we enjoy, and that they so looked upon it, and not as an evil merely confining itself to the States where it is situated; and while we agree that, by the Constitution we assented to, in the States where it exists we have no right to interfere with it, because it is in the Constitution; and we are by both duty and inclination to stick by that Constitution, in all its letter and spirit, from beginning to end.

So much then as to my disposition—my wish—to have all the State Legislatures blotted out, and to have one consolidated government, and a uniformity of domestic regulations in all the States, by which I suppose it is meant, if we raise corn here, we must make sugar-cane grow here too, and we must make those which grow North grow in the South. All this, I suppose, he understands I am in favor of doing. Now, so much for all this nonsense—for I must call it so. The Judge can have no issue with me on a question of establishing uniformity in the domestic regulations of the States.

A little now on the other point—the Dred Scott decision. Another of the issues, he says, that is to be made with me, is upon his devotion to the Dred Scott decision, and my opposition to it.

I have expressed, heretofore, and I now repeat, my opposition to the Dred Scott decision, but I should be allowed to state the nature of that opposition, and I ask your indulgence while I do so. What is fairly implied by the term Judge Douglas has used, "resistance to the decision ?" I do not resist it. If I wanted to take Dred Scott from his master, I would be interfering with property, and that terrible difficulty that Judge Douglas speaks of, of interfering with property would arise. But I am doing no such thing as that, but all that I am doing is refusing to obey it as a political rule. If I were in Congress, and a vote should come up on a question whether slavery should be prohibited in a new territory, in spite of the Dred Scott decision, I would vote that it should. That is what I would do. Judge Douglas said, last night, that before the decision he might advance his opinion, and it might be contrary to the decision when it was made ; but after it was made he would abide by it until it was reversed. Just so! We let this property abide by the decision, but we will try to reverse that decision. We will try to put it where Judge Douglas would not object, for he says he will obey it until it is reversed. Somebody has to reverse that decision, since it is made, and we mean to reverse it, and we mean to do it peaceably.

What are the uses of decisions of courts? They have two uses. As rules of property they have two uses. First—they decide upon the question before the court. They decide in this case that Dred Scott is a slave. Nobody resists that. Not only that, but they say to everybody else, that persons standing just as Dred Scott stands, is as he is. That is, they say that when a question comes up upon another person, it

will be so decided again, unless the court decides in another
way, unless the court overrules its decision. Well, we mean
to do what we can to have the court decide the other way.
That is one thing we mean to try to do.

The sacredness that Judge Douglas throws around this decision, is a degree of sacredness that has never been before
thrown around any other decision. I have never heard of
such a thing. Why, decisions apparently contrary to that
decision, or that good lawyers thought were contrary to that
decision, have been made by that very court before. It is
the first of its kind; it is an astonisher in legal history. It
is a new wonder of the world. It is based upon falsehood in
the main as to the facts—allegations of facts upon which it
stands are not facts at all in many instances, and no decision
made on any question—the first instance of a decision made
under so many unfavorable circumstances; thus placed, has ever
been held by the profession as law, and it has always needed
confirmation before the lawyers regarded it as settled law.
But Judge Douglas will have it that all hands must take this
extraordinary decision, made under these extraordinary circumstances, and give their vote in Congress in accordance with
it, yield to it, and obey it in every possible sense. Circumstances alter cases. Do not gentlemen here remember the
case of that same Supreme Court, some twenty-five or thirty
years ago, deciding that a National Bank was constitutional?
I ask, if somebody does not remember that a National Bank
was declared to be constitutional? Such is the truth, whether
it be remembered or not. The bank charter ran out, and a
recharter was granted by Congress. That recharter was laid
before General Jackson. It was urged upon him, when he
denied the constitutionality of the bank, that the Supreme
Court had decided that it was constitutional.; and that General
Jackson then said that the Supreme Court had no right to lay
down a rule to govern a co-ordinate branch of the Government, the members of which had sworn to support the Constitution—that each member had sworn to support that Constitution as he understood it. I will venture here to say, that
I have heard Judge Douglas say that he approved of General
Jackson for that act. What has now become of all his tirade
about " resistance to the Supreme Court ?"

My fellow-citizens, getting back a little, for I pass from

these points, when Judge Douglas makes his threat of anni-
hilation upon the " alliance," he is cautious to say that that
warfare of his is to fall upon the leaders of the Republican
party. Almost every word he utters, and every distinction he
makes, has its significance. He means for the Republicans,
who do not count themselves as leaders, to be his friends ; he
makes no fuss over them; it is the leaders that he is making
war upon. He wants it understood that the mass of the Republican party are really his friends. It is only the leaders
that are doing something, that are intolerant, and that require
extermination at his hands. As this is clearly and unquestionably the light in which he presents that matter, I want to ask
your attention, addressing myself to the Republicans here, that
I may ask you some questions, as to where you, as the Republican party, would be placed if you sustained Judge Douglas in his present position by a re-election? I do not claim,
gentlemen, to be unselfish; I do not pretend that I would not
like to go the United States Senate, I make no such hypocritical pretence, but I do say to you that in this mighty issue, it is
nothing to you—nothing to the mass of the people of the
nation—whether or not Judge Douglas or myself shall ever be
heard of after this night ; it may be a trifle to either of us, but
in connection with this mighty question, upon which hangs
the destinies of the nation, perhaps, it is absolutely nothing ; but where will you be placed if you re-endorse Judge
Douglas? Don't you know how apt he is—how exceedingly
anxious he is at all times to seize upon anything and everything to persuade you that something *he* has done *you* did
yourselves? Why, he tried to persuade you last that night our
Illinois Legislature instructed him to introduce the Nebraska
bill. There was nobody in that Legislature ever thought of
such thing ; and when he first introduced the bill, he never
thought of it ; but still he fights furiously for the proposition,
and that he did it because there was a standing instruction to
our Senators to be always introducing Nebraska bills. He tells
you he is for the Cincinnati platform, he tells you he is for the
Dred Scott decision. He tells you, not in his speech last
night, but substantially in a former speech, that he cares not
if slavery is voted up or down—he tells you the struggle on
Lecompton is past—it may come up again or not, and if it
does he stands where he stood when, in spite of him and his

opposition, you built up the Republican party. If you endorse him, you tell him you do not care whether slavery be voted up or down, and he will close, or try to close your mouths with his declaration, repeated by the day, the week, the month, and the year. Is that what you mean ? [Cries of " no," one voice, " yes."] Yes, I have no doubt you have always been for him, if you mean that. No doubt of that, soberly I have said, and I repeat it. I think, in the position in which Judge Douglas stood in opposing the Lecompton Constitution, he was right ; he does not know that it will return, but if it does we may know where to find him, and if it does not we may know where to look for him, and that is on the Cincinnati platform. Now, I could ask the Republican party, after all the hard names that Judge Douglas has called them by—all his repeated charges of their inclination to marry with and hug negroes —all his declarations of Black Republicanism—by the way, we are improving, the black has got rubbed off—but with all that, if he be endorsed by Republican votes, where do you stand ? Plainly, you stand ready saddled, bridled, and harnessed, and waiting to be driven over to the slavery extension camp of the nation—just ready to be driven over, tied together in a lot—to be driven over, every man with a rope around his neck, that halter being held by Judge Douglas. That is the question. If Republican men have been in earnest in what they have done, I think they had better not do it ; but I think that the Republican party is made up of those who, as far as they can peaceably, will oppose the extension of slavery, and who will hope for its ultimate extinction. If they believe it is wrong in grasping up the new lands of the continent, and keeping them from the settlement of free white laborers, who want the land to bring up their families upon ; if they are in earnest, although they may make a mistake, they will grow restless, and the time will come when they will come back again and reorganize, if not by the same name, at least upon the same principles as their party now has. It is better, then, to save the work while it is begun. You have done the labor ; maintain it—keep it. If men choose to serve you, go with them ; but as you have made up your organization upon principle, stand by it ; for, as surely as God reigns over you, and has inspired your mind, and given you a sense of propriety, and continues to give you hope, so surely will you still cling to these ideas, and you will at last come back again after your wanderings, merely to do your work over again.

We were often—more than once at least—in the course of Judge Douglas's speech last night, reminded that this government was made for white men—that he believed it was made for white men. Well, that is putting it into a shape in which no one wants to deny it; but the Judge then goes into his passion for drawing inferences that are not warranted. I protest, now and forever, against that counterfeit logic which presumes that because I did not want a negro woman for a slave, I do necessarily want her for a wife. My understanding is that I need not have her for either, but, as God made us separate, we can leave one another alone, and do one another much good thereby. There are white men enough to marry all the white women, and enough black men to marry all the black women, and in God's name let them be so married. The Judge regales us with the terrible enormities that take place by the mixture of races; that the inferior race bears the superior down. Why, Judge, if we do not let them get together in the territories they won't mix there.

A voice—"Three cheers for Lincoln." (The cheers were given with a hearty good will.)

Mr. Lincoln—I should say at least that that is a self-evident truth.

Now, it happens that we meet together once every year, sometimes about the 4th of July, for some reason or other. These 4th of July gatherings I suppose have their uses. If you will indulge me, I will state what I suppose to be some of them.

We are now a mighty nation; we are thirty, or about thirty millions of people, and we own and inhabit about one fifteenth part of the dry land of the whole earth. We run our memory back over the pages of history for about eighty-two years, and we discover that we were then a very small people in point of numbers, vastly inferior to what we are now, with a vastly less extent of country, with vastly less of everything we deem desirable among men—we look upon the change as exceedingly advantageous to us and to our posterity, and we fix upon something that happened away back, as in some way or other being connected with this rise of prosperity. We find a race of men living in that day whom we claim as our fathers and grandfathers; they were iron

men ; they fought for the principle that they were contending
for ; and we understood that by what they then did it has followed that the degree of prosperity which we now enjoy has
come to us. We hold this annual celebration to remind ourselves of all the good done in this process of time, of how it
was done and who did it, and how we are historically connected with it ; and we go from these meetings in better humor with ourselves—we feel more attached the one to the
other, and more firmly bound to the country we inhabit. In
every way we are better men in the age, and race, and country in which we live, for these celebrations. But after we
have done all this we have not yet reached the whole. There
is something else connected with it. We have besides these,
men—descended by blood from our ancestors—among us, perhaps half our people, who are not descendants at all of these
men ; they are men who have come from Europe—German,
Irish, French, and Scandinavian—men that have come from
Europe themselves, or whose ancestors have come hither and
settled here, finding themselves our equals in all things. If
they look back through this history to trace their connection
with those days by blood, they find they have none, they cannot carry themselves back into that glorious epoch and make
themselves feel that they are part of us, but when they look
through that old Declaration of Independence, they find·that
those old men say that " We hold these truths to be self-evident, that all men are created equal," and then they feel that
that moral sentiment taught in that day evidences their relation to those men, that it is the father of all moral principle
in them, and that they have a right to claim it as though they
were blood of the blood, and flesh of the flesh, of the men who
wrote that Declaration, and so they are. That is the electric
cord in that Declaration that links the hearts of patriotic and
liberty-loving men together, that will link those patriotic
hearts as long as the love of freedom exists in the minds of
men throughout the world.
    Now, sirs, for the purpose of squaring things with this idea
of " don't care if slavery is voted up or voted down," for sustaining the Dred Scott decision, for holding that the Declaration of Independence did not mean anything at all, we have
Judge Douglas giving his exposition of what the Declaration
of Independence means, and we have him saying that the

8*

people of America are equal to the people of England. According to his construction, you Germans are not connected with it. Now I ask you in all soberness, if all these things, if indulged in, if ratified, if confirmed and endorsed, if taught to our children, and repeated to them, do not tend to rub out the sentiment of liberty in the country, and to transform this government into a government of some other form? Those arguments that are made, that the inferior race are to be treated with as much allowance as they are capable of enjoying; that as much is to be done for them as their condition will allow. What are these arguments? They are the arguments that kings have made for enslaving the people in all ages of the world. You will find that all the arguments in favor of king-craft were of this class ; they always bestrode the necks of the people, not that they wanted to do it, but because the people were better off for being ridden. That is their argument, and this argument of the Judge is the same old serpent that says you work and I eat, you toil and I will enjoy the fruits of it. Turn in whatever way you will—whether it come from the mouth of a king, an excuse for enslaving the people of his country, or from the mouth, of men of one race as a reason for enslaving the men of another race, it is all the same old serpent, and I hold if that course of argumentation that is made for the purpose of convincing the public mind that we should not care about this, should be granted, it does not stop with the negro. I should like to know if, taking the old Declaration of Independence, which declares that all men are equal upon principle, and making exceptions to it, where will it stop? If one man says it does not mean a negro, why not another say it does not mean some other man? If that declaration is not the truth, let us get the statute book in which we find it, and tear it out. Who is so bold as to do it ? If it is not true, let us tear it out! (Cries of "No, no!") Let us stick to it then, let us stand firmly by it then.

It may be argued that there are certain conditions that make necessities and impose them upon us, and to the extent that a necessity is imposed upon a man, he must submit to it. I think that was the condition in which we found ourselves when we established this government. We had slavery among us, we could not get our Constitution unless we permitted them to remain in slavery, we could not secure the good we did secure if we grasped for more, and having by necessity submitted to that much, it does not destroy the principle that is the charter of our liberties. Let that charter stand as our standard.

My friend has said to me that I am a poor hand to quote Scripture. I will try it again, however. It is said in one of the admonitions of our Lord, " As your Father in Heaven is perfect, be ye also perfect." The Savior, I suppose, did not expect that any human creature could be perfect as the Father in Heaven ; but He said, " As your Father in Heaven is perfect, be ye also perfect." He set that up as a standard, and he who did most toward reaching that standard, attained the highest degree of moral perfection. So I say, in relation to the principle that all men are created equal, let it be as nearly reached as we can. If we cannot give freedom to every creature, let us do nothing that will impose slavery upon any other creature. Let us then turn this government back into the channel in which the framers of the Constitution originally placed it. Let us stand firmly by each other. If we do not do so we are turning in the contrary direction, that our friend Judge Douglas proposes—not intentionally—as·working in the traces tends to make this one universal slave nation. He is one that runs in that direction, and as such I resist him.

My friends, I have detained you about as long as I desired to do, and I have only to say, let us discard all this quibbling about this man and the other man—this race and that race and the other race being inferior, and therefore they must be placed in an inferior position—discarding our standard that we have left us. Let us discard all these things, and unite as one people throughout this land, until we shall once more stand up declaring that all men are created equal.

My friends, I could not, without launching off upon some new topic, which would detain you too long, continue to-night. I thank you for this most extensive audience that you have furnished me to-night. I leave you, hoping that the lamp of liberty will burn in your bosoms until there shall no longer be a doubt that all men are created free and equal.

SPEECH OF MR. LINCOLN,

DELIVERED in SPRINGFIELD, *Saturday evening, July* 17, 1858.
(*Mr. Douglas was not present.*)

FELLOW-CITIZENS: Another election, which is deemed an important one, is approaching, and, as I suppose, the Republicans will, without much difficulty, elect their State ticket. But in regard to the Legislature, we, the Republicans, labor under some disadvantages. In the first place, we have a Legislature to elect upon an apportionment of the representation made several years ago, when the proportion of the population was far greater in the South (as compared with the North) than it now is; and inasmuch as our opponents hold almost entire sway in the South, and we a correspondingly large majority in the North, the fact that we are now to be represented as we were years ago, when the population was different, is, to us, a very great disadvantage.   We had in the year 1855, according to law, a census or enumeration of the inhabitants taken for the purpose of a new apportionment of representation.   We know what a fair apportionment of representation upon that census would give us.   We know that it could not, if fairly made, fail to give the Republican party from six to ten more members of the Legislature than they can probably get as the law now stands.   It so happened at the last session of the Legislature, that our opponents, holding the control of both branches of the Legislature, steadily refused to give us such an apportionment as we were rightly entitled to have upon the census already taken. The Legislature steadily refused to give us such an apportionment as we were rightfully entitled to have upon the census taken of the population of the State.   The Legislature would pass no bill upon that subject, except such as was at least as unfair to us as the old one, and in which, in some instances, two men in the Democratic regions were allowed to go as far toward sending a member to the Legislature as three were in the Republican regions. Comparison was made at the time as to representative and senatorial districts, which completely demonstrated that such was the fact. Such a bill was passed and tendered to the Republican Governor for his signature; but principally for the reasons I have stated, he withheld his approval, and the bill fell without becoming a law.

Another disadvantage under which we labor is, that there are one or two Democratic Senators who will be members of the next Legislature, and will vote for the election of Senator, who are holding over in districts in which we could, on all reasonable calculation, elect men of our own, if we only had the chance of an election. When we consider that there are but twenty-five Senators in the Senate, taking two from the side where they rightfully belong and adding them to the other, is to us a disadvantage not to be lightly regarded. Still, so it is; we have this to contend with. Perhaps there is no ground of complaint on our part. In attending to the many things involved in the last general election for President, Governor, Auditor, Treasurer, Superintendent of Public Instruction, Members of Congress, of the Legislature, County Officers, and so on, we allowed these things to happen by want of sufficient attention, and we have no cause to complain of our adversaries, so far as this matter is concerned. But we have some cause to complain of the refusal to give us a fair apportionment.

There is still another disadvantage under which we labor, and to which I will ask your attention. It arises out of the relative positions of the two persons who stand before the State as candidates for the Senate. Senator Douglas is of world-wide renown. All the anxious politicians of his party, or who have been of his party for years past, have been looking upon him as certainly, at no distant day, to be the President of the United States. They have seen in his round, jolly, fruitful face, post-offices, land-offices, marshalships, and cabinet appointments, chargeships, and foreign missions, bursting and sprouting out in wonderful exuberance, ready to be laid hold of by their greedy hands. And as they have been gazing upon this attractive picture so long, they cannot, in the little distraction that has taken place in the party, bring themselves to give up the charming hope; but with greedier anxiety they rush about him, sustain him, and give him marches, triumphal entries, and receptions beyond what, even in the days of his highest prosperity, they could have brought about in his favor. On the contrary, nobody has ever expected me to be President. In my poor, lean, lank face, nobody has ever seen that any cabbages were sprouting out. These are disadvantages, all taken together, that the Republicans labor under. We have to fight this battle upon principle, and upon principle alone. I am, in a certain sense, made the standard-bearer in be half of the Republicans. I was made so merely because there had to be some one so placed—I being in nowise preferable to any other one of the twenty-five—perhaps a hundred we have in the Republican ranks. Then I say I wish it to be distinctly understood and borne in mind that we have to fight this battle without many— perhaps without any— of the external aids which are brought to bear against us. So I hope those with whom I am surrounded have principle enough to nerve themselves for the task, and leave nothing undone, that can be fairly done, to bring about the right result.

After Senator Douglas left Washington, as his movements were made known by public prints, he tarried a considerable time in the city of New-York ; and it was heralded that, like another Napoleon, he was lying by and framing the plan of his campaign. It was telegraphed to Washington City, and published in the *Union*, that he was framing his plan for the purpose of going to Illinois to pounce upon and annihilate the treasonable and disunion speech which Lincoln had made here on the 16th of June. Now, I do suppose that the Judge really spent some time in New-York maturing the plan of the campaign, as his friends heralded for him. I have been able, by noting his movements since his arrival in Illinois, to discover evi dences confirmatory of that allegation. I think I have been able to see what are the material points of that plan. I will, for a little while, ask your attention to some of them. What I shall point out, though not showing the whole plan, are, nevertheless, the main points, as I suppose.

They are not very numerous. The first is popular sovereignty. The second and third are attacks upon my speech made on the 16th of June. Out of these three points—drawing within the range of popular sovereignty the question of the Lecompton constitution — he makes his principal assault. Upon these his successive speeches are substantially one and the same. On this matter of popular sovereignty I wish to be a little careful. Auxiliary to these main points, to be sure, are their thunderings of cannon, their marching and music, their fizzle-gigs and fire-works ; but I will not waste time with them. They are but the little trappings of the campaign.

Coming to the substance—the first point—popular sovereignty. It is to be labeled upon the cars in which he travels ; put upon the hacks he rides in ; to be flaunted upon the arches he passes under, and the banners which wave over him. It is to be dished up in as many varieties as a French cook can produce soups from potatoes. Now, as this is so great a staple of the plan of the campaign, it is worth while to examine it carefully ; and if we examine only a very little, and do not allow ourselves to be misled, we shall be able to see that the whole thing is the most arrant Quixotism that was ever enacted before a community. What is the matter of popular sovereignty? The first thing, in order to understand it, is to get a good definition of what it is, and after that to see how it is applied.

I suppose almost every one knows that, in this controversy, whatever has been said has had reference to the question of negro slavery. We have not been in a controversy about the right of the people to govern themselves in the *ordinary* matters of domestic concern in the States and territories. Mr. Buchanan, in one of his late messages (I think when he sent up the Lecompton constitution), urged that the main point to which the public attention had been directed, was not in regard to the great variety of small domestic matters, but was directed to the question of negro slavery ; and he asserts, that if the people had had a fair chance to vote on that question, there was no reasonable ground of objection in regard to minor questions. Now, while I think that the people had *not* had given, or offered them, a fair chance upon that slavery question ; still, if there had been a fair submission to a vote upon that main question, the President's proposition would have been true to the uttermost. Hence, when hereafter I speak of popular sovereignty, I wish to be understood as applying what I say to the question of slavery only, not to other minor domestic matters of a territory or a State.

Does Judge Douglas, when he says that several of the past years of his life have been devoted to the question of " popular sovereignty," and that all the remainder of his life shall be devoted to it, does he mean to say that he has been devoting his

life to securing to the people of the territories the right to exclude slavery from the territories ? If he means so to say, he
means to deceive ; because he and every one knows that the
decision of the Supreme Court, which he approves and makes
especial ground of attack upon me for disapproving, forbids
the people of a territory to exclude slavery. This covers the
whole ground, from the settlement of a territory till it reaches
the degree of maturity entitling it to form a State constitution.
So far as all that ground is concerned, the Judge is not sustaining popular sovereignty, but absolutely.opposing it.   He
sustains the decision which declares that the popular will of
the territories has no constitutional power to exclude slavery
during their territorial existence. This being so, the period
of time from the first settlement of a territory till it reaches
the point of forming a State constitution, is not the thing that
the Judge has fought for, or is fighting for, but, on the contrary, he has fought for, and is fighting for, the thing that anni-
hilates and crushes out that same popular sovereignty.

Well, so much being disposed of, what is left ? Why, he
is contending for the right of the people, when they come to
make a State constitution, to make it for themselves, and precisely as best suits themselves. I say again, that is Quixotic.
I defy contradiction when I declare that the Judge can find no
one to oppose him on that proposition. I repeat, there is nobody opposing that proposition on *principle*. Let me not be
misunderstood. I know that, with reference to the Lecompton constitution, I may be misunderstood ; but when you understand me correctly, my proposition will be true and accurate. Nobody is opposing, or has opposed, the right of the
people, when they form a constitution, to form it for themselves. Mr. Buchanan and his friends have not done it ; they,
too, as well as the Republicans and the Anti-Lecompton
Democrats, have not done it ; but, on the contrary, they
together have insisted on the right of the people to form a
constitution for themselves. The difference between the Buchanan men on the one hand, and the Douglas men and the
Republicans on the other, has not been on a question of principle, but on a question of *fact*.

The dispute was upon the question of fact, whether the
Lecompton constitution had been fairly formed by the people
or not. Mr. Buchanan and his friends have not contended

for the contrary principle any more than the Douglas men or
the Republicans. They have insisted that whatever of small
irregularities existed in getting up the Lecompton constitution
were such as happen in the settlement of all new territories.
The question was, was it a fair emanation of the people? It
was a question of fact and not of principle. As to the principle, all were agreed. Judge Douglas voted with the Republicans upon that matter of fact.

He and they, by their voices and votes, denied that it was
a fair emanation of the people. The administration affirmed
that it was. With respect to the evidence bearing upon that
question of fact, I readily agree that Judge Douglas and the
Republicans had the right on their side, and that the administration was wrong. But I state again, as a matter of principle, there is no dispute upon the right of a people in a territory, merging into a State to form a constitution for themselves, without outside interference from any quarter. This
being so, what is Judge Douglas going to spend his life for?
Is he going to spend his life in maintaining a principle that
nobody on earth opposes? Does he expect to stand up in
majestic dignity, and go through his *apotheosis* and become a
god, in the maintaining of a principle which neither man nor
mouse in all God's creation is opposing? Now, something in
in regard to the Lecompton constitution more specially; for I
pass from this other question of popular sovereignty as the
most arrant humbug that has ever been attempted on an intelligent community.

As to the Lecompton constitution, I have already said that,
on the question of fact as to whether it was a fair emanation
of the people or not, Judge Douglas with the Republicans and
some Americans, had greatly the argument against the administration ; and while I repeat this, I wish to know what there
is in the opposition of Judge Douglas, to the Lecompton constitution that entitles him to be considered the only opponent
to it—as being *par excellence* the very *quintessence* of that opposition. I agree to the rightfulness of his opposition. He in
the Senate and his class of men there formed the number
three and no more. In the House of Representatives his class
of men—the Anti-Lecompton Democrats—formed a number
of about twenty. It took one hundred and twenty to defeat the
measure, against one hundred and twelve. Of the votes of

that one hundred and twenty, Judge Douglas's friends furnished twenty, to add to which there were six Americans and ninety-four Republicans. I do not say that I am precisely accurate in their numbers, but I am sufficiently so for any use I am making of it.

Why is it that twenty shall be entitled to all the credit of doing that work, and the hundred none of it? Why, if, as Judge Douglas says, the honor is to be divided, and due credit is to be given to other parties, why is just so much given as is consonant with the wishes, the interests, and advancement of the twenty? My understanding is, when a common job is done, or a common enterprise prosecuted, if I put in five dollars to your one, I have a right to take out five dollars to your one. But he does not so understand it. He declares the dividend of credit for defeating Lecompton upon a basis which seems unprecedented and incomprehensible.

Let us see. Lecompton in the raw was defeated. It afterward took a sort of cooked-up shape, and was passed in the English bill. It is said by the Judge that the defeat was a good and proper thing. If it was a good thing, why is he entitled to more credit than others, for the performance of that good act, unless there was something in the antecedents of the Republicans that might induce every one to expect them to join in that good work, and at the same time, something leading them to doubt that he would? Does he place his superior claim to credit, on the ground that he performed a good act which was never expected of him? He says I have a proneness for quoting scripture. If I should do so now, it occurs that perhaps he places himself somewhat upon the ground of the parable of the lost sheep, which went astray upon the mountains, and when the owner of the hundred sheep found the one that was lost, and threw it upon his shoulders, and came home rejoicing, it was said that there was more rejoicing over the one sheep that was lost, and had been found, than over the ninety and nine in the fold. The application is made by the Savior in this parable, thus : " Verily, I say unto you, there is more rejoicing in heaven over one sinner that repenteth, than over ninety and nine just persons that need no repentance."

·And now, if the Judge claims the benefit of this parable, *let him repent* Let him not come up here and say : " I am

the only just person ; and you are the ninety-nine sinners !"
Repentance before *forgiveness* is a provision of the Christian
system, and on that condition alone will the Republicans grant
his forgiveness.

How will he prove that we have ever occupied a different
position in regard to the Lecompton constitution, or any principle in it ? He says he did not make his opposition on the
ground as to whether it was a free or slave constitution, and
he would have you understand that the Republicans made their
opposition because it ultimately became a slave constitution.
To make proof in favor of himself on this point, he reminds
us that he opposed Lecompton before the vote was taken declaring whether the State was to be be free or slave. But he
forgets to say that our Republican Senator, Trumbull, made
a speech against Lecompton even before he did.

Why did he oppose it ? Partly, as he declares, because the
members of the convention who framed it were not fairly
elected by the people ; that the people were not allowed to
vote unless they had been registered ; and that the people of
whole counties, in some instances, were not registered. For
these reasons he declares the constitution was not an emanation, in any sense, from the people. He also has an additional
objection as to the mode of submitting the constitution back
to the people. But bearing on the question of whether the
delegates were fairly elected, a speech of his, made something
more than twelve months ago, from this stand, becomes important. It was made a little while before the election of the
delegates who made Lecompton. In that speech, he declared
there was every reason to hope and believe the election would
be fair ; and if any one failed to vote, it would be his own
culpable fault.

I, a few days after, made a sort of answer to that speech.
In that answer, I made, substantially, the very argument with
which he combated his Lecompton adversaries in the Senate
last winter. I pointed to the facts that the people could not
vote without being registered, and that the time for registering
had gone by. I commented on it as wonderful that Judge
Douglas could be ignorant of these facts, which every one else
in the nation so well knew.

I now pass from popular sovereignty and Lecompton. I
may have occasion to refer to one or both.

When he was preparing his plan of campaign, Napoleon-like, in New-York, as appears by two speeches I have heard him deliver since his arrival in Illinois, he gave special attention to a speech of mine, delivered here on the 16th of June last. He says that he carefully read that speech. He told us that at Chicago, a week ago last night, and he repeated it at Bloomington last night. Doubtless, he repeated it again to-day, though I did not hear him. In the first two places—Chicago and Bloomington—I heard him ; to-day I did not. He said he had carefully examined that speech ; *when*, he did not say ; but there is no reasonable doubt it was when he was in New-York, preparing his plan of campaign. I am glad he did read it carefully. He says it was evidently prepared with great care. I freely admit it was prepared with care. I claim not to be more free from errors than others—perhaps scarcely so much ; but I was very careful not to put anything in that speech as a matter of fact, or make any inferences which did not appear to me to be true, and fully warrantable. If I had made any mistake I was willing to be corrected ; if I had drawn any inference in regard to Judge Douglas, or any one else, which was not warranted, I was fully prepared to modify it as soon as discovered. I planted myself upon the truth, and the truth only, so far as I knew it, or could be brought to know it.

Having made that speech with the most kindly feelings toward Judge Douglas, as manifested therein, I was gratified when I found that he had carefully examined it, and had detected no error of fact, nor any inference against him, nor any misrepresentations, of which he thought fit to complain. In neither of the two speeches I have mentioned, did he make any such complaint. I will thank any one who will inform me that he, in his speech to-day, pointed out anything I had stated, respecting him, as being erroneous. I presume there is no such thing. I have reason to be gratified that the care and caution used in that speech, left it so that he, most of all others interested in discovering error, has not been able to point out one thing against him which he could say was wrong. He seizes upon the doctrines he supposes to be included in that speech, and declares that upon them will turn the issues of this campaign. He then quotes, or attempts to quote, from my speech. I will not say that he wilfully misquotes, but he does fail to quote accurately. His attempt at quoting is from a passage which I believe I can quote accurately from memory. I shall make the quotation now, with some comments upon it, as I have already said, in order that the Judge shall be left entirely without excuse for misrepresenting me. I do so now, as I hope, for the last time. I do this in great caution, in order that if he repeats his misrepresentation, it shall be plain to all that he does so wilfully. If, after all, he still persists, I shall be compelled to reconstruct the course I have marked out for myself, and draw upon such humble resources as I have, for a new course, better suited to the real exigencies of the case. I set out, in this campaign, with the intention of conducting it strictly as a gentleman, in substance at least, if not in the outside polish. The latter I shall never be, but that which constitutes the inside of a gentleman I hope I understand, and am not less inclined to practise than others. It was my purpose and expectation, that this canvass would be conducted upon principle, and with fairness upon both sides, and it shall not be my fault if this purpose and expectation shall be given up.

He charges, in substance, that I invite a war of sections; that I propose all the local institutions of the different States shall become consolidated and uniform. What is there in the language of that speech which expresses such purpose, or bears such construction? I have again and again said that I would not enter into any of the States to disturb the institution of slavery. Judge Douglas said, at Bloomington, that I used language most able and ingenious for concealing what I really meant; and that while I had protested against entering into the slave States, I nevertheless did mean to go on the banks of the Ohio and throw missiles into Kentucky, to disturb them in their domestic institutions.

I said, in that speech, and I meant no more, that the institution of slavery ought to be placed in the very attitude where the framers of this government placed it and left it. I do not understand that the framers of our Constitution left the people of the free States in the attitude of firing bombs or shells into the slave States. I was not using that passage for the purpose for which he infers I did use it. I said: "We are now far advanced into the fifth year since a policy was created for the avowed object and with the confident promise of putting an end to slavery agitation. Under the operation of that policy, that agitation has not only not ceased, but has constantly augmented. In my opinion it will not cease till a crisis shall have been reached and passed. ' A house divided against itself cannot stand.' I believe that this government cannot endure permanently half slave and half free. It will become all one thing or all the other. Either the opponents of slavery will arrest the further spread of it, and place it where the public mind shall rest in the belief that it is in the course of ultimate extinction, or its advocates will push it forward till it shall become alike lawful in all the States, old as well as new, North as well as South."

Now you all see, from that quotation, I did not express my *wish* on anything. In that passage I indicated no wish or purpose of my own; I simply expressed my *expectation*. Cannot the Judge perceive a distinction between a *purpose* and an *expectation?* I have often expressed an expectation to die, but I never expressed a *wish* to die. I said at Chicago, and now repeat, that I am quite aware this government has endured, half slave and half free, for eighty-two years. I understand that little bit of history. I expressed the opinion I did, because I perceived—or thought I perceived—a new set of causes introduced. I did say at Chicago, in my speech there, that I do wish to see the spread of slavery arrested, and to see it placed where the public mind shall rest in the belief that it is in the course of ultimate extinction. I said that because I supposed, when the public mind shall rest in that belief, we shall have peace on the slavery question. I have believed—and now believe—the public mind did rest on that belief up to the introduction of the Nebraska bill.

Although I have ever been opposed to slavery, so far I rested in the hope and belief that it was in the course of ultimate extinction. For that reason, it had been a minor question with me. I might have been mistaken; but I had believed, and now believe, that the whole public mind—that is, the mind of the great majority—had rested in that belief up to the repeal of the Missouri compromise. But upon that event, I became convinced that either I had been resting in a delusion, or the institution was being placed on a new basis—a basis for making it perpetual, national, and universal. Subsequent events have greatly confirmed me in that belief. I believe that bill to be the beginning of a conspiracy for that purpose. So believing, I have since then considered that question a paramount one. So believing, I thought the public mind will never rest till the power of Congress to restrict the spread of it shall again be acknowledged and exercised on the one hand, or on the other, all resistance be entirely crushed out. I have expressed that opinion, and I entertain it to-night. It is denied that there is any tendency to the nationalization of slavery in these States.

Mr. Brooks, of South Carolina, in one of his speeches, when they were presenting him canes, silver plate, gold pitchers, and the like, for assaulting Senator Sumner, distinctly affirmed his opinion that when this Constitution was formed, it was the belief of no man that slavery would last to the present day.

He said, what I think, that the framers of our Constitution placed the institution of slavery where the public mind rested in the hope that it was in the course of ultimate extinction. But he went on to say that the men of the present age, by their experience, have become wiser than the framers of the Constitution ; and the invention of the cotton-gin had made the perpetuity of slavery a necessity in this country.

As another piece of evidence tending to this same point : Quite recently in Virginia, a man—the owner of slaves— made a will, providing that, after his death, certain of his slaves should have their freedom, if they should so choose, and go to Liberia, rather than remain in slavery. They chose to be liberated. But the persons to whom they would descend as property, claimed them as slaves. A suit was instituted, which finally came to the Supreme Court of Virginia, and was therein decided against the slaves, upon the ground that a negro cannot make a choice—that they had no legal power to choose—could not perform the condition upon which their freedom depended.

I do not mention this with any purpose of criticising it, but to connect it with the arguments as affording additional evidence of the change of sentiment upon this question of slavery in the direction of making it perpetual and national. I argue now, as I did before, that there is such a tendency, and I am backed not merely by the facts, but by the open confession in the slave States.

And now, as to the Judge's inference, that because I wish
to see slavery placed in the course of ultimate extinction—
placed where our fathers originally placed it—I wish to
annihilate the State Legislatures—to force cotton to grow on
the tops of the Green Mountains—to freeze ice in Florida—
to cut lumber on the broad Illinois prairies—that I am in
favor of all these ridiculous and impossible things.

It seems to me it is a complete answer to all this to ask, if,
when Congress did have the fashion of restricting slavery
from free territory—when courts did have the fashion of deciding that taking a slave into a free country made him
free—I say it is a sufficient answer to ask, if any of this
ridiculous nonsense about consolidation, and uniformity, did
actually follow? Who heard of any such thing, because of
the Ordinance of '87? because of the Missouri restriction?
because of the numerous court decisions of that character?

Now, as to the Dred Scott decision; for upon that he
makes his last point at me. He boldly takes ground in favor
of that decision.

This is one half the onslaught, and one third of the entire
plan of the campaign. I am opposed to that decision in a
certain sense, but not in the sense which he puts on it. I say
that in so far as it decided in favor of Dred Scott's master,
and against Dred Scott and his family, I do not propose to
disturb or resist the decision.

I never have proposed to do any such thing. ɪ think, that
in respect for judicial authority, my humble history would not
suffer in comparison with that of Judge Douglas. He would
have the citizen conform his vote to that decision; the member of Congress, ʜɪs; the President, his use of the veto power.
He would make it a rule of political action for the people and
all the departments of government. I would not. By resisting it as a political rule, I disturb no right of property,
create no disorder, excite no mobs.

When he spoke at Chicago, on Friday evening of last week,
he made this same point upon me. On Saturday evening I
replied, and reminded him of a Supreme Court decision which
he opposed for at least several years. Last night, at Bloomington, he took some notice of that reply; but entirely forgot
to remember that part of it.

He renews his onslaught upon me, forgetting to remember

that I have turned the tables against himself on that very point. I renew the effort to draw his attention to it. I wish to stand erect before the country, as well as Judge Douglas, on this question of judicial authority; and therefore I add something to the authority in favor of my own position. I wish to show that I am sustained by authority, in addition to that heretofore presented. I do not expect to convince the Judge. It is part of the plan of his campaign, and he will cling to it with a desperate gripe. Even, turn it upon him— the sharp point against him, and gaff him through—he will still cling to it till he can invent some new dodge to take the place of it.

In public speaking it is tedious reading from documents ; but I must beg to indulge the practice to a limited extent. I shall read from a letter written by Mr. Jefferson in 1820, and now to be found in the seventh volume of his correspondence, at page 177. It seems he had been presented by a gentleman of the name of Jarvis with a book, or essay, or periodical, called the "Republican," and he was writing in acknowledgment of the present, and noting some of its contents. After expressing the hope that the work will produce a favorable effect upon the minds of the young, he proceeds to say :

"That it will have this tendency may be expected, and for that reason I feel an urgency to note what I deem an error in it, the more requiring notice as your opinion is strengthened by that of many others. You seem, in pages 84 and 148, to consider the judges as the ultimate arbiters of all constitutional questions—a very dangerous doctrine indeed, and one which would place us under the despotism of an oligarchy. Our judges are as honest as other men, and not more so. They have, with others, the same passions for party, for power, and the privilege of their corps. Their maxim is, 'boni judicis est ampliare jurisdictionem ;' and their power is the more dangerous as they are in office for life, and not responsible, as the other functionaries are, to the elective control. The Constitution has erected no such single tribunal, knowing that, to whatever hands confided, with the corruptions of time and party, its members would become despots. It has more wisely made all the departments coequal and cosovereign with themselves."

Thus we see the power claimed for the Supreme Court by

9

Judge Douglas, Mr. Jefferson holds, would reduce us to the despotism of an oligarchy.

Now, I have said no more than this—in fact, never quite so much as this—at least I am sustained by Mr. Jefferson.

Let us go a little farther. * You remember we once had a National Bank. Some one owed the bank a debt; he was sued and sought to avoid payment, on the ground that the bank was unconstitutional. The case went to the Supreme Court, and therein it was decided that the bank was constitutional. The whole democratic party revolted against that decision. General Jackson himself asserted that he, as President, would not be bound to hold a National Bank to be constitutional, even though the court had decided it to be so. He fell in precisely with the view of Mr. Jefferson, and acted upon it under his official oath, in vetoing a charter for a National Bank. The declaration that Congress does not possess this constitutional power to charter a bank, has gone into the democratic platform, at their national conventions, and was brought forward and reaffirmed in their last convention at Cincinnati. They have contended for that declaration, in the very teeth of the Supreme Court, for more than a quarter of a century. In fact, they have reduced the decision to an absolute nullity. That decision, I repeat, is repudiated in the Cincinnati platform; and still, as if to show that effrontry can go no farther, Judge Douglas vaunts in the very speeches in which he denounces me for opposing the Dred Scott decision, that he stands on the Cincinnati platform.

Now, I wish to know what the Judge can charge upon me, with respect to decisions of the Supreme Court, which does not lie in all its length, breadth, and proportions at his own door. The plain truth is simply this : Judge Douglas is *for* Supreme Court decisions when he likes and against them when he does not likes them. He is for the Dred Scott decision because it tends to nationalize slavery—because it is part of the original combination for that object. It so happens, singularly enough, that I never stood opposed to a decision of the Supreme Court till this. On the contrary, I have no recollection that he was ever particularly in favor of one till this. He never was in favor of any, nor opposed to any, till the present one, which helps to nationalize slavery.

Free men men of Sangamon—free men of Illinois—free

men everywhere—judge ye between him and me, upon this issue.

He says this Dred Scott case is a very small matter at most —that it has no practical effect ; that at best, or rather, I suppose, at worst, it is but an abstraction. I submit that the proposition, that the thing which determines whether a man is free or a slave, is rather *concrete* and *abstract*. I think you would conclude that it was, if your liberty depended upon it, and so would Judge Douglas if his liberty depended upon it. But suppose it was on the question of spreading slavery over the new territories that he considers it as being merely an abstract matter, and one of no practical importance. How has the planting of slavery in new countries always been effected ? It has now been decided that slavery cannot be kept out of our new territories by any legal means. In what does our new territories now differ in this respect from the old colonies when slavery was first planted within them? It was planted, as Mr. Clay once declared, and as history proves true, by individual men in spite of the wishes of the people ; the mother government refusing to prohibit it, and withholding from the people of the colonies the authority to prohibit it for themselves. Mr. Clay says this was one of the great and just causes of complaint against Great Britain by the colonies, and the best apology we can now make for having the institution among us. In that precise condition our Nebraska politicians have at last succeeded in placing our own new territories ; the government will not prohibit slavery within them, nor allow the people to prohibit it.

I defy any man to find any difference between the policy which originally planted slavery in these colonies and that policy which now prevails in our new territories. If it does not go into them, it is only because no individual wishes it to go. The Judge indulged himself, doubtless to-day, with the question as to what I am going to do with or about the Dred Scott decision. Well, Judge, will you please to tell me what you did about the bank decision ? Will you not graciously allow us to do with the Dred Scott decision precisely as you did with the bank decision ? You succeeded in breaking down the moral effect of that decision ; did you find it necessary to amend the Constitution ? or to set up a court of negroes in order to do it ?

There is one other point.   Judge Douglas has a very affectionate leaning toward the Americans and Old Whigs.   Last evening, in a sort of weeping tone, he described to us a death-bed scene.   He had been called to the side of Mr. Clay, in his last moments, in order that the genius of " popular sovereignty" might duly descend from the dying man and settle upon him, the living and most worthy successor.   He could do no less than promise that he would devote the remainder of his life to " popular sovereignty ;" and then the great statesman departs in peace.   By this part of the " plan of the campaign," the Judge has evidently promised himself that tears shall be drawn down the cheeks of all Old Whigs, as large as half-grown apples.

Mr. Webster, too, was mentioned ; but it did not quite come to a death-bed scene, as to him.   It would be amusing, if it were not disgusting, to see how quick these compromise-breakers administer on the political effects of their dead adversaries, trumping up claims never before heard of, and dividing the assets among themselves.   If I should be found dead to-morrow morning, nothing but my insignificance could prevent a speech being made on my authority, before the end of next week.   It so happens that in·that " popular sovereignty" with which Mr. Clay was identified, the Missouri Compromise was expressly reserved ; and it was a little singular if Mr. Clay cast his mantle upon Judge Douglas on purpose to have that compromise repealed.

Again, the Judge did not keep faith with Mr. Clay when he first brought in his Nebraska bill.   He left the Missouri Compromise unrepealed, and in his report accompanying the bill, he told the world he did it on purpose.   The manes of Mr. Clay must have been in great agony, till thirty days later, when " popular sovereignty" stood forth in all its glory.

One more thing.   Last night Judge Douglas tormented himself with horrors about my disposition to make negroes perfectly equal with white men in social and political relations. He did not stop to show that I have said any such thing, or that it legitimately follows from anything I have said, but he rushes on with his assertions.   I adhere to the Declaration of Independence.   If Judge Douglas and his friends are not willing to stand by it, let them come up and amend it.   Let them make it read that all men are created equal except ne-

groes. Let us have it decided, whether the Declaration of
Independence, in this blessed year of 1858, shall be thus
amended. In his construction of the Declaration last year,
he said it only meant that Americans in America were equal
to Englishmen in England. Then, when I pointed out to him
that by that rule he excludes the Germans, the Irish, the Por-
tuguese, and all the other people who have come among us
since the Revolution, he reconstructs his construction. In his
last speech he tells us it meant Europeans.

I press him a little further, and ask if it meant to include the
Russians in Asia? or does he mean to exclude that vast population from the principles of our Declaration of Independence?
I expect ere long he will introduce another amendment to his
definition. He is not at all particular. He is satisfied with
anything which does not endanger the nationalizing of negro
slavery. It may draw white men down, but it must not lift
negroes up. Who shall say, " I am the superior, and you are
the inferior ?"

My declarations upon this subject of negro slavery may be
misrepresented, but cannot be misunderstood. I have said
that I do not understand the Declaration to mean that all
men were created equal in all respects. They are not our
equal in color; but I suppose that it does mean to declare that
all men are equal in some respects; they are equal in their
right to " life, liberty, and the pursuit of happiness." Certainly the negro is not our equal in color—perhaps not in
many other respects; still, in the right to put into his mouth
the bread that his own hands have earned, he is the equal of
every other man, white or black. In pointing out that more
has been given you, you cannot be justified in taking away the
little which has been given him. All I ask for the negro is
that if you do not like him, let him alone. If God gave him
but little, that little let him enjoy.

When our government was established, we had the institution of slavery among us. We were in a certain sense compelled to tolerate its existence. It was a sort of necessity.
We had gone through our struggle and secured our own independence. The framers of the Constitution found the institution of slavery among their other institutions at the time.
They found that by an effort to eradicate it, they might lose
much of what they had already gained. They were obliged

to bow to the necessity. They gave power to Congress to abolish the slave trade at the end of twenty years. They also prohibited it in the territories where it did not exist. They did what they could and yielded to the necessity for the rest. I also yield to all which follows from that necessity. What I wou!d most desire would be the separation of the white and black races.

One more point on this Springfield speech which Judge Douglas says he has read so carefully. I expressed my be- lief in the existence of a conspiracy to perpetuate and nation- alize slavery. I did not profess to know it, nor do I now. I showed the part Judge Douglas had played in the string of facts, constituting to my mind the proof of that conspiracy. I showed the parts played by others.

I charged that the people had been deceived into carrying the last Presidential election, by the impression that the peo- dle of the territories might exclude slavery if they chose, when it was known in advance by the conspirators, that the court was to decide that neither Congress nor the people could so exclude slavery. These charges are more distinctly made than anything else in the speech.

Judge Douglas has carefully read and re-read that speech. He has not, so far as I know, contradicted those charges. In the two speeches which I heard, he certainly did not. On his own tacit admission I renew that charge. I charge him as having been a party to that conspiracy and to that deception for the sole purpose of nationalizing slavery.

MR. LINCOLN'S SPEECH,

AT GALESBURGH, *Oct.* 7, 1858.

My FELLOW-CITIZENS : A very large portion of the speech which Judge Douglas has addressed to you has previously been delivered and put in print. I do not mean that for a hit upon .the Judge at all. If I had not been interrupted I was going to say that such an answer as I was able to make to a very large portion of it, had already been more than once made and published. There has been an opportunity afforded to the public to see our respective views upon the topics discussed in a large portion of the speech which he has just delivered. I make these remarks for the purpose of excusing myself for not passing over the entire ground that the Judge has traversed. I, however, desire to take up some of the points that he has attended to, and ask your attention to them, and I shall follow him backward upon some notes which I have taken, reversing the order by beginning where he concluded.

The Judge has alluded to the Declaration of Independence, and insisted that negroes are not included in that Declaration; and that it is a slander upon the framers of that instrument, to suppose that negroes were meant therein; and he asks you : Is it possible to believe that Mr. Jefferson, who penned the immortal paper, could have supposed himself applying the language of that instrument to the negro race, and yet held a portion of that race in slavery? Would he not at once have freed them? I only have to remark upon this part of the Judge's speech (and that, too, very briefly, for I shall not detain myself, or you, upon that point for any great length of time), that I believe the entire records of the world, from the date of the Declaration of Independence up to within three years ago, may be searched in vain for one single affirmation, from one single man, that the negro was not included in the Declaration of Independence; I think I may defy Judge Douglas to show that he ever said so, that Washington ever said so, that any President ever said so, that any member of Congress ever said so, or that any living man upon the whole earth ever said so, until the necessities of the present policy of the Democratic party, in regard to slavery, had to invent that affirmation. And I will remind Judge Douglas and this audience, that while Mr. Jefferson was the owner of slaves, as undoubtedly he was, in speaking upon this very subject, he used the strong language that "he trembled for his country when he remembered that God was just;" and I will offer the highest premium in my power to Judge Douglas if he will show that he, in all his life, ever uttered a sentiment at all akin to that of Jefferson.

The next thing to which I will ask your attention is the Judge's comments upon the fact, as he assumes it to be, that we cannot call our public meetings as Republican meetings; and he instances Tazewell county as one of the places where

the friends of Lincoln have called a public meeting and have
not dared to name it a Republican meeting. He instances
Monroe county as another where Judge Trumbull and Jehu
Baker addressed the persons whom the Judge assumes to be
the friends of Lincoln, calling them the " Free Democracy."
I have the honor to inform Judge Douglas that he spoke in
that very county of Tazewell last Saturday, and I was there
on Tuesday last, and when he spoke there he spoke under a
call not venturing to use the word " Democrat." [Turning
to Judge Douglas.] What think you of this?

So again, there is another thing to which I would ask the
Judge's attention upon this subject. In the contest of 1856
his party delighted to call themselves together as the " National Democracy," but now, if there should be a notice put up
anywhere, for a meeting of the " National Democracy," Judge
Douglas and his friends would not come. They would not
suppose themselves invited. They would understand that it
was a call for those hateful post-masters whom he talks about.

Now a few words in regard to these extracts from speeches
of mine, which Judge Douglas has read to you, and which he
supposes are in very great contrast to each other. Those
speeches have been before the public for a considerable time,
and if they have any inconsistency in them, if there is
any conflict in them, the public have been able to detect it.
When the Judge says, in speaking on this subject, that I make
speeches of one sort for the people of the northern end of the
State, and of a different sort for the southern people, he assumes that I do not understand that my speeches will be put
in print and read north and south. I knew all the while that the
speech that I made at Chicago, and the one I made at Jonesboro and the one at Charleston, would all be put in print and
all the reading and intelligent men in the community would
see them and know all about my opinions. And I have not supposed, and do not now suppose, that there is any conflict whatever between them. But the Judge will have it that if we do
not confess that there is a sort of inequality between the white
and black races, which justifies us in making them slaves, we
must, then, insist that there is a degree of equality that requires us to make them our wives. Now, I have all the while
taken a broad distinction in regard to that matter ; and that
is all there is in these different speeches which he arrays here,
and the entire reading of either of the speeches will show that

that distinction was made. Perhaps by taking two parts of the same speech, he could have got up as much of a conflict as the one he has found. I have all the while maintained, that in so far as it should be insisted that there was an equality between the white and black races that should produce a perfect social and political equality, it was an impossibility. This you have seen in my printed speeches, and with it I have said, that in their right to "life, liberty and the pursuit of happiness," as proclaimed in that old Declaration, the inferior races are our equals. And these declarations I have constantly made in reference to the abstract moral question, to contemplate and consider when we are legislating about any new country which is not already cursed with the actual presence of the evil—slavery. I have never manifested any impatience with the necessities that spring from the actual presence of black people mong us, and the actual existence of slavery among, us where it does already exist; but I have insisted that, in legislating for new countries, where it does not exist, there is no just rule other than that of moral and abstract right! With reference to those new countries, those maxims as to the right of a people to "life, liberty and the pursuit of happiness," were the just rules to be constantly referred to. There is no misunderstanding this, except by men interested to misunderstand it. I take it that I have to address an intelligent and reading community, who will peruse what I say, weigh it, and then judge whether I advance improper or unsound views, or whether I advance hypocritical, and deceptive, and contrary views in different portions of the country. I believe myself to be guilty of no such thing as the latter, though, of course, I cannot claim that I am entirely free from all error in the opinions I advance.

The Judge has also detained us a while in regard to the distinction between his party and our party. His he assumes to be a national party—ours a sectional one. He does this in asking the question whether this country has any interest in the maintenance of the Republican party? He assumes that our party is altogether sectional—that the party to which he adheres is national; and the argument is, that no party can be a rightful party—can be based upon rightful principles—unless it can announce its principles everywhere. I presume that Judge Douglas could not go into Russia and announce the doctrine of our national Democracy; he could not denounce the doctrine of kings, and emperors, and monarchies, in Russia; and it may be true of this country, that in some places we may not be able to proclaim a doctrine as clearly true as the truth of Democracy, because there is a section so directly opposed to it that they will not tolerate us in doing so. Is it the true test of the soundness of a doctrine, that in some places people won't let you proclaim it? Is that the way to test the truth of any doctrine? Why, I understood that at one time the people of Chicago would not let Judge Douglas preach a certain favorite doctrine of his. I commend to his consideration the question, whether he takes that as a test of the unsoundness of what he wanted to preach.

There is another thing to which I wish to ask attention for a little while on this occasion. What has always been the evidence brought forward to prove that the Republican party is a sectional party? The main one was that in the Southern portion of the Union the people did not let the Republicans proclaim their doctrines among them. That has been the main evidence brought forward—that they had no supporters, or substantially none, in the slave States. The South have not taken hold of our principles as we announce them; nor does Judge Douglas now grapple with those principles. We have a Republican State platform, laid down in Springfield in June last, stating our position all the way through the questions before the country. We are now far advanced in this canvass. Judge Douglas and I have made perhaps forty speeches apiece, and we have now for the fifth time met face to face in debate, and up to this day I have not found either Judge Douglas or any friend of his taking hold of the Republican platform or laying his fingers upon anything in it that is wrong. I ask you all to recollect that. Judge Douglas turns away from the platform of principles to the fact that he can find people somewhere who will not allow us to announce those principles. If he had great confidence that our principles were wrong, he would take hold of them and demonstrate them to be wrong. But he does not do so. The only evidence he has of their being wrong is in the fact that there are people who won't allow us to preach them. I ask again is that the way to test the soundness of a doctrine?

I ask his attention also to the fact that by the rule of nationality he is himself. fast becoming sectional. I ask his attention to the fact that his speeches would not go as current now south of the Ohio river as they have formerly gone there. I ask his attention to the fact that he felicitates himself to-day that all the Democrats of the free States are agreeing with him, while he omits to tell us that the Democrats of any slave State agree with him. If he has not thought of this, I commend to his consideration the evidence of his own declaration, on this day, of his becoming sectional too. I see it rapidly approaching. Whatever may be the result of this ephemeral contest between Judge Douglas and myself, I see the day rapidly approaching when his pill of sectionalism, which he has been thrusting down the throats of Republicans for years past, will be crowded down his own throat.

Now in regard to what Judge Douglas said (in the beginning of his speech) about the Compromise of 1850, containing the principle of the Nebraska bill, although I have often presented my views upon that subject, yet as I have not done so in this canvass, I will, if you please, detain you a little with them. I have always maintained, so far as I was able, that there was nothing of the principle of the Nebraska bill in the Compromise of 1850 at all—nothing whatever. Where can you find the principle of the Nebraska bill in that Compromise? If anywhere, in the two pieces of the Compromise organizing the territories of New-Mexico and Utah. It was expressly provided in these two acts, that, when they came to be admitted into the Union, they should be admitted with or without slavery, as they should choose, by their own constitutions. Nothing was said in either of those acts as to what was to be done in relation to slavery during the territorial existence of those territories, while Henry Clay constantly made the declaration (Judge Douglas recognizing him as a leader) that, in his opinion, the old Mexican laws would control that question during the territorial existence, and that these old Mexican laws excluded slavery. How can that be used as a principle for declaring that during the territorial existence as well as at the time of framing the Constitution, the people, if you please, might have slaves if they wanted them? I am not discussing the question whether it is right or wrong; but how are the New-Mexican and Utah laws patterns for the Nebraska bill? I maintain that the organization of Utah and

New-Mexico *did not* establish a general principle at all. It had no feature of establishing a general principle. The acts to which I have referred were a part of a general system of Compromises. They did not lay down what was proposed as a regular policy for the territories; only an agreement in this particular case to do in that way, because other things were done that were to be a compensation for it. They were allowed to come in in that shape, because in another way it was paid for—considering that as a part of that system of measures called the Compromise of 1850, which finally included half a dozen acts. It included the admission of California as a free State, which was kept out of the Union for half a year because it had formed a free Constitution. It included the settlement of the boundary of Texas, which had been undefined before, which was in itself a slavery question : for, if you pushed the line farther west, you made Texas larger, and made more slave territory ; while, if you drew the line toward the east, you narrowed the boundary and diminished the domain of slavery, and by so much increased free territory. It included the abolition of the slave-trade in the District of Columbia. It included the passage of a new Fugitive Slave law.

All these things were put together, and though passed in separate acts, were nevertheless in legislation (as the speeches• at the time will show), made to depend upon each other. Each got votes, with the understanding that the other measures were to pass, and by this system of compromise, in that series of measures, those two bills—the New-Mexico and Utah bills—were passed; and I say for that reason they could not be taken as models, framed upon their own intrinsic principle, for all future territories. And I have the evidence of this in the fact that Judge Douglas, a year afterward, or more than a year afterward, perhaps, when he first introduced bills for the purpose of framing new territories, did not attempt to follow these bills of New Mexico and Utah ; and even when he introduced this Nebraska bill, I think you will discover that he did not exactly follow them. But I do not wish to dwell at great length upon this branch of the discussion. My own opinion is, that a thorough investigation will show most plainly that the New-Mexico and Utah bills were part of a system of compromise, and not designed as patterns for future territorial legislation ; and that this Nebraska bill did not follow them as a pattern at all.

The Judge tells, in proceeding, that he is opposed to making any odious distinctions between free and slave States. I am altogether unaware that the Republicans are in favor of making any odious distinctions between the free and slave States. But there still is a difference, I think, between Judge Douglas and the Republicans in this. I suppose that the real difference between Judge Douglas and his friends, and the Republicans on the contrary, is, that the Judge is not in favor of making any difference between slavery and liberty—that he is in favor of eradicating, of pressing out of view, the questions of preference in this country for free or slave institutions ; and consequently every sentiment he utters discards the idea that there is any wrong in slavery. Everything that emanates from him or his coadjutors in their course of policy, carefully excludes the thought that there is anything wrong in slavery. All their arguments, if you will consider them, will be seen to exclude the thought that there is anything whatever wrong in slavery. If you will take the Judge's speeches, and select the short and pointed sentences expressed by him— as his declaration that he " don't care whether slavery is voted up or down"—you will see at once that this is perfectly logical, if you do not admit that slavery is wrong. If you do admit that it is wrong, Judge Douglas cannot logically say he don't care whether a wrong is voted up or voted down. Judge Douglas declares that if any community want slavery they have a right to have it. He can say that logically, if he says that there is no wrong in slavery ; but if you admit that there is a wrong in it, he cannot logically say that anybody has a right to do wrong. He insists that, upon the score of equality, the owners of slaves and owners of property—of horses and every other sort of property—should be alike and hold them alike in a new territory. That is perfectly logical, if the two species of property are alike and are equally founded in right. But if you admit that one of them is wrong, you cannot institute any equality between right and wrong. And from this difference of sentiment—the belief on the part of one that the institution is wrong, and a policy springing from that belief which looks to the arrest of the enlargement of that wrong ; and this other sentiment, that it is no wrong, and a policy sprung from that sentiment which will tolerate no idea of preventing that wrong from growing larger, and looks to

there never being an end of it through all the existence of
things, arises the real difference between Judge Douglas and
his friends on the one hand, and the Republicans on the other.
Now, I confess myself as belonging to that class in the country who contemplate slavery as a moral, social, and political
evil, having due regard for its actual existence among us,
and the difficulties of getting rid of it in any satisfactory way,
and to all the constitutional obligations which have been
thrown about it ; but, nevertheless, desire a policy that looks
to the prevention of it as a wrong, and looks hopefully to the
time when as a wrong it may come to an end.

Judge Douglas has again, for, I believe, the fifth time, it
not the seventh, in my presence, reiterated his charge of a
conspiracy or combination between the National Democrats
and Republicans. What evidence Judge Douglas has upon
this subject, I know not, inasmuch as he never favors us with
any. I have said upon a former occasion, and I do not choose
to suppress it now, that I have no objection to the division in
the Judge's party. He got it up himself. It was all his and
their work. He had, I think, a great deal more to do with
the steps that led to the Lecompton constitution than Mr. Buchanan had ; though at last, when they reached it, they quar-
reled over it, and their friends divided upon it. I am very
free to confess to Judge Douglas that I have no objection to
the division ; but I defy the Judge to show any evidence that
I have in any way promoted that division, unless he insists on
being a witness himself, in merely saying so. I can give all
fair friends of Judge Douglas here to understand exactly the
view that Republicans take in regard to that division. Don't
you remember how, two years ago, the opponents of the Democratic party were divided between Fremont and Fillmore?
I guess you do. Any Democrat who remembers that division,
will remember also, that he was at the time very glad of it,
and then he will be able to see all there is between the National Democrats and the Republicans. What we now think
of the two divisions of Democrats, you then thought of the
Fremont and Fillmore divisions. That is all there is of it.

But, if the Judge continues to put forward the declaration
that there is an unholy and unnatural alliance between the
Republican and the National Democrats, I now want to enter
my protest against receiving him as an entirely competent wit-

ness upon that subject. I want to call to the Judge's attention an attack he made upon me, in the first one of these debates, at Ottawa, on the 21st of August. In order to fix extreme Abolitionism upon me, Judge Douglas read a set of resolutions, which he declared had been passed by a Republican State Convention, in October, 1854, at Springfield, Illinois, and he declared I had taken part in that Convention. It turned out that, although a few men calling themselves an anti-Nebraska State Convention, had sat at Springfield about that time, yet neither did I take any part in it, nor did it pass the resolutions, or any such resolutions, as Judge Douglas read. So apparent had it become that the resolutions which he read had not been passed at Springfield at all, nor by a State Convention in which I had taken part, that seven days afterward, at Freeport, Judge Douglas declared that he had been misled by Charles H. Lanphier, editor of the *State Register*, and Thomas L. Harris, member of Congress in that District, and he promised in that speech that when he went to Springfield he would investigate the matter. Since then Judge Douglas has been to Springfield, and I presume has made the investigation; but a month has passed since he has been there, and, so far as I know, he has made no report of the result of his investigation. I have waited, as I think, sufficient time for the report of that investigation, and I have some curiosity to see and hear it. A fraud—an absolute forgery was committed, and the perpetration of it was traced to the three— Lanphier, Harris, and Douglas. Whether it can be narrowed in any way so as to exonerate any one of them, is what Judge Douglas's report would probably show.

It is true that the set of resolutions read by Judge Douglas were published in the Illinois *State Register*, on the 16th of October, 1854, as being the resolutions of an anti-Nebraska Convention, which had sat in that same month of October, at Springfield. But it is also true, that the publication in the *Register* was a forgery then, and the question is still behind, which of the three, if not all of them, committed that forgery? The idea that it was done by mistake, is absurd. The article in the Illinois *State Register* contains part of the real proceedings of that Springfield Convention, showing that the writer of the article had the real proceedings before him, and purposely threw out the genuine resolutions passed by the Convention, and fraudulently substituted the others. Lanphier then, as now, was the editor of the *Register*, so there seems to be but little room for his escape. But then it is to be borne in mind that Lanphier had less interest in the object of that forgery than either of the other two. The main object of that forgery, at that time, was to beat Yates and elect Harris to Congress, and that object was known to be exceedingly dear to Judge Douglas at that time. Harris and Douglas were both in Springfield when the Convention was in session, and although they both left before the fraud appeared in the *Register*, subsequent events show that they have both had their eyes fixed upon that Convention.

The fraud having been apparently successful upon the occasion, both Harris and Douglas have more than once since then been attempting to put it to new uses. As the fisherman's wife, whose drowned husband was brought home with his body full of eels, said when she was asked, "What was to be done with him?" "*Take the eels out and set him again;*" so Harris and Douglas have shown a disposition to take the eels out of that stale fraud by which they gained Harris's election, and set the fraud again more than once. On the 9th of July, 1856, Douglas attempted a repetition of it upon Trumbull on the floor of the Senate of the United States, as will appear from the appendix of the *Congressional Globe* of that date.

On the 9th of August, Harris attempted it again upon Norton in the House of Representatives, as will appear by the same documents—the appendix to the *Congressional Globe* of that date. On the 21st of August last, all three—Lanphier, Douglas, and Harris—reattempted it upon me at Ottawa. It has been clung to and played out again and again as an exceedingly high trump by this blessed trio. And now that it has been discovered publicly to be a fraud, we find that Judge Douglas manifests no surprise at it at all. He makes no complaint of Lanphier, who must have known it to be a fraud from the beginning. He, Lanphier, and Harris, are just as cozy now, and just as active in the concoction of new schemes as they were before the general discovery of this fraud. Now all this is very natural if they are all alike guilty in that fraud, and it is very unnatural if any one of them is innocent. Lanphier perhaps insists that the rule of honor among thieves does not quite require him to take all upon himself, and con-

sequently my friend Judge Douglas finds it difficult to make a
satisfactory report upon his investigation.   But meanwhile
the three are agreed that each is " *a most honorable man.*"

Judge Douglas requires an endorsement of his truth and
honor by a re-election to the United States Senate, and he
makes and reports against me and against Judge Trumbull,
day after day, charges which we know to be utterly untrue,
without for a moment seeming to think that this one unexplained fraud, which he promised to investigate, will be the
least drawback to his claim to belief.   Harris ditto.   He asks
a re-election to the lower House of Congress without seeming
to remember at all that he is involved in this dishonorable
fraud !   The Illinois *State Register*, edited by Lanphier, then,
as now, the central organ of both Harris and Douglas, continues to din the public ear with this assertion without seeming
to suspect that these assertions are at all lacking in title to belief.

After all, the question still recurs upon us, how did that
fraud originally get into the *State Register* ?   Lanphier then, as
now, was the editor of that paper.   Lanphier knows.   Lanphier cannot be ignorant of how and by whom it was originally concocted.   Can he be induced to tell, or if he has told,
can Judge Douglas be induced to tell how it originally was
concocted ?   It may be true that Lanphier insists that the
two men for whose benefit it was originally devised, shall at
least bear their share of it !   How that is, I do not know,
and while it remains unexplained, I hope to be pardoned if I
insist that the mere fact of Judge Douglas making charges
against Trumbull and myself is not quite sufficient evidence to
establish them !

While we were at Freeport, in one of these joint discussions, I answered certain interrogatories which Judge Douglas
had propounded to me, and there in turn propounded some to
him, which he in a sort of way answered.   The third one of
these interrogatories I have with me, and wish now to make
some comments upon it.   It was in these words : " If the
Supreme Court of the United States shall decide that the
States cannot exclude slavery from their limits, are you in
favor of acquiescing in, adhering to, and following such decision, as a rule of political action ?"

To this interrogatory Judge Douglas made no answer, in
any just sense of the word.   He contented himself with
sneering at the thought that it was possible for the Supreme

Court ever to make such a decision. He sneered at me for propounding the interrogatory. I had not propounded it without some reflection, and I wish now to address to this audience some remarks upon it.

In the second clause of the sixth article, I believe it is, of the Constitution of the United States, we find the following language: "This Constitution and the laws of the United States which shall be made in pursuance thereof; and all treaties made, or which shall be made under the authority of the United States, shall be the supreme law of the land; and the judges in every State shall be bound thereby,-anything in the Constitution or laws of any State to the contrary, notwithstanding."

The essence of the Dred Scott case is compressed into the sentence which I will now read: "Now, as we have already said in an earlier part of this opinion, upon a different point, the right of property in a slave is distinctly and expressly affirmed in the Constitution." I repeat it, "*The right of property in a slave is distinctly and expressly affirmed in the Constitution!*" What is it to be "*affirmed*" in the Constitution? Made firm in the Constitution—so made that it cannot be separated from the Constitution without breaking the Constitution—durable as the Constitution, and part of the Constitution. Now, remembering the provision of the Constitution which I have read, affirming that that instrument is the supreme law of the land; that the judges of every State shall be bound by it, any law or constitution of any State to the contrary, notwithstanding; that the right of property in a slave is affirmed in that Constitution, is made, formed into, and cannot be separated from it without breaking it; durable as the instrument; part of the instrument;—what follows as a short and even syllogistic argument from it? I think it follows, and I submit to the consideration of men capable of arguing, whether as I state it, in syllogistic form, the argument has any fault in it?

Nothing in the constitution or laws of any State can destroy a right distinctly and expressly affirmed in the Constitution of the United States.

The right of property in a slave is distinctly and expressly affirmed in the Constitution of the United States.

Therefore, nothing in the Constitution or laws of any State can destroy the right of property in a slave.

I believe that no fault can be pointed out in that argument ; assuming the truth of the premises, the conclusion, so far as I have capacity at all to understand it, follows inevitably. There is a fault in it as I think, but the fault is not in the reasoning ; but the falsehood in fact is a fault of the premises. I believe that the right of property in a slave *is not* distinctly and expressly affirmed in the Constitution, and Judge Douglas thinks it *is*. I believe that the Supreme Court and the advocates of that decision may search in vain for the place in the Constitution where the right of a slave is distinctly and expressly affirmed. I say, therefore, that I think one of the premises is not true in fact. But it is true with Judge Douglas. It is true with the Supreme Court who pronounced it. They are estopped from denying it, and being estopped from denying it, the conclusion follows that the Constitution of the United States being the supreme law, no constitution or law can interfere with it. It being affirmed in the decision that the right of property in a slave is distinctly and expressly affirmed in the Constitution, the conclusion inevitably follows that no State law or constitution can destroy that right. I then say to Judge Douglas and to all others, that I think it will take a better answer than a sneer to show that those who have said that the right of property in a slave is distinctly and expressly affirmed in the Constitution, are not prepared to show that no constitution or law can destroy that right. I say I believe it will take a far better argument than a mere sneer to show to the minds of intelligent men that whoever has so said, is not prepared, whenever public sentiment is so far advanced as to justify it, to say the other.

This is but an opinion, and the opinion of one very humble man ; but it is my opinion that the Dred Scott decision, as it is, never would have been made in its present form if the party that made it had not been sustained previously by the elections. My own opinion is, that the new Dred Scott decision, deciding against the right of the people of the States to exclude slavery, will never be made, if that party is not sustained by the elections. I believe, further, that it is just as sure to be made as to-morrow is to come, if that party shall be sustained. I have said, upon a former occasion, and I repeat it now, that the course of argument that Judge Douglas makes use of upon this subject (I charge not his motives in this), is preparing the public mind for that new Dred Scott decision. I have asked him again to point out to me the reasons for his first adherence to the Dred Scott decision as it is. I have turned his attention to the fact that General Jackson differed with him in regard to the political obligation of a Supreme Court decision. I have asked his attention to the fact that Jefferson differed with him in regard to the political obligation of a Supreme Court decision. Jefferson said, that "Judges are as honest as other men, and not more so." And he said, substantially, that "whenever a free people should give up in absolute submission to any department of government, retaining for themselves no appeal from it, their liberties are gone." I have asked his attention to the fact that the Cincinnati platform, upon which he says he stands, disregards a time-honored decision of the Supreme Court, in denying the power of Congress to establish a National Bank. I have asked his attention to the fact that he himself was one of the most active instruments at one time in breaking down the Supreme Court of the State of Illinois, because it had made a decision distasteful to him—a struggle ending in the remarkable circumstance of his sitting down as one of the new Judges who were to overslaugh that decision—getting his title of Judge in that very way.

So far in this controversy I can get no answer at all from Judge Douglas upon these subjects. Not one can I get from him, except that he swells himself up and says, "All of us who stand by the decision of the Supreme Court are the friends of the Constitution ; all you fellows that dare question it in any way are the enemies of the Constitution." Now, in this very devoted adherence to this decision, in opposition to all the great political leaders whom he has recognized as leaders—in opposition to his former self and history, there is something very marked. And the manner in which he adheres to it—not as being right upon the merits, as he conceives (because he did not discuss that at all), but as being absolutely obligatory upon every one, simply because of the source whence it comes—as that which no man can gainsay, whatever it may be—this is another marked feature of his adherence to that decision. It marks it in this respect, that it commits him to the next decision, whenever it comes, as being as obligatory as this one, since he does not investigate it, and won't inquire whether this opinion is right or wrong.

So he takes the next one without inquiring whether it is right or wrong. He teaches men this doctrine, and in doing so prepares the public mind to take the next decision when it comes, without any inquiry. In this I think I argue fairly (without questioning motives at all), that Judge Douglas is most ingeniously and powerfully preparing the public mind to take that decision when it comes ; and not only so, but he is doing it in various other ways. In these general maxims about liberty—in his assertions that he " don't care whether slavery is voted up or down;" that " whoever wants slavery has a right to have it ;" that " upon principles of equality it should be allowed to go everywhere ;" that " there is no inconsistency between free and slave institutions." In this, he is also preparing (whether purposely or not) the way for making the institution of slavery national! I repeat again, for I wish no misunderstanding, that I do not charge that he means it so ; but I call your minds to inquire, if you were going to get the best instrument you could, and then set it to work in the most ingenious way, to prepare the public mind for this movement, operating in the free States, where there is now an abhorrence of the institution of slavery, could you find an instrument so capable of doing it as Judge Douglas? or one employed in so apt a way to do it?

I have said once before, and I will repeat it now, that Mr. Clay, when he was once answering an objection to the Colonization Society, that it had a tendency to the ultimate emancipation of the slaves, said that " those who would repress all tendencies to liberty and ultimate emancipation must do more than put down the benevolent efforts of the Colonization Society—they must go back to the era of our liberty and independence, and muzzle the cannon that thunders its annual joyous return—they must blot out the moral lights around us—they must penetrate the human soul, and eradicate the light of reason and the love of liberty!" And I do think—I repeat, though I said it on a former occasion—that Judge Douglas, and whoever like him teaches that the negro has no share, humble though it may be, in the Declaration of Independence, is " going back to the era of our liberty and independence, and, so far as in him lies, muzzling the cannon that thunders its annual joyous return ;" that he is blowing out the moral lights around us, when he contends that whoever wants slaves has a right to hold them; that he is penetrating, so far as lies in his power, the human soul, and eradicating the light of reason and the love of liberty, when he is in every possible way preparing the public mind, by his vast influence, for making the institution of slavery perpetual and national.

There is, my friends, only one other point to which I will call your attention for the remaining time that I have left me, and, perhaps, I shall not occupy the entire time that I have, as that one point may not take me clear through it.

Among the interrogatories that Judge Douglas propounded to me at Freeport, there was one in about this language : " Are you opposed to the acquisition of any further territory to the United States, unless slavery shall first be prohibited therein ?" I answered as I thought, in this way, that I am not generally opposed to the acquisition of additional territory, and that I would support a proposition for the .acquisition of additional territory, according as my supporting it was or was not calculated to aggravate this slavery question among us. I then proposed to Judge Douglas another interrogatory, which was correlative to that : " Are you in favor of acquiring additional territory in disregard of how it may affect us upon the slavery question ?" Judge Douglas answered, that is, in his own way he answered it. I believe that, although he took a great many words to answer it, it was a little more fully answered than any other. The substance of his answer was, that this country would continue to expand—that it would need additional territory—that it was as absurd to suppose that we could continue upon our present territory, enlarging in population as we are, as it would be to hoop a boy twelve years of age, and expect him to grow to man's size without bursting the hoops. I believe it was something like that. Consequently he was in favor of the acquisition of further territory, as fast as we might need it, in disregard of how it might affect the slavery question. I do not say this as giving his exact language, but he said so substantially, and he would leave the question of slavery where the territory was acquired, to be settled by the people of the acquired territory. [" That's the doctrine."] May be it is ; let us consider that for a while. This will probably, in the run of things, become one of the concrete manifestations of this slavery question. If Judge Douglas's policy upon this question succeeds and gets fairly settled down, until all opposition is crushed out, the next thing will be a grab for the territory of poor Mexico, and an invasion of the rich lands of South America, then the adjoining islands will follow, each one of which promises additional slave fields. And this question is to be left to the people of those countries for settlement. When we shall get Mexico, I don't know whether the Judge will be in favor of the Mexican people that we get with it settling that question for themselves and all others ; because we know the Judge has a great horror for mongrels, and I understand that the people of Mexico are most decidedly a race of mongrels. I understand that there is not more than one person there out of eight who is pure white, and I suppose from the Judge's previous declaration that when we get Mexico or any considerable portion of it, that he will be in favor of these mongrels settling the question, which would bring him somewhat into collision with his horror of an inferior race.

It is to remembered, though, that this power of acquiring additional territory is a power confided to the President and Senate of the United States. It is a power not under the control of the representatives of the people any further than they, the President and the Senate, can be considered representatives of the people. Let me illustrate that by a case we have in our history. When we acquired the territory from Mexico in the Mexican war, the House of Representatives, composed of the immediate representatives of the people, all the time insisted that the territory thus to be acquired should be brought in upon condition that slavery should be forever prohibited therein, upon the terms and in the language that slavery had been prohibited from coming into this country. That was insisted upon constantly, and never failed to call forth an assurance that any territory thus acquired should have that prohibition in it, so far as the House of Representatives was concerned. But at last the President and the Senate acquired the territory without asking the House of Representatives anything about it, and took it without that prohibition. They have the power of acquiring territory without the immediate representatives of the people being called upon to say anything about it, and thus furnishing a very apt and powerful means of bringing new territory into the Union, and when it is once brought into the country, involving us anew in this slavery agitation. It is, therefore, as I think, a very important question for the consideration of the American people, whether the policy of bringing in additional territory, without considering at all how it will operate upon the safety of the Union, in reference to this one great disturbing element in our national politics, shall be adopted as the policy of the country. You will bear in mind that it is to be acquired, according to the Judge's view, as fast as it is needed, and the indefinite part of this proposition is that we have only Judge Douglas and his class of men to decide how fast it is needed. We have no clear and certain way of determining or demonstrating how fast territory is needed by the necessities of the country. Whoever wants to go out filibustering, then, thinks that more territory is needed. Whoever wants wider slave fields, feels sure that some additional territory is needed as slave territory. Then it is as easy to show the necessity of additional slave territory as it is to assert anything that is incapable of absolute demonstration. Whatever motive a man or a set of men may have for making annexation of property or territory, it is very to easy assert, but much less to disprove, that it is necessary for the wants of the country.

And now it only remains for me to say that I think it is a very grave question for the people of this Union to consider whether, in view of the fact that this slavery question has been the only one that has ever endangered our Republican institutions—the only one that has ever threatened or menaced a dissolution of the Union—that has ever disturbed us in such a way as to make us fear for the perpetuity of our liberty—in view of these facts, I think it is an exceedingly interesting and important question for this people to consider, whether we shall engage in the policy of acquiring additional territory, discarding altogether from our consideration, while obtaining new territory, the question how it may affect us in regard to this the only endangering element to our liberties and national greatness. The Judge's view has been expressed. I, in my answer to his question, have expressed mine. I think it will become an important and practical question. Our views are before the public. I am willing and anxious that they should consider them fully—that they should turn it about and consider the importance of the question, and arrive at a just conclusion as to whether it is or it is not wise in the people of this Union, in the acquisition of new territory, to consider whether it will add to the disturbance that is existing among us—whether it will add to the one only danger that has ever threatened the perpetuity of the Union or of our own liberties. I think it is extremely important that they shall decide, and rightly decide, that question before entering upon that policy.

And now, my friends, having said the little I wish to say upon this head, whether I have occupied the whole of the remnant of my time or not, I believe I could not enter upon any new topics so as to treat it fully without transcending my time, which I would not for a moment think of doing. I give way to Judge Douglas.

MR. LINCOLN'S SPEECH,

At Quincy, Ill., *October* 13, 1858.

LADIES AND GENTLEMEN: I have had no immediate conference with Judge Douglas, but I will venture to say that he and I will perfectly agree that your entire silence, both when I speak and when he speaks, will be most agreeable to us.

In the month of May, 1856, the elements of the State of Illinois, which have since been consolidated into the Republican party, assembled together in a State Convention at Bloomington. They adopted at that time, what, in political language, is called a platform. In June of the same year, the elements of the Republican party in the nation assembled together in a National Convention at Philadelphia. They adopted what is called the National Platform. In June, 1858 —the present year—the Republicans of Illinois re-assembled at Springfield, in State Convention, and adopted again their platform, as I suppose, not differing in any essential particular from either of the former ones, but perhaps adding something in relation to the new developments of political progress in the country.

The Convention that assembled in June last did me the honor, if it be one, and I esteem it such, to nominate me as their candidate for the United States Senate. I have sup-

10

posed that, in entering upon this canvass, I stood generally upon these platforms. We are now met together on the 13th of October of the same year, only four months from the adoption of the last platform, and I am unaware that in this canvass, from the beginning until to-day, any one of our adversaries has taken hold of our platforms, or laid his finger upon anything that he calls wrong in them.

In the very first one of these joint discussions between Senator Douglas and myself, Senator Douglas, without alluding at all to these platforms, or any one of them, of which I have spoken, attempted to hold me responsible for a set of resolutions passed long before the meeting of either one of these Conventions of which I have spoken. And as a ground for holding me responsible for these resolutions, he assumed that they had been passed at a State Convention of the Republican party, and that I took part in that Convention. It was discovered afterward that this was erroneous, that the resolutions which he endeavored to hold me responsible for, had not been passed by any State Convention anywhere, had not been passed at Springfield, where he supposed they had, or assumed that they had, and that they had been passed in no Convention in which I had taken part. The Judge, nevertheless, was not willing to give up the point that he was endeavoring to make upon me, and he therefore thought to still hold me to the point that he was endeavoring to make, by showing that the resolutions that he read, had been passed at a local Convention in the northern part of the State, although it was not a local Convention that embraced my residence at all, nor one that reached, as I suppose, nearer than one hundred and fifty or two hundred miles of where I was when it met, nor one in which I took any part at all. He also introduced other resolutions, passed at other meetings, and by combining the whole, although they were all antecedent to the two State Conventions, and the one National Convention I have mentioned, still he insisted and now insists, as I understand, that I am in some way responsible for them.

At Jonesboro, on our third meeting, I insisted to the Judge that I was in no way rightfully held responsible for the proceedings of this local meeting or Convention, in which I had taken no part, and in which I was in no way embraced ; but I insisted to him that if he thought I was responsible for every

man or every set of men everywhere, who happen to be my
friends, the rule ought to work both ways, and he ought to be
responsible for the acts and resolutions of all men or sets of
men who were and are now his supporters and friends, and
gave him a pretty long string of resolutions, passed by men
who are now his friends, and announcing doctrines for which
he does not desire to be held responsible.

This still does not satisfy Judge Douglas. He still adheres
to his proposition, that I am responsible for what some of my
friends in different parts of the State have done ; but that he
is not responsible for what his have done. At least, so I understand him. But in addition to that, the Judge, at our meeting in Galesburgh, last week, undertakes to establish that I
am guilty of a species of double-dealing with the public—that
I make speeches of a certain sort in the north, among the
Abolitionists, which I would not make in the south, and that
I make speeches of a certain sort in the south which I would
not make in the north. I apprehend, in the course I have
marked out for myself, that I shall not have to dwell at very
great length upon this subject.

As this was done in the Judge's opening speech at Galesburgh, I had an opportunity, as I had the middle speech there,
of saying something in answer to it. He brought forward a
quotation or two from a speech of mine, delivered at Chicago,
and then, to contrast with it, he brought forward an extract
of a speech of mine at Charleston, in which he insisted that I
was greatly inconsistent, and insisted that his conclusion followed that I was playing a double part, and speaking in one
region one way, and in another region another way. I have
not time now to dwell on this as long as I would like, and
wish only now to requote that portion of my speech at Charleston, which the Judge quoted, and then make some comments
upon it. This he quotes from me as being delivered at Charleston, and I believe correctly : " I will say, then, that I am
not, nor ever have been, in favor of bringing about, in any
way, the social and political equality of the white and black
races—that I am not, nor ever have been, in favor of making
voters or jurors of negroes, nor of qualifying them to hold office, nor to intermarry with white people ; and I will say in addition to this, that there is a physical difference between the white
and black races which will ever forbid the two races living to-

gether on terms of social and political equality. And inasmuch as they cannot so live, while they do remain together, there must be the position of superior and inferior. I am as much as any other man in favor of having the superior position assigned to the white race." This, I believe, is the entire quotation from the Charleston speech, as Judge Douglas made it. His comments are as follows:

" Yes, here you find men who hurrah for Lincoln, and say he is right when he discards all distinction between races, or when he declares that he discards the doctrine that there is such a thing as a superior and inferior race ; and Abolitionists are required and expected to vote for Mr. Lincoln because he goes for the equality of races, holding that in the Declaration of Independence the white man and negro were declared equal, and endowed by law with equality. And down south with the old line Whigs, with the Kentuckians, the Virginians, and the Tennesseans, he tells you there is a physical difference between the races, making the one superior, the other inferior, and he is in favor of maintaining the superiority of the white race over the negro."

Those are the Judge's comments. Now I wish to show you, that a month—or, only lacking three days of a month—before I made the speech at Charleston, which the Judge quotes from, he had, himself, heard me say substantially the same thing. It was in our first meeting, at Ottawa—and I will say a word about where it was, and the atmosphere it was in, after awhile —but at our first meeting, at Ottawa, I read an extract from an old speech of mine, made nearly four years ago, not merely to show my sentiments, but to show that my sentiments were long entertained and openly expressed; in which extract I expressly declared that my own feelings would not admit a social and political equality between the white and black races, and that even if my own feelings would admit of it, I still knew that the public sentiment of the country would not, and that such a thing was an utter impossibility, or substantially that. That extract from my old speech, the reporters, by some sort of accident, passed over, and it was not reported. I lay no blame upon anybody. I suppose they thought that I would hand it over to them, and dropped reporting while I was reading it, but afterward went away without getting it from me. At the end of that quotation from my old speech, which I read at Ottawa, I made the comments which were reported at that time, and which I will now read, and ask you to notice how very nearly they are the same as Judge Douglas says were delivered by me, down in Egypt. After reading I added these words : " Now, gentlemen, I don't wan't to read at any great length, but this is the true complexion of all I have ever said in regard to the institution of slavery or the black race, and this is the whole of it ; anything that argues me into his idea of perfect social and political equality with the negro, is but a specious and fantastical arrangement of words by which a man can prove a horse-chestnut to be a chestnut-horse. I will say here, while upon this subject, that I have no purpose, directly or indirectly, to interfere with the institution in the States where it exists. I believe I have no right to do so. I have no inclination to do so. I have no purpose to introduce political and social equality between the white and black races. There is a physical difference between the two, which, in my judgment, will probably forever forbid their living together on the footing of perfect equality, and inasmuch as it becomes a necessity that there must be a difference, I, as well as Judge Douglas, am in favor of the race to which I belong having the superior position. I have never said anything to the contrary, but I hold that, notwithstanding all this, there is no reason in the world, why the negro is not entitled to all the rights enumerated in the Declaration of Independence—the right of life, liberty, and the pursuit of happiness. I hold that he is as much entitled to these as the white man. I agree with Judge Douglas, that he is not my equal in many respects, certainly not in color—perhaps not in intellectual and moral endowments; but in the right to eat the bread without the leave of anybody else, which his own hand earns, he is my equal, and the equal of Judge Douglas, and the equal of every other man. "

I have chiefly introduced this for the purpose of meeting the Judge's charge that the quotation he took from my Charleston speech was what I would say' down south among the Kentuckians, the Virginians, etc., but would not say in the regions in which was supposed to be more of the abolition element. I now make this comment : That speech, from which I have now read the quotation, and which is there given correctly, perhaps too much so for good taste, was made away up north in the abolition district of this State *par excellence*—in the Lovejoy District—in the personal presence of Lovejoy, for he was on the stand with us when I made it. It had been made and put in print in that region only three days less than a month before the speech made at Charleston, the like of which Judge Douglas thinks I would not make where there was any Abolition element. I only refer to this matter to say that I am altogether unconscious of having attempted any double-dealing anywhere—that upon one occasion I may say one thing and leave other things unsaid, and *vice versa ;* but that I have said anything on one occasion that is inconsistent with what I have said elsewhere, I deny—at least I deny it so far as the intention is concerned. I find that I have devoted to this topic a larger portion of my time than I had intended. I wished to show, but I will pass it upon this occasion, that in the sentiment I have occasionally advanced upon the Declaration of Independence, I am entirely borne out by the sentiments advanced by our old Whig leader, Henry Clay, and I have the book here to show it from ; but because I have already occupied more time than I intended to do on that topic, I pass over it.

At Galesburgh I tried to show that by the Dred Scott decision, pushed to its legitimate consequences, slavery would be established in all the States as well as in the territories. I did this because, upon a former occasion, I had asked Judge Douglas, whether, if the Supreme Court should make a decision declaring that the States had not the power to exclude slavery from their limits, he would adopt and follow that decision as a rule of political action ; and because he had not directly answered that question, but had merely contented himself with sneering at it, I again introduced it, and tried to show that the conclusion that I stated followed inevitably and logically from the proposition already decided by the court. Judge Douglas had the privilege of replying to me at Galesburgh, and again he gave me no direct answer as to whether he would or would not sustain such a decision if made. I give him this third chance to say yes or no. ·He is not obliged to do either—probably he will not do either—but I give him the third chance. I tried to show then that this result— this conclusion inevitably followed from the point already decided by the court. The Judge, in his reply, again sneers at

the thought of the court making any such decision, and in the course of his remarks upon this subject, uses the language which I will now read. Speaking of me the Judge says:
" He goes on and insists that the Dred Scott decision would carry slavery into the free States, notwithstanding the decision itself says the contrary." And he adds : " Mr. Lincoln knows that there is no member of the Supreme Court that holds that doctrine. He knows that every one of them in their opinions held the reverse."

I especially introduce this subject again for the purpose of saying that I have the Dred. Scott decision here, and I will thank Judge Douglas to lay his finger upon the place in the entire opinions of the court where any of them " says the contrary." It is very hard to affirm a negative with entire confidence. I say, however, that I have examined that decision with a good deal of care, as a lawyer examines a decision, and so far as I have been able to do so, the court has nowhere in its opinions said that the States have the power to exclude slavery, nor have they used other language substantially that. I also say, so far as I can find, not one of the concurring Judges has said that the States can exclude slavery, nor said anything that was substantially that. The nearest approach that any one of them has made to it, so far as I can find, was by Judge Nelson, and the approach he made to it was exactly, in substance, the Nebraska bill—that the States had the exclusive power over the question of slavery, so far as they are not limited by the Constitution of the United States. I asked the question therefore, if the non-concurring Judges, McLean or Curtis, had asked to get an express declaration that the States could absolutely exclude slavery from their limits, what reason have we to believe that it would not havebeen voted down by the majority of the Judges, just as Chase's amendment was voted down by Judge Douglas and his compeers when it was offered to the Nebraska bill.

Also at Galesburgh, I said something in regard to those Springfield resolutions that Judge Douglas attempted to use upon me at Ottawa, and commented at some length upon the fact that they were, as presented, not genuine. Judge Douglas in his reply to me seemed to be somewhat exasperated. He said he would never have believed that Abraham Lincoln, as he kindly called me, would have attempted such a thing as

I had attempted upon that occasion; and among other expressions which he used toward me, was that I dared to say forgery—that I had *dared* to say forgery [turning to Judge Douglas]. Yes, Judge, I did dare to say forgery. But in this political canvass, the Judge ought to remember that I was not the first who *dared* to say forgery. At Jacksonville Judge Douglas made a speech in answer to something said by Judge Trumbull, and at the close of what he said upon that subject, he *dared* to say that Trumbull had forged his evidence. He said, too, that he should not concern himself with Trumbull any more, but thereafter he should hold Lincoln responsible for the slanders upon him. When I met him at Charleston after that, although I think that I should not have noticed the subject if he had not said he would hold me responsible for it, I spread out before him the statements of the evidence that Judge Trumbull had used, and I asked Judge Douglas, piece by piece, to put his finger upon one piece of all that evidence that he would say was a forgery! When I went through with each and every piece, Judge Douglas did not *dare* then to say that any piece of it was a forgery. So it seems that there are some things that Judge Douglas dares to do, and some that he dares not to do.

A voice—" It's the same thing with you."

Mr. Lincoln—Yes, sir, it's the same thing with me. I do dare to say forgery when it's true, and don't dare to say forgery when it's false. Now, I will say here to the audience and to Judge Douglas, I have not dared to say he committed a forgery, and I never shall until I know it; but I did dare to say—just to suggest to the Judge—that a forgery had been committed, which by his own showing had been traced to him and two of his friends. I dared to suggest to him that he had expressly promised in one of his public speeches to investigate that matter ; and I dared to suggest to him that there was an implied promise that when he investigated it he would make known the result. I dared to suggest to the Judge that he could not expect to be quite clear of suspicion of that fraud, for since the time that promise was made he had been with those friends, and had not kept his promise in regard to the investigation and the report upon it. I am not a very daring man, but I dared that much, Judge, and I am not much scared about it yet. When the Judge says he wouldn't have

believed of Abraham Lincoln that he would have made such an
attempt as that, he reminds me of the fact that he entered
upon this canvass with the purpose to treat me courteously;
that touched me somewhat. It sets me to thinking. I was
aware, when it was first agreed that Judge Douglas and I
were to have these seven-joint discussions, that they were
the successive acts of a drama—perhaps I should say, to be
enacted not merely in the face of audiences like this, but in
the face of the nation, and to some extent, by my relation to
him, and not from anything in myself, in the face of the
world: and I am anxious that they should be conducted with
dignity and in the good temper which would be befitting the
vast audience before which they were conducted. But when
Judge Douglas got home from Washington and made his first
speech in Chicago, the evening afterward I made some sort of a
reply to it. His second speech was made at Bloomington, in
which he commented upon my speech at Chicago, and said that
I had used language ingeniously contrived to conceal my intentions, or words to that effect. Now, I understand that this
is an imputation upon my veracity and my candor. I do not
know what the Judge understood by it; but in our first discussion at Ottawa, he led off by charging a bargain, somewhat
corrupt in its character, upon Trumbull and myself—that we
had entered into a bargain, one of the terms of which was that
Trumbull was to abolitionize the old Democratic party, and I
(Lincoln) was to abolitionize the old Whig party—I pretending to be as good an old line Whig as ever. Judge Douglas
may not understand that he implicated my truthfulness and
my honor, when he said I was doing one thing and pretending
another; and I misunderstood him if he thought he was treating me in a dignified way, as a man of honor and truth, as he
now claims he was disposed to treat me. Even after that
time, at Galesburgh, when he brings forward an extract from
a speech made at Chicago, and an extract from a speech
made at Charleston, to prove that I was trying to play a
double part—and that I was trying to cheat the public, and
get votes upon one set of principles at one place and upon
another set of principles at another place—I do not understand but what he impeaches my honor, my veracity, and
my candor, and because *he* does this, I do not understand that
I am bound, if I see a truthful ground for it, to keep my

hands off him. As soon as I learned that Judge Douglas was disposed to treat me in this way, I signified in one of my speeches that I should be driven to draw upon whatever of humble resources I might have—to adopt a new course with him. I was not entirely sure that I should be able to hold my own with him, but I at least had the purpose made to do as well as I could upon him ; and now I say that I will not be the first to cry "hold." I think it originated with the Judge, and if he quits, I probably will. But I shall not ask any favors at all. He asks me, as he asks the audience, if I wish to push this matter to the point of personal difficulty. I tell him, no. He did not make a mistake, in one of his early speeches, when he calls me an "amiable" man, though perhaps he did when he called me an "intelligent" man. It really hurts me very much to suppose that I have wronged anybody on earth. I again tell him, no! I very much prefer, when this canvass shall be over, however it may result, that we at least part without any bitter recollections of personal difficulties.

The Judge, in his concluding speech at Galesburgh, says that I was pushing this matter to a personal difficulty, to avoid the responsibility for the enormity of my principles. I say to the Judge and this audience now, that I will again state our principles as well as I hastily can in all their enormity, and if the Judge hereafter chooses to confine himself to a war upon these principles, he will probably not find me departing from the same course.

We have in this nation this element of domestic slavery. It is a matter of absolute certainty that it is a disturbing element. It is the opinion of all the great men who have expressed an opinion upon it, that it is a dangerous element. We keep up a controversy in regard to it. That controversy necessarily springs from difference of opinion, and if we can learn exactly—can reduce to the lowest elements—what that difference of opinion is, we perhaps shall be better prepared for discussing the different systems of policy that we would propose in regard to that disturbing element. I suggest that the difference of opinion, reduced to its lowest terms, is no other than the difference between the men who think slavery a wrong and those who do not think it wrong. The Republican party think it wrong—we think it is a moral, a social, and a political wrong. We think it is a wrong not confining itself merely to the persons or the States where it exists, but that it is a wrong in its tendency, to say the least, that extends itself to the existence of the whole nation. Because we think it wrong, we propose a course of policy that shall deal with it as a wrong. We deal with it as with any other wrong, in so far as we can prevent its growing any larger, and so deal with it that in the run of time there may be some promise of an end to it. We have a due regard to the actual presence of it among us and the difficulties of getting rid of it in any satisfactory way, and all the constitutional obligations thrown about it. I suppose that in reference both to its actual existence in the nation, and to our constitutional obligations, we have no right at all to disturb it in the States where it exists, and we profess that we have no more inclination to disturb it than we have the right to do it. We go farther than that ; we don't propose to disturb it where, in one instance, we think the Constitution would permit us. We think the Constitution would permit us to disturb it in the District of Columbia. Still we do not propose to do that, unless it should be in terms which I don't suppose the nation is very likely soon to agree to—the terms of making the emancipation gradual and compensating the unwilling owners. Where we suppose we have the constitutional right, we restrain ourselves in reference to the actual existence of the institution and the difficulties thrown about it. We also oppose it as an evil so far as it seeks to spread itself. We insist on the policy that shall restrict it to its present limits. We don't suppose that in doing this we violate anything due to the actual presence of the institution, or anything due to the constitutional guaranties thrown around it.

We oppose the Dred Scott decision in a certain way, upon which I ought, perhaps, to address you a few words. We do not propose that when Dred Scott has been decided to be a slave, by the court, we, as a mob, will decide him to be free. We do not propose that, when any other one, or one thousand, shall be decided by that court to be slaves, we will in any violent way disturb the rights of property thus settled ; but we nevertheless do oppose that decision as a political rule, which shall be binding on the voter to vote for nobody who thinks it wrong, which shall be binding on the members of Congress or

the President to favor no measure that does not actually concur with the principles of that decision. We do not propose
to be bound by it as a political rule in that way, because we
think it lays the foundation not merely of enlarging and
spreading out what we consider an evil, but it lays the foundation for spreading that evil into the States themselves. We
propose so resisting it as to have it reversed if we can, and a
new judicial rule established upon this subject.

I will add this, that if there be any man who does not believe that slavery is wrong in the three aspects which I have
mentioned, or in any one of them, that man is misplaced, and
ought to leave us. While, on the other hand, if there be any
man in the Republican party who is impatient over the necessity springing from its actual presence, and is impatient of
the constitutional guaranties thrown around it, and would act
in disregard of these, he too is misplaced, standing with us.
He will find his place somewhere else ; for we have a due regard, so far as we are capable of understanding them, for all
these things. This, gentlemen, as well as I can give it, is a
plain statement of our principles in all their enormity.

I will say now, that there is a sentiment in the country contrary to me—a sentiment which holds that slavery is not
wrong, and therefore it goes for the policy that does not propose dealing with it as a wrong. That policy is the Democratic policy, and that sentiment is the Democratic sentiment.
If there be a doubt in the mind of any one of this vast audience
that this is really the central idea of the Democratic party, in
relation to this subject, I ask him to bear with me while I
state a few things tending, as I think, to prove that proposition. In the first place, the leading man—I think I may do
my friend, Judge Douglas, the honor of calling him such—
advocating the present Democratic policy, never himself says
it is wrong. He has the high distinction, so far as I know, of
never having said slavery is either right or wrong. Almost
everybody else says one or the other, but the Judge never does.
If there be a man in the Democratic party who thinks it is
wrong, and yet clings to that party, I suggest to him in the first
place that his leader don't talk as he does, for he never says that
it is wrong. In the second place, I suggest to him that if
he will examine the policy proposed to be carried forward, he
will find that he carefully excludes the idea that there is any-

thing wrong in it. If you will examine the arguments that are made on it, you will find that every one carefully excludes the idea that there is anything wrong in slavery. Perhaps that Democrat who says he is as much opposed to slavery as I am, will tell me that I am wrong about this. . I wish him to examine his own course in regard to this matter a moment, and then see if his opinion will not be changed a little. You say it is wrong ; but don't you constantly object to anybody else saying so ? Do you not constantly argue that this is not the right place to oppose it ? You say it must not be opposed in the free States, because slavery is not here ; it must not be opposed in the slave States, because it is there ; it must not be opposed in politics, because that will make a fuss ; it must not be opposed in the pulpit, because it is not religion. Then where is the place to oppose it ? There is no suitable place to oppose it. There is no plan in the country to oppose this evil overspreading the continent, which you say yourself is coming. Frank Blair and Gratz Brown tried to get up a system of gradual emancipation in Missouri, had an election in August and got beat, and you, Mr. Democrat, threw up your hat, and halloed " Hurrah for Democracy." So, I say again, that in regard to the arguments that are made, when Judge Douglas says he " don't care whether slavery is voted up or voted down," whether he means that as an individual expression of sentiment, or only as a sort of statement of his views on national policy, it is alike true to say that he can thus argue logically if he don't see anything wrong in it ; but he cannot say so logically if he admits that slavery is wrong. He cannot say that he would as soon see a wrong voted up as voted down. When Judge Douglas says, that whoever or whatever community wants slaves, they have a right to have them, he is perfectly logical if there is nothing wrong in the institution ; but if you admit that it is wrong, he cannot logically say that anybody has a right to do wrong. When he says that slave property and horse and hog property are alike, to be allowed to go into the territories, upon the principle of equality, he is reasoning truly, if there is no difference between them as property ; but if the one is property, held rightfully, and the other is wrong, then there is no equality between the right and wrong ; so that, turn it in any way you can, in all the arguments sustaining the Democratic policy, and in that policy it-

self, there is a careful, studied exclusion of the idea that there
is anything wrong in slavery.   Let us understand this.   I am
not, just here, trying to prove that we are right and they are
wrong.   I have been stating where we and they stand, and
trying to show what is the real difference between us ; and I
now say, that whenever we can get the question distinctly
stated—can get all these men who believe that slavery is in
some of these respects wrong, to stand and act with us in
treating it as a wrong—then, and not till then, I think we will
in some way come to an end of this slavery agitation.

MR. LINCOLN'S REPLY TO MR. DOUGLAS,

At Alton, Ill., *October* 15, 1858.

Ladies and Gentlemen : I have been somewhat, in my
own mind, complimented by a large portion of Judge Douglas's speech—I mean that portion which he devotes to the controversy between himself and the present Administration.
This is the seventh time Judge Douglas and myself have met
in these joint discussions, and he has been gradually improving in regard to his war with the Administration.   At Quincy,
day before yesterday, he was a little more severe upon the Administration than I had heard him upon any occasion, and I took
pains to compliment him for it.   I then told him to "Give it
to them with all the power he had ;" and as some of them
were present, I told them I would be very much obliged if
they would *give it to him* in about the same way.   I take it he
has now vastly improved upon the attack he made then upon,
the Administration.   I flatter myself he has really taken my
advice on this subject.   All I can say now is to recommend
to him and to them what I then commended—to prosecute
the war against one another in the most vigorous manner.   I
say to them again—" Go it, husband !—Go it, bear !"

There is one other thing I will mention before I will leave
this branch of the discussion—although I do not consider it
much of my business, any way.   I refer to that part of the
Judge's remarks where he undertakes to involve Mr. Buchanan
in an inconsistency.   He reads something from Mr. Buchanan,
from which he undertakes to involve him in an inconsistency ;

and he gets something of a cheer for having done so.   I
would only remind the Judge that while he is very valiantly
fighting for the Nebraska bill and the repeal of the Missouri
Compromise, it has been but a little while since he was the
valiant advocate of the Missouri Compromise.   I want to
know if Buchanan has not as much right to be inconsistent as
Douglas has?   Has Douglas the *exclusive right*, in this country,
of being *on all sides of all questions?*   Is nobody allowed that
high privilege but himself?   Is he to have an entire *monopoly*
on that subject?

So far as Judge Douglas addressed his speech to me, or so
far as it was about me, it is my business to pay some attention to it.   I have heard the Judge state two or three times
what he has stated to-day—that in a speech which I made at
Springfield, Illinois, I had in a very especial manner complained that the Supreme Court in the Dred Scott case had decided that a negro could never be a citizen of the United
States.   I have omitted, by some accident, heretofore, to an-
alyze this statement, and it is required of me to notice it now.
In point of fact it is *untrue.*   I never have complained *especially*
of the Dred Scott decision because it held that a negro could
not be a citizen, and the Judge is always wrong when he says
I ever did so complain of it.   I have the speech here, and I
will thank him, or any of his friends, to show where I
said that a negro should be a citizen, and complained especially of the Dred Scott decision because it declared he
could not be one.   I have done no such thing, and Judge
Douglas so persistently insisting that I have done so, has
strongly impressed me with the belief of a predetermination
on his part to misrepresent me.   He could not get his foundation for insisting that I was in favor of this negro equality
anywhere else as well as he could by assuming that untrue
proposition.   Let me tell this audience what is true in regard
to that matter ; and the means by which they may correct me
if I do not tell them truly is by a recurrence to the speech
itself.   I spoke of the Dred Scott decision in my Springfield
speech, and I was then endeavoring to prove that the Dred
Scott decision was a portion of a system, or scheme, to make
slavery national in this country.   I pointed out what things
had been decided by the court.   I mentioned as a fact that
they had decided that a negro could not be a citizen—that

they had done so, as I supposed, to deprive the negro, under all circumstances, of the remotest possibility of ever becoming a citizen and claiming the rights of a citizen of the United States under a certain clause of the Constitution. I stated that, without making any complaint of it at all. I then went on and stated the other points decided in the case, namely : that the bringing of a negro in the State of Illinois and holding him in slavery for two years here was a matter in regard to which they would not decide whether it would make him free or not; that they decided the further point that taking him into a United States Territory where slavery was prohibited by act of Congress, did not make him free, because that act of Congress, as they held, was unconstitutional. I mentioned these three things as making up the points decided in that case. I mentioned them in a lump taken in connection with the introduction of the Nebraska bill, and the amendment of Chase, offered at the time, declaratory of the right of the people of the Territories to *exclude slavery*, which was voted down by the friends of the bill. I mentioned all these things together, as evidence tending to prove a combination and conspiracy to make the institution of slavery national. In that connection and in that way I mentioned the decision on the point that a negro could not be a citizen, and in no other connection.

Out of this, Judge Douglas builds up his beautiful fabrication—of my purpose to introduce a perfect, social, and political equality between the white and black races. His assertion that I made an " especial objection" (that is his exact language) to the decision on this account, is untrue in point of fact.

Now, while I am upon this subject, and as Henry Clay has been alluded to, I desire to place myself, in connection with Mr. Clay, as nearly right before this people as may be. I am quite aware what the Judge's object is here by all these allusions. He knows that we are before an audience, having strong sympathies southward by relationship, place of birth, and so on. He desires to place me in an extremely Abolition attitude. He read upon a former occasion, and alludes without reading to-day, to a portion of a speech which I delivered in Chicago. In his quotations from that speech, as he has made them upon former occasions, the extracts were taken in

such a way as, I suppose, brings them within the definition of
what is called *garbling*—taking portions of a speech which,
when taken by themselves, do not present the entire sense of
the speaker as expressed at the time. I propose, therefore,
out of that same speech, to show how one portion of it which
he skipped over (taking an extract before and an extract after)
will give a different idea, and the true idea I intended to convey. It will take me some little time to read it, bnt I believe
I will occupy the time that way.

You have heard him frequently allude to my controversy
with him in regard to the Declaration of Independence. I
confess that I have had a struggle with Judge Douglas on that
matter, and I will try briefly to place myself right in regard
to it on this occasion. I said—and it is between the extracts
Judge Douglas has taken from this speech, and put in his published speeches :

"It may be argued that there are certain conditions that
make necessities and impose them upon us, and to the extent
that a necessity is imposed upon a man he must submit to it.
I think that was the condition in which we found ourselves
when we established this government. We had slaves among
us ; we could not get our Constitution unless we permitted
them to remain in slavery ; we could not secure the good we
did secure if we grasped for more ; and having, by necessity,
submitted to that much, it does not destroy the principle that
is the charter of our liberties. Let the charter remain as our
standard."

Now I have upon all occasions declared as strongly as Judge
Douglas against the disposition to interfere with the existing
institution of slavery. You hear me read it from the same
speech from which he takes garbled extracts for the purpose
of proving upon me a disposition to interfere with the institution of slavery, and establish a perfect social and political
equality between negroes and white people.

Allow me, while upon this subject, briefly to present one
other extract from a speech of mine, more than a year ago, at
Springfield, in discussing this very same question, soon after
Judge Douglas took his ground that negroes were not included
in the Declaration of Independence :

"I think the authors of that notable instrument intended to
include *all* men, but they did not mean to declare all men

equal *in all respects.* They did not mean to say all men were equal in color, size, intellect, moral development, or social capacity. They defined with tolerable distinctness in what they did consider all men created equal—equal in certain inalienable rights, among which are life, liberty, and the pursuit of, happiness. This they said, and this they meant. They did not mean to assert the obvious untruth, that all were then actually enjoying that equality, or yet, that they were about to confer it immediately upon them. In fact they had no power to confer such a boon. They meant simply to declare the *right,* so that the *enforcement* of it might follow as fast as circumstances should permit.

"They meant to set up a standard maxim for free society which should be familiar to all: constantly looked to, constantly labored for, and even, though never perfectly attained, constantly approximated, and thereby constantly spreading and deepening its influence, and augmenting the happiness and value of life to all people, of all colors, everywhere."

There again are the sentiments I have expressed in regard to the Declaration of Independence upon a former occasion—sentiments which have been put in print and read wherever anybody cared to know what so humble an individual as myself chose to say in regard to it.

At Galesburgh, the other day, I said in answer to Judge Douglas, that three years ago there never had been a man, so far as I knew or believed, in the whole world, who had said that the Declaration of Independence did not include negroes in the term "all men." I re-assert it to-day. I assert that Judge Douglas and all his friends may search the whole records of the country, and it will be a matter of great astonishment to me if they shall be able to find that one human being, three years ago, had ever uttered the astounding sentiment that the term "all men" in the Declaration did not include the negro. Do not let me be misunderstood. I know that more than three years ago there were men who, finding this assertion constantly in the way of their schemes to bring about the ascendency and perpetuation of slavery, *denied the truth of it.* I know that Mr. Calhoun and all the politicians of his school denied the truth of the Declaration. I know that it ran along in the mouths of some Southern men for a period of years, ending at last in that shameful, though rather

forcible, declaration of Pettit, of Indiana, upon the floor of the
United States Senate, that the Declaration of Independence
was, in that respect, "a self-evident lie," rather than a self-
evident truth. But I say, with a perfect knowledge of all this
hawking at the Declaration without directly attacking it, that
three years ago there never had lived a man who had ventured
to assail it in the sneaking way of pretending to believe it and
then asserting it did not include the negro. I believe the first
man who ever said it was Chief Justice Taney in the Dred
Scott case, and the next to him was our friend, Stephen A.
Douglas. And now it has become the catchword of the
entire party. I would like to call upon his friends everywhere
to consider how they have come in so short a time to view this
matter in a way so entirely different from their former belief?
to ask whether they are not being borne along by an irresistible current—whither, they know not?

In answer to my proposition at Galesburgh, last week, I
see that some man in Chicago has got up a letter, addressed to
the Chicago *Times*, to show, as he professes, that somebody *had*
said so before ; and he signs himself " An Old-Line Whig," if
I remember correctly In the first place, I would say he *was
not* an old-line Whig. I am somewhat acquainted with old-
line Whigs. I was with the old-line Whigs from the origin
to the end of that party ; I became pretty well acquainted
with them, and I know they always had some sense, whatever
else you could ascribe to them. I know there never was one
who had not more sense than to try to show by the evidence
he produces that some man had, prior to the time I named,
said that negroes were not included in the term "all men" in
the Declaration of Independence. What is the evidence he
produces? I will bring forward *his* evidence, and let you see
what *he* offers by way of showing that somebody more than
three years ago had said negroes were not included in the Declaration. He brings forward part of a speech from Henry
Clay—*the* part of *the* speech of Henry Clay which I used to
bring forward to prove precisely the contrary. I guess we are
surrounded to some extent to-day by the old friends of Mr.
Clay, and they will be glad to hear anything from that authority. While he was in Indiana a man presented a petition to
liberate his negroes, and he (Mr. Clay) made a speech in answer to it, which I suppose he carefully wrote out himself and

caused to be published. I have before me an extract from that speech, which constitutes the evidence this pretended "Old-Line Whig" at Chicago brought forward to show that Mr. Clay didn't suppose the negro was included in the Declaration of Independence. Hear what Mr. Clay said:

"And what is the foundation of this appeal to me in Indiana, to liberate the slaves under my care in Kentucky? It is a general declaration in the act announcing to the world the independence of the thirteen American colonies, that all men are created equal. Now, as an abstract principle, *there is no doubt of the truth of that declaration;* and it is desirable, *in the original construction of society, and in organized societies,* to keep it in view as a great fundamental principle. But, then, I apprehend that in no society that ever did exist, or ever shall be formed, was or can the equality asserted among the members of the human race, be practically enforced and carried out. There are portions, large portions, women, minors, insane, culprits, transient sojourners, that will always probably remain subject to the government of another portion of the community.

" That declaration, whatever may be the extent of its import, was made by the delegations of the thirteen States. In most of them slavery existed, and had long existed, and was established by law. It was introduced and forced upon the colonies by the paramount law of England. Do you believe, that in making that declaration the States that concurred in it intended that it should be tortured into a virtual emancipation of all the slaves within their respective limits? Would Virginia and other Southern States have ever united in a declaration which was to be interpreted into an abolition of slavery a.nong them? Did any one of the thirteen colonies entertain such a design or expectation? To impute such a secret and unavowed purpose, would be to charge a political fraud upon the noblest band of patriots that ever assembled in council—a fraud upon the Confederacy of tne Revolution—a fraud upon the union of those States whose constitution not only recognized the lawfulness of slavery, but permitted the importation of slaves from Africa until the year 1808."

This is the entire quotation brought forward to prove that somebody previous to three years ago had said the negro was not included in the term "all men" in the Declaration. How does it do so? In what way has it a tendency to prove that? Mr. Clay says *it is true as an abstract principle* that all men are created equal, but that we cannot apply it practically in all cases. He illustrates this by bringing forward the cases of females, minors, and insane persons, with whom it cannot be enforced; but he says it is true as an abstract principle in the organization of society as well as in organized society, and it should be kept in view as a fundamental principle. Let me read a few words more before I add some comments of my own. Mr. Clay says a little further on:

"I desire no concealment of my opinions in regard to the institution of slavery. I look upon it as a great evil, and deeply lament that we have derived it from the parental government, and from our ancestors. But here they are, and the question is, how can they be best dealt with? If a state of nature existed, and we were about to lay the foundations of society, *no man would be more strongly opposed than I should be*, to *incorporating the institution of slavery among its elements.*"

Now, here in this same book—in this same speech—in this same extract brought forward to prove that Mr. Clay held that the negro was not included in the Declaration of Independence—no such statement on his part, but the declaration *that it is a great fundamental truth*, which should be constantly kept in view in the organization of society and in societies already organized. But if I say a word about it—if I attempt, as Mr. Clay said all good men ought to do, to keep it in view —if in this "organized society," I ask to have the public eye turned upon it—if I ask, in relation to the organization of new territories, that the public eye should be turned upon it —forthwith I am vilified as you hear me to-day. What have I done, that I have not the license of Henry Clay's illustrious example here in doing? Have I done aught that I have not his authority for, while maintaining that in organizing new territories and societies, this fundamental principle should be regarded, and in organized society holding it up to the public view and reorganizing what *he* recognized as the great principle of free government?

And when this new principle—this new proposition that no human being ever thought of three years ago—is brought forward, *I combat it* as having an evil tendency, if not an evil design. I combat it as having a tendency to dehumanize the negro—to take away from him the right of ever striving to be a man. I combat it as being one of the thousand things constantly done in these days to prepare the public mind to make property, and nothing but property, of the *negro in all the States of this Union.*

But there is a point that I wish, before leaving this part of the discussion, to ask attention to. I have read and I repeat the words of Henry Clay :

" I desire no concealment of my opinions in regard to the institution of slavery. I look upon it as a great evil, and deeply lament that we have derived it from the parental government and from our ancestors. I wish every slave in the United States was in the country of his ancestors. But here they are ; the question is how they can best be dealt with ? If a state of nature existed, and we were about to lay the foundations of society, no man would be more strongly opposed than I should be, to incorporate the institution of slavery among its elements."

The principle upon which I have insisted in this canvass, is in relation to laying the foundations of new societies. I have never sought to apply these principles to the old States, for the purpose of abolishing slavery in those States. It is nothing but a miserable perversion of what I *have* said, to assume that I have declared Missouri, or any other slave State, shall emancipate her slaves. I have proposed no such thing. But when Mr. Clay says that in laying the foundations of societies in our territories where it does not exist, he would be opposed to the introduction of slavery as an element, I insist that we have *his warrant*—his license for insisting upon the exclusion of that element which he declared in such strong and emphatic language *was most hateful to him.*

Judge Douglas has again referred to a Springfield speech in which I said "a house divided against itself cannot stand." The Judge has so often made the entire quotation from that speech that I can make it from memory   I used this language:

" We are now far into the fifth year, since a policy was initiated with the avowed object and confident promise of putting an end to the slavery agitation. Under the operation of this policy, that agitation has not only not ceased, but has constantly augmented. In my opinion it will not cease until a crisis shall have been reached and passed. 'A house divided against itself cannot stand.' I believe this government cannot endure permanently half slave and half free. I do not expect the house to fall—but I do expect it will cease to be divided. It will become all one thing, or all the other. Either the opponents of slavery will arrest the further spread of it, and place it where the public mind shall rest in the belief that it is in the course of ultimate extinction, or its advocates will push it forward till it shall become alike lawful in all the States—old as well as new, North as well as South."

That extract and the sentiments expressed in it, have been extremely offensive to Judge Douglas. He has warred upon them as Satan wars upon the Bible. His perversions upon it are endless. Here now are my views upon it in brief.

I said we are now far into the fifth year, since a policy was initiated with the avowed object and confident promise of putting an end to the slavery agitation. Is it not so? When that Nebraska bill was brought forward four years ago last January, was it not for the " avowed object " of putting an end to the slavery agitation? We were to have no more agitation in Congress—it was all to be banished to the territories. By the way, I will remark here that, as Judge Douglas is very fond of complimenting Mr. Crittenden in these days, Mr. Crittenden has said there was a falsehood in that whole business, for there was *no slavery agitation at the time to allay.* We were for a little while *quiet* on the troublesome thing, and that very allaying plaster of Judge Douglas' stirred it up again. But was it not understood or intimated with the " confident promise " of putting an end to the slavery agitation? Surely it was. In every speech you heard Judge Douglas make, until he got into this " imbroglio," as they call it, with the administration about the Lecompton constitution, every speech on that Nebraska bill was full of his felicitations that we were *just at the end* of the slavery agitation. The last tip of the last joint of the old serpent's tail was just drawing out of view. But has it proved so? I have asserted that under that policy that agitation " has not only not ceased, but has constantly augmented." When was there ever a greater agitation in Congress than last winter? When was it as great in the country as to-day?

There was a collateral object in the introduction of that

Nebraska policy which was to clothe the people of the
territories with a superior degree of self-government, beyond
what they had ever had before. The first object, and the
main one, of conferring upon the people a higher degree
of "self-government," is a question of fact to be determined
by you in answer to a single question. Have you ever heard
or known of a people anywhere on earth who had as little to
do, as, in the first instance of its use, the people of Kansas
had with this same right of "self-government?" In its main
policy, and in its collateral object, *it has been nothing but a living, creeping lie from the time of its introduction till to-day.*

I have intimated that I thought the agitation would not
cease until a crisis should have been reached and passed. I
have stated in what way I thought it would be reached and
passed. I have said that it might go one way or the other.
We might, by arresting the further spread of it, and placing
it where the fathers originally placed it, put it where the
public mind should rest in the belief that it was in the course
of ultimate extinction. Thus the agitation may cease. It
may be pushed forward until it shall become alike lawful in
all the States, old as well as new, North as well as South.
I have said, and I repeat, my wish is that the further spread
of it may be arrested, and that it may be placed where the
public mind shall rest in the belief that it is in the course of
ultimate extinction. I have expressed that as my wish. I
entertain the opinion upon evidence sufficient to my mind,
that the fathers of this government placed that institution
where the public mind *did* rest in the belief that it was in the
course of ultimate extinction. Let me ask why they made
provision that the source of slavery—the African slave-
trade—should be cut off at the end of twenty years? Why
did they make provision that in all the new territory we owned
at that time, slavery should be forever inhibited? Why stop
its spread in one direction, and cut off its source in another,
if they did not look to its being placed in the course of ultimate extinction?

Again; the institution of slavery is only mentioned in the
Constitution of the United States two or three times, and in
neither of these cases does the word "slavery" or "negro
race" occur; but covert language is used each time, and for
a purpose full of significance. What is the language in re-

gard to the prohibition of the African slave-trade? It runs in about this way: "The migration or importation of such persons as any of the States now existing shall think proper to admit, shall not be prohibited by the Congress prior to the year one thousand eight hundred and eight."

The next allusion in the Constitution to the question of slavery and the black race, is on the subject of the basis of representation, and there the language used is, "Representatives and direct taxes shall be apportioned among the several States which may be included within this Union, according to their respective numbers, which shall be determined by adding to the whole number of free persons, including those bound to service for a term of years, and excluding Indians not taxed—three fifths of all other persons."

It says "persons," not slaves, not negroes; but this "three fifths" can be applied to no other class among us than the negroes.

Lastly, in the provision for the reclamation of fugitive slaves, it is said: "No person held to service or labor in one State, under the laws thereof, escaping into another, shall in consequence of any law or regulation therein, be discharged from such service or labor, but shall be delivered up, on claim of the party to whom such service or labor may be due." There again there is no mention of the word "negro" or of slavery. In all three of these places, being the only allusions to slavery in the instrument, covert language is used. Language is used not suggesting that slavery existed or that the black race were among us. And I understand the contemporaneous history of those times to be that covert language was used with a purpose, and that purpose was that in our Constitution, which it was hoped and is still hoped will endure forever—when it should be read by intelligent and patriotic men, after the institution of slavery had passed from among us—there should be nothing on the face of the great charter of liberty suggesting that such a thing as negro slavery had ever existed among us. This is part of the evidence that the fathers of the government expected and intended the institution of slavery to come to an end. They expected and intended that it should be in the course of ultimate extinction. And when I say that I desire to see the further spread of it arrested, I only say I desire to see that done which the fathers have first done.

When I say I desire to see it placed where the public mind will rest in the belief that it is in the course of ultimate extinction, I only say I desire to see it placed where they placed it. It is not true that our fathers, as Judge Douglas assumes, made this government part slave and part free. Understand the sense in which he put sit. He assumes that slavery is a rightful thing within itself—was introduced by the framers of the Constitution. The exact truth is that they found the institution existing among us, and they left it as they found it. But in making the government they left this institution with many clear marks of disapprobation upon it. They found slavery among them, and they left it among them because of the difficulty—the absolute impossibility of its immediate removal. And when Judge Douglas asks me why we cannot let it remain part slave and part free, as the fathers of the government made it, he asks a question based upon an assumption which is itself a falsehood ; and I turn upon him and ask him the question, when the policy that the fathers of the government had adopted in relation to this element among us was the best policy in the world—the only wise policy—the only policy that we can ever safely continue upon—that will ever give us peace, unless this dangerous element masters us all and becomes a national institution—*I turn upon him and ask him why he could not leave it alone?* I turn and ask him why he was driven to the necessity of introducing a *new policy* in regard to it? He has himself said he introduced a new policy. He said so in his speech on the 22d of March of the present year, 1858. I ask him why he could not let it remain where our fathers placed it? I ask, too, of Judge Douglas and his friends why we shall not again place this institution upon the basis on which the fathers left it? I ask you, when he infers that I am in favor of setting the free and slave States at war, when the institution was placed in that attitude by those who made the Constitution *did they make any war?* If we had no war out of it, when thus placed, wherein is the ground of belief that we shall have war out of it, if we return to that policy? Have we had any peace upon this matter springing from any other basis? I maintain that we have not. I have proposed nothing more than a return to the policy of the fathers.

I confess, when I propose a certain measure of policy, it is not enough for me that I do not intend anything evil in the result, but it is incumbent on me to show that it has not a

tendency to that result. I have met Judge Douglas in that
point of view. I have not only made the declaration that I
do not *mean* to produce a conflict between the States, but I
have tried to show by fair reasoning, and I think I have
shown to the minds of fair men, that I propose nothing but
what has a most peaceful tendency. The quotation that I
happened to make in that Springfield speech, that "a house
divided against itself cannot stand," and which has proved so
offensive to the Judge, was part and parcel of the same thing.
He tries to show that variety in the domestic institutions of
the different States is necessary and indispensable. I do not
dispute it. I have no controversy with Judge Douglas about
that. I shall very readily agree with him that it would be
foolish for us to insist upon having a cranberry law here, in
Illinois, where we have no cranberries, because they have a
cranberry law in Indiana, where they have cranberries. I
should insist that it would be exceedingly wrong in us to deny
to Virginia the right to enact oyster laws, where they have
oysters, because we want no such laws here. I understand, I
hope, quite as well as Judge Douglas, or anybody else, that
the variety in the soil and climate and face of the country,
and consequent variety in the industrial pursuits and produc-
tions of a country, require systems of law conforming to this
variety in the natural features of the country. I understand,
quite as well as Judge Douglas, that if we here raise a barrel
of flour more than we want, and the Louisianians raise a barrel of sugar more than they want, it is of mutual advantage to
exchange. That produces commerce, brings us together, and
makes us better friends. We like one another the more for it.
And I understand, as well as Judge Douglas, or anybody else,
that these mutual accommodations are the cements which
bind together the different parts of this Union—that instead
of being a thing to "divide the house"—figuratively expressing the Union—they tend to sustain it; they are the props of
the house tending always to hold it up.

But when I have admitted all this, I ask if there is any
parallel between these things and this institution of slavery?
I do not see that there is any parallel at all between them.
Consider it. When have we had any difficulty or quarrel
among ourselves about the cranberry laws of Indiana, or the
oyster laws of Virginia, or the pine lumber laws of Maine, or

the fact that Louisiana produces sugar, and Illinois flour? When have we had any quarrels over these things? When have we had perfect peace in regard to this thing which I say is an element of discord in this Union? We have sometimes had peace, but when was it? It was when the institution of slavery remained quiet where it was. We have had difficulty and turmoil whenever it has made a struggle to spread itself where it was not. I ask, then, if experience does not speak in thunder-tones, telling us that the policy which has given peace to the country heretofore, being returned to, gives the greatest promise of peace again. You may say, and Judge Douglas has intimated the same thing, that all this difficulty in regard to the institution of slavery is the mere agitation of office-seekers and ambitious northern politicians. He thinks we want to get "his place," I suppose. I agree that there are office-seekers among us. The Bible says somewhere that we are desperately selfish. I think we would have discovered that fact without the Bible. I do not claim that I am any less so than the average of men, but I do claim that I am not more selfish than Judge Douglas.

But is it true that all the difficulty and agitation we have in regard to this institution of slavery springs from office-seeking —from the mere ambition of politicians? Is that the truth? How many times have we had danger from this question? Go back to the day of the Missouri Compromise. Go back to the Nullification question, at the bottom of which lay this same slavery question. Go back to the time of the Annexation of Texas. Go back to the troubles that led to the Compromise of 1850. You will find that every time, with the single exception of the Nullification question, they sprung from an endeavor to spread this institution. There never was a party in the history of this country, and there probably never will be, of sufficient strength to disturb the general peace of the country. Parties themselves may be divided and quarrel on minor questions, yet it extends not beyond the parties themselves. But does *not* this question make a disturbance outside of political circles? Does it not enter into the churches and rend them asunder? What divided the great Methodist Church into two parts, North and South? What has raised this constant disturbance in every Presbyterian General Assembly that meets? What disturbed the

Unitarian Church in this very city two years ago? What
has jarred and shaken the great American Tract Society recently, not yet splitting it, but sure to divide it in the end?
Is it not this same mighty, deep-seated power, that somehow
operates on the minds of men, exciting and stirring them up
in every avenue of society—in politics, in religion, in litera-
ture, in morals, in all the manifold relations of life? Is this
the work of politicians? Is that irresistible power, which for
fifty years has shaken the government and agitated the people
to be stilled and subdued by pretending that it is an exceedingly simple thing, and we ought not to talk about it? If
you will get everybody else to stop talking about it, I assure
you I will quit before they have half done so. But where is
the philosophy or statesmanship which assumes that you can
quiet that disturbing element in our society which has disturbed us for more than half a century, which has been the
only serious danger that has threatened our institutions—I
say, where is the philosophy or the statesmanship based on the
assumption that we are to quit talking about it, and that the
public mind is all at once to cease being agitated by it? Yet
this is the policy here in the north that Douglas is advocating
—that we are to care nothing about it! I ask you if it is not
a false philosophy? Is it not a false statesmanship that undertakes to build up a system of policy upon the basis of
caring nothing about *the very thing that everybody does care the
most about?*—a thing which all experience has shown we care
a very great deal about?
  The Judge alludes very often in the course of his remarks
to the exclusive right which the States have to decide the
whole thing for themselves. I agree with him very readily
that the different States have that right. He is but fighting a
man of straw when he assumes that I am contending against
the right of the States to do as they please about it. Our controversy with him is in regard to the new territories. We
agree that when the States come in as States they have the
right and the power to do as they please. We have no power
as citizens of the free States or in our federal capacity as
members of the Federal Union through the general government, to disturb slavery in the States where it exists. We
profess constantly that we have no more inclination than
belief in the power of the government to disturb it; yet we

are driven constantly to defend ourselves from the assumption that we are warring upon the rights of the States. What I insist upon is, that the new territories shall be kept free from it while in the territorial condition. Judge Douglas assumes that we have no interest in them—that we have no right whatever to interfere. I think we have some interest. I think that as white men we have. Do we not wish for an outlet for our surplus population, if I may so express myself? Do we not feel an interest in getting to that outlet with such institutions as we would like to have prevail there? If you go to the territory opposed to slavery, and another man comes upon the same ground with his slave, upon the assumption that the things are equal, it turns out that he has the equal right all his way and you have no part of it your way. If he goes in and makes it a slave territory, and by consequence a slave State, is it not time that those who desire to have it a free State were on equal ground. Let me suggest it in a different way. How many Democrats are about here ["A thousand"] who have left slave States and come into the free State of Illinois to get rid of the institution of slavery? [Another voice—"A thousand and one."] I reckon there are a thousand and one. I will ask you, if the policy you are now advocating had prevailed when this country was in a territorial condition, where would you have gone to get rid of it? Where would you have found your free State or territory to go to? And when hereafter, for any cause, the people in this place shall desire to find new homes, if they wish to be rid of the institution, where will they find the place to go to?

Now, irrespective of the moral aspect of this question as to whether there is a right or wrong in enslaving a negro, I am still in favor of our new territories being in such a condition that white men may find a home—may find some spot where they can better their condition—where they can settle upon new soil and better their condition in life. I am in favor of this not merely (I must say it here as I have elsewhere) for our own people who are born among us, but as an outlet for *free white people everywhere*, the world over—in which Hans, and Baptiste, and Patrick, and all other men from all the world, may find new homes and better their conditions in life.

I have stated on former occasions, and I may as well state

again, what I understand to be the real issue in this controversy between Judge Douglas and myself. On the point of my wanting to make war between the free and the slave States, there has been no issue between us. So, too, when he assumes that I am in favor of introducing a perfect social and political equality between the white and black races. These are false issues, upon which Judge Douglas has tried to force the controversy. There is no foundation in truth for the charge that I maintain either of these propositions. The real issue in this controversy—the one pressing upon every mind—is the sentiment on the part of one class that looks upon the institution of slavery as a wrong, and of another class that *does not* look upon it as a wrong. The sentiment that contemplates the institution of slavery in this country as a wrong, is the sentiment of the Republican party. It is the sentiment around which all their actions — all their arguments circle —from which all their propositions radiate. They look upon it as being a moral, social, and political wrong; and while they contemplate it as such, they nevertheless have due regard for its actual existence among us, and the difficulties of getting rid of it in any satisfactory way and to all the constitutional obligations thrown about it. Yet having a due regard for these, they desire a policy in regard to it that looks to its not creating any more danger. They insist that it should, as far as may be, *be treated* as a wrong, and one of the methods of treating it as a wrong is to *make provision that it shall grow no larger.* They also desire a policy that looks to a peaceful end of slavery at sometime, as being wrong. These are the views they entertain in regard to it, as I understand them; and all their sentiments—all their arguments and propositions are brought within this range. I have said and I repeat it here, that if there be a man among us who does not think that the institution of slavery is wrong in any one of the aspects of which I have spoken, he is misplaced and ought not to be with us. And if there be a man among us who is so impatient of it as a wrong as to disregard its actual presence among us and the difficulty of getting rid of it suddenly in a satisfactory way, and to disregard the constitutional obligations thrown about it, that man is misplaced if he is on our platform. We disclaim sympathy with him in practical action. He is not placed properly with us.

On this subject of treating it as a wrong, and limiting its spread let me say a word. Has anything ever threatened the existence of this Union save and except this very institution of slavery? What is it that we hold most dear among us? Our own liberty and prosperity. What has ever threatened our liberty and prosperity save and except this institution of slavery? If this is true, how do you propose to improve the condition of things by enlarging slavery—by spreading it out and making it bigger? You may have a wen or cancer upon your person and not be able to cut it out lest you bleed to death; but surely it is no way to cure it, to engraft it and spread it over your whole body. That is no proper way of treating what you regard a wrong. You see this peaceful way of dealing with it as a wrong—restricting the spread of it, and not allowing it to go into new countries where it has not already existed. This is the peaceful way, the old-fashioned way, the way in which the fathers themselves set us the example.

On the other hand, I have said there is a sentiment which treats it as *not* being wrong. That is the Democratic sentiment of this day. I do not mean to say that every man who stands within that range positively asserts that it is right. That class will include all who positively assert that it is right, and all who, like Judge Douglas, treat it as indifferent and do not say it is either right or wrong. These two classes of men fall within the general class of those who do not look upon it as a wrong. And if there be among you anybody who suppose that he, as a Democrat, can consider himself " as much opposed to slavery as anybody," I would like to reason with him. You never treat it as a wrong. What other thing that you consider as a wrong, do you deal with as you deal with that? Perhaps you *say* it is wrong, *but your leader never does, and you quarrel with anybody who says it is wrong.* Although you pretend to say so yourself, you can find no fit place to deal with it as a wrong. You must not say anything about it in the free States, *because it is not here.* You must not say anything about it in the slave States, *because it is there.* You must not say anything about it in the pulpit, because that is religion and has nothing to do with it. You must not say anything about it in politics, *because that will disturb the security of " my place."* There is no place to talk about it as being a wrong, although you say yourself it *is* a wrong. But finally you will screw yourself up to the belief that if the people of the slave States should adopt a system of gradual emancipation on the slavery question, you would be in favor of it. You would be in favor of it. You say that is getting it in the right place, and you would be glad to see it succeed. But you are deceiving yourself. You all know that Frank Blair and Gratz Brown, down there in St. Louis, undertook to introduce that system in Missouri. They fought as valiantly as they could for the system of gradual emancipation which you pretend you would be glad to see succeed. Now I will bring you to the test. After a hard fight they were beaten, and when the news came over here you threw up your hats and *hurrahed for Democracy*. More than that, take all the argument made in favor of the system you have proposed, and it carefully excludes the idea that there is anything wrong in the institution of slavery. The arguments to sustain that policy carefully excluded it. Even here, to-day, you heard Judge Douglas quarrel with me because I uttered a wish that it might sometime come to an end. Although Henry Clay could say he wished every slave in the United States was in the country of his ancestors, I am denounced by those pretending to respect Henry Clay for uttering a wish that it might sometime, in some peaceful way, come to an end. The Democratic policy in regard to that institution will not tolerate the merest breath, the slightest hint, of the least degree of wrong about it. Try it by some of Judge Douglas' arguments. He says he "don't care whether it is voted up or voted down" in the territories. I do not care myself in dealing with that expression, whether it is intended to be expressive of his individual sentiments on the subject, or only of the national policy he desires to have established. It is alike valuable for my purpose. Any man can say that who does not see anything wrong in slavery, but no man can logically say it who does see a wrong in it; because no man can logically say he don't care whether a wrong is voted up or voted down. He may say he don't care whether an indifferent thing is voted up or down, but he must logically have a choice between a right thing and a wrong thing. He contends that whatever community wants slaves has a right to have them. So they have if it is not a wrong. But if it is a wrong, he cannot say people have a right to do wrong. He

11

says that upon the score of equality, slaves should be allowed to go in a new territory, like other property. This is strictly logical if there is no difference between it and other property. If it and other property are equal, his argument is entirely logical. But if you insist that one is wrong and the other right, there is no use to institute a comparison between right and wrong. You may turn over everything in the Democratic policy from beginning to end, whether in the shape it takes on the statute-book, in the shape it takes in the Dred Scott decision, in the shape it takes in conversation, or the shape it takes in short maxim-like arguments—it everywhere carefully excludes the idea that there is anything wrong in it.

That is the real issue. That is the issue that will continue in this country when these poor tongues of Judge Douglas and myself shall be silent. It is the eternal struggle between these two principles—right and wrong—throughout the world. They are the two principles that have stood face to face from the beginning of time; and will ever continue to struggle. The one is the common right of humanity and the other the divine right of kings. It is the same principle, in whatever shape it develops itself. It is the same spirit that says, "You work and toil and earn bread, and I'll eat it" No matter in what shape it comes, whether from the mouth of a king who seeks to bestride the people of his own nation and live by the fruit of their labor, or from one race of men as an apology for enslaving another race, it is the same tyrannical principle. I was glad to express my gratitude at Quincy, and I re-express it here to Judge Douglas—*that he looks to no end to the institution of slavery.* That will help the people to see where the struggle really is. It will hereafter place with us all men who really do wish the wrong may have an end. And whenever we can get rid of the fog which obscures the real question— when we can get Judge Douglas and his friends to avow a policy looking to its perpetuation—we can get out from among that class of men and bring them to the side of those who treat it as a wrong. Then there will soon be an end of it, and that end will be its "ultimate extinction." Whenever the issue can be distinctly made, and all extraneous matter thrown out so that men can fairly see the real difference between the parties, this controversy will soon be settled, and it will be done peaceably too. There will be no war, no violence. It will be placed again where the wisest and best men of the world placed it. Brooks of South Carolina once declared that when this Constitution was framed, its framers did not look to the institution existing until this day. When he said this, I think he stated a fact that is fully borne out by the history of the times. But he also said they were better and wiser men than the men of these days; yet the men of these days had experience which they had not, and by the invention of the cotton-gin it became a necessity in this country that slavery should be perpetual. I now say that, willingly or unwillingly, purposely or without purpose, Judge Douglas has been the most prominent instrument in changing the position of the institution of slavery which the fathers of the government expected to come to an end ere this—*and putting it upon Brooks' cotton-gin basis*—placing it where he openly confesses he has no desire there shall ever be an end of it.

I understand I have ten minutes yet. I will employ it in saying something about this argument Judge Douglas uses, while he sustains the Dred Scott decision, that the people of the territories can still somehow exclude slavery. The first thing I ask attention to is the fact that Judge Douglas constantly said, before the decision, that whether they could or not, *was a question for the Supreme Court.* But after the court has made the decision he virtually says it is *not* a question for the Supreme Court, but for the people. And how is it he tells us they can exclude it? He says it needs "police regulations," and that admits of "unfriendly legislation." Although it is a right established by the Constitution of the United States to take a slave into a territory of the United States and hold him as property, yet unless the territorial legislature will give friendly legislation, and, more especially, if they adopt unfriendly legislation, they can practically exclude him. Now, without meeting this proposition as a matter of fact, I pass to consider the real constitutional obligation. Let me take the gentleman who looks me in the face before me, and let us suppose that he is a member of the territorial legislature. The first thing he will do will be to swear that he will support the Constitution of the United States. His neighbor by his side in the territory has slaves and needs territorial legislation to enable him to enjoy that constitutional right. Can he withhold the legislation which his neighbor needs for the enjoyment of a right which is fixed in his favor in the Constitution of the United States which he has sworn to support? Can he withhold it without violating his oath? And more especially can he pass unfriendly legislation to violate his oath? Why, this is a *monstrous* sort of talk about the Constitution of the United States! *There his never been as outlandish or lawless a doctrine from the mouth of any respectable man on earth.* I do not believe it is a constitutional right to hold slaves in a territory of the United States. I believe the decision was improperly made and I go for reversing it. Judge Douglas is furious against those who go for reversing a decision. But he is for legislating it out of all force while the law itself stands. I repeat that there has never been so monstrous a doctrine uttered from the mouth of at respectable man.

I suppose most of us (I know it of myself) believe that the people of the Southern States are entitled to a Congressional Fugitive Slave law—that is a right fixed in the Constitution. But it cannot be made available to them without Congressional legislation. In the Judge's language, it is a "barren right" which needs legislation before it can become efficient and valuable to the persons to whom it is guaranteed. And as the right is constitutional I agree that the legislation shall be granted to it—and that not that we like the institution of slavery. We profess to have no taste for running and catching niggers—at least I profess no taste for that job at all. Why then do I yield support to a Fugitive Slave law? Because I do not understand that the Constitution, which guarantees that right, can be supported without it. And if I believed that the right to hold a slave in a territory was equally fixed in the Constitution with the right to reclaim fugitives, I should be bound to give it the legislation necessary to support it. I say that no man can deny his obligation to give the necessary legislation to support slavery in a territory, who believes it is a constitutional right to have it there. No man can, who does not give the Abolitionists an argument to deny the obligation enjoined by the Constitution to enact a Fugitive Slave law. Try it now. It is the strongest Abolition argument ever made. I say if that Dred Scott decision is correct, then the right to hold slaves in a territory is equally a constitutional right with the right of a slaveholder to have his runaway returned. No one can show the distinction between them. The one is express, so that we cannot deny it. The other is construed to be in the Constitution, so that he who believes the decision to be correct believes in the right. And the man who argues that by unfriendly legislation, in spite of that constitutional right, slavery may be driven from the territories, cannot avoid furnishing an argument by which Abolitionists may deny the obligation to return fugitives, and claim the power to pass laws unfriendly to the right of the slaveholder to reclaim his fugitive. I do not know how such an argument may strike a popular assembly like this, but I defy anybody to go before a body of men whose minds are educated to estimating evidence and reasoning, and show that there is an iota of difference between the constitutional right to reclaim a fugitive, and the constitutional right to hold a slave, in a territory, provided this Dred Scott decision is correct. I defy any man to make an argument that will justify unfriendly legislation to deprive a slaveholder of his right to hold his slave in a territory, that will not equally, in all its length, breadth, and thickness, furnish an argument for nullifying the Fugitive Slave law. Why, there is not such an Abolitionist in the nation as Douglas, after all.

SPEECH OF MR. LINCOLN,

At Columbus, Ohio, *September*, 1859.

Fellow-Citizens of the State of Ohio : I cannot fail to remember that I appear for the first time before an audience in this now great State—an audience that is accustomed to hear such speakers as Corwin and Chase, and Wade, and many other renowned men ; and, remembering this, I feel that it will be well for you, as for me, that you should not raise your expectations to that standard to which you would have been justified in raising them had one of these distinguished men appeared before you. You would perhaps be only preparing a disappointment for yourselves, and, as a consequence of your disappointment, mortification to me. I hope, therefore, that you will commence with very moderate expectations ; and perhaps, if you will give me your attention, I shall be able to interest you to a moderate degree.

Appearing here for the first time in my life, I have been somewhat embarrassed for a topic by way of introduction to my speech ; but I have been relieved from that embarrassment by an introduction which the *Ohio Statesman* newspaper gave me this morning. In this paper I have read an article, in which, among other statements, I find the following :

" In debating with Senator Douglas during the memorable contest of last fall, Mr. Lincoln declared in favor of negro suffrage, and attempted to defend that vile conception against the Little Giant."

I mention this now, at the opening of my remarks, for the purpose of making three comments upon it. The first I have already announced--it furnishes me an introductory topic ; the second is to show that the gentleman is mistaken ; thirdly, to give him an opportunity to correct it.

In the first place, in regard to this matter being a mistake. I have found that it is not entirely safe, when one is misrepresented under his very nose, to allow the misrepresentation to go uncontradicted. I therefore propose, here at the outset, not only to say that this is a misrepresentation, but to show conclusively that it is so ; and you will bear with me while I read a couple of extracts from that very "memorable" debate with Judge Douglas last year, to which this newspaper refers. In the first pitched battle which Senator Douglas and myself had, at the town of Ottawa, I used the language which I will now read. Having been previously reading an extract, I continued as follows :

" Now, gentlemen, I don't want to read at any greater length, but this is the true complexion of all I have ever said in regard to the institution of slavery and the black race. This is the whole of it, and anything that argues me into his idea of perfect social and political equality with the negro, is but a specious and fantastic arrangement of words, by which a man can prove a horse-chestnut to be a chestnut horse. I will say here, while upon this subject, that I have no purpose directly or indirectly to interfere with the institution of slavery in the States where it exists. I believe I have no lawful right to do so, and I have no inclination to do so. I have no purpose to introduce political and social equality between the white and black races. There is a physical difference between the two, which, in my judgment, will probably forbid their ever living together upon the footing of perfect equality, and inasmuch as it becomes a necessity that there must be a difference, I, as well as Judge Douglas, am in favor of the race to which I belong having the superior position. I have never said anything to the contrary, but I hold that, notwithstanding all this, there is no reason in the world why the negro is not entitled to all the natural rights enumerated in the Declaration of Independence, the right to life, liberty, and the pursuit of happiness. I hold that he is as much entitled to these as the white man. I agree with Judge Douglas, he is not my equal in many respects—certainly not in color, perhaps not in moral or intellectual endowments. But in the right to eat the bread, without leave of anybody else, which his own hand earns, *he is my equal, and the equal of Judge Douglas, and the equal of every living man.*"

Upon a subsequent occasion, when the reason for making a statement like this recurred, I said :

"While I was at the hotel to-day, an elderly gentleman called upon me to know whether I really was in favor of producing perfect equality between the negroes and white people. While I had not proposed to myself on this occasion to say much on that subject, yet as the question was asked me, I thought I would occupy perhaps five minutes in saying something in regard to it. I will say then, that I am not or ever have been in favor of bringing about, in any way, the social and political equality of the white and black races—that I am not or ever have been in favor of making voters or jurors of negroes, nor of qualifying them to hold office, or intermarry with the white people ; and I will say in addition to this that there is a physical difference between the white and the black races which I believe will forever forbid the two races living together on terms of social and political equality. And, inasmuch as they cannot so live, while they do remain together there must be the position of superior and inferior, and I, as much as any other man, am in favor of having the superior position assigned to the white race. I say upon this occasion I do not perceive that because the white man is to have the superior position, the negro should be denied everything. I do not understand that because I do not want a negro woman for a slave, I must necessarily want her for a wife. My understanding is that I can just let her alone. I am now in my fiftieth year, and I certainly never have had a black woman for either a slave or a wife. So it seems to me quite possible for us to get along without making either slaves or wives of negroes. I will add to this that I have never seen, to my knowledge, a man, woman, or child, who was in favor of producing perfect equality, social and political, between negroes and white men. I recollect of but one distinguished instance that I ever heard of so frequently as to be satisfied of its correctness—and that is the case of Judge Douglas's old friend, Col. Richard M. Johnson. I will also add to the remarks I have made (for I am not going to enter at large upon this subject), that I have never had the least apprehension that I or my friends would marry negroes, if there was no law to keep them from it ; but as Judge Douglas and his friends seem to be in great apprehension lest they might, if there were no law to keep them from it, I give him the most solemn pledge that I will to the very last stand by the law of the State, which forbids the marrying of white people with negroes."

There, my friends, you have briefly, what I have, upon former occasions, said upon the subject to which this newspaper, to the extent of its ability, has drawn the public attention. In it you not only perceive, as a probability, that in that contest I did not at any time say I was in favor of negro suffrage ; but the absolute proof that twice—once substantially and once expressly—I declared against it. Having shown you this, there remains but a word of comment upon that newspaper article. It is this : that I presume the editor of that paper is an honest and truth-loving man, and that he will be greatly obliged to me for furnishing him thus early an opportunity to correct the misrepresentation he has made, before it has run so long that malicious people can call him a liar.

The Giant himself has been here recently. I have seen a brief report of his speech. If it were otherwise unpleasant to me to introduce the subject of the negro as a topic for discussion, I might be somewhat relieved by the fact that he dealt exclusively in that subject while he was here. I shall, therefore, without much hesitation or diffidence, enter upon this subject.

The American people, on the first day of January, 1854, found the African slave-trade prohibited by a law of Congress. In a majority of the States of this Union, they found African slavery, or any other sort of slavery, prohibited by State constitutions. They also found a law existing, supposed to be valid, by which slavery was' excluded from almost all the territory the United States then owned. This was the condition of the country, with reference to the institution of slavery, on the first of January, 1854. A few days after that, a bill was introduced into Congress, which ran through its regular course in the two branches of the National Legislature, and finally passed into a law in the month of May, by which the act of Congress prohibiting slavery from going into the territories of the United States was repealed. In connection with the law itself, and, in fact, in the terms of the law, the then existing prohibition was not only repealed, but there was a declaration of a purpose on the part of Congress never thereafter to exercise any power that they might have, real or supposed, to prohibit the extension or spread of slavery. This was a very great change ; for the law thus repealed was of more than thirty years' standing. Following rapidly upon the heels of this action of Congress, a decision of the Supreme Court is made, by which it is declared that Congress, if it desires to prohibit the spread of slavery into the territories, has no constitutional power to do so. Not only so, but that decision lays down principles, which, if pushed to their logical conclusion—I say pushed to their logical conclusion—would decide that the constitutions of free States, forbidding slavery, are themselves unconstitutional. Mark me, I do not say the Judge said this, and let no man say I affirm the Judge used these words ; but I only say it is my opinion that what they did say, if pressed to its logical conclusion, will inevitably result thus.

Looking at these things, the Republican party, as I understand its principles and policy, believe that there is great danger of the institution of slavery being spread out and extended, until it is ultimately made alike lawful in all the States of this Union ; so believing, to prevent that incidental and ultimate consummation, is the original and chief purpose of the Repub-

lican organization. I say " chief purpose" of the Republican
organization ; for it is certainly true, that if the National
House shall fall into the hands of the Republicans, they will
have to attend to all the other matters of national house-
keeping, as well as this. The chief and real purpose of the
Republican party is eminently conservative. It proposes
nothing save and except to restore this government to its
original tone in regard to this element of slavery, and there
to maintain it, looking for no further change in reference to it,
than that which the original framers of the government themselves expected and looked forward to.

The chief danger to this purpose of the Republican party is
not just now the revival of the African slave-trade, or the passage of a Congressional slave-code, or the declaring of a second
Dred Scott decision, making slavery lawful in all the States.
These are not pressing us just now. They are not quite
ready yet. The authors of these measures know that we are
too strong for them ; but they will be upon us in due time,
and we will be grappling with them hand to hand, if they are
not now headed off. They are not now the chief danger to
the purpose of the Republican organization ; but the most im-
minent danger that now threatens that purpose is the insidious
Douglas popular sovereignty. This is the miner and sapper.
While it does not propose to revive the African slave-trade,
nor to pass a slave-code, nor to make a second Dred Scott decision, it is preparing us for the onslaught and charge of these
ultimate enemies when they shall be ready to come on and the
word of command for them to advance shall be given. I say
this Douglas popular sovereignty—for there is a broad distinction, as I now understand it, between that article and a
genuine popular sovereignty.

I believe there is a genuine popular sovereignty. I think a
definition of genuine popular sovereignty, in the abstract,
would be about this : That each man shall do precisely as he
pleases with himself, and with all those things which exclusively concern him. Applied to government, this principle
would be, that a general government shall do all those things
which pertain to it, and all the local governments shall do
precisely as they please in respect to those matters which exclusively concern them. I understand that this government of
the United States, under which we live, is based upon this

principle ; and I am misunderstood if it is supposed that I
have any war to make upon that principle.

Now, what is Judge Douglas's popular sovereignty ? It is,
as a principle, no other than that, if one man chooses to make
a slave of another man, neither that other man nor anybody
else has a right to object. Applied to government, as he seeks
to apply it, it is this: If, in a new territory into which a few
people are beginning to enter for the purpose of making their
homes, they choose to either exclude slavery from their limits or
to establish it there, however one or the other may affect the
persons to be enslaved, or the infinitely greater number of persons who are afterward to inhabit that territory, or the other
members of the families of communities, of which they are but
an incipient member, or the general head of the family of
States as parent of all—however their action may affect one
or the other of these, there is no power or right to interfere.
That is Douglas's popular sovereignty applied.

He has a good deal of trouble with popular sovereignty.
His explanations explanatory of explanations explained are interminable. The most lengthy, and, as I suppose, the most
maturely considered of his long series of explanations, is his
great essay in Harper's Magazine. I will not attempt to enter on any very thorough investigation of his argument, as
there made and presented. I will, nevertheless, occupy a good
portion of your time here in drawing your attention to certain
points in it. Such of you as may have read this document
will have perceived that the Judge, early in the document,
quotes from two persons as belonging to the Republican party,
without naming them, but who can readily be recognized as
being Gov. Seward of New-York and myself. It is true, that
exactly fifteen months ago this day, I believe, I for the first
time expressed a sentiment upon this subject, and in such a
manner that it should get into print, that the public might see
it beyond the circle of my hearers ; and my expression of it at
that time is the quotation that Judge Douglas makes. He
has not made the quotation with accuracy, but justice to him
requires me to say that it is sufficiently accurate not to change
its sense.

The sense of that quotation condensed is this—that this slavery element is a durable element of discord among us, and
that we shall probably not have perfect peace in this country

with it until it either masters the free principle in our government, or is so far mastered by the free principle as for the public mind to rest in the belief that it is going to its end. This sentiment, which I now express in this way, was, at no great distance of time, perhaps in different language, and in connection with some collateral ideas, expressed by Gov. Seward. Judge Douglas has been so much annoyed by the expression of that sentiment that he has constantly, I believe, in almost all his speeches since it was uttered, been referring to it. I find he alluded to it in his speech here, as well as in the copyright essay. I do not now enter upon this for the purpose of making an elaborate argument to show that we were right in the expression of that sentiment. In other words, I shall not stop to say all that might properly be said upon this point ; but I only ask your attention to it for the purpose of making one or two points upon it.

If you will read the copyright essay, you will discover that Judge Douglas himself says a controversy between the American colonies and the government of Great Britain began on the slavery question, in 1699, and continued from that time until the Revolution ; and, while he did not say so, we all know that it has continued with more or less violence ever since the Revolution.

Then we need not appeal to history, to the declarations of the framers of the government, but we know from Judge Douglas himself that slavery began to be an element of discord among the white people of this country as far back as 1699, or one hundred and sixty years ago, or five generations of men —counting thirty years to a generation. Now, it would seem to me that it might have occurred to Judge Douglas, or anybody who had turned his attention to these facts, that there was something in the nature of that thing, slavery, somewhat durable for mischief and discord.

There is another point I desire to make in regard to this matter, before I leave it. From the adoption of the Constitution down to 1820 is the precise period of our history when we had comparative peace upon this question—the precise period of time when we came nearer to having peace about it than any other time of that entire hundred and sixty years, in which he says it began, or of the eighty years of our own Constitution. Then it would be worth our while to stop and examine into the probable reason of our coming nearer to having peace then than at any other time. This was the precise period of time in which our fathers adopted, and during which they followed, a policy restricting the spread of slavery, and the whole Union was acquiescing in it. The whole country looked forward to the ultimate extinction of the institution. It was when a policy had been adopted and was prevailing, which led all just and right-minded men to suppose that slavery was gradually coming to an end, and that they might be quiet about it, watching it as it expired. I think Judge Douglas might have perceived that, too, and whether he did or not, it is worth the attention of fair-minded men, here and elsewhere, to consider whether that is not the truth of the case. If he had looked at these two facts, that this matter had been an element of discord for one hundred and sixty years among this people, and that the only comparative peace we have had about it was when that policy prevailed in this government, which he now wars upon, he might then perhaps have been brought to a more just appreciation of what I said fifteen months ago—that " a house divided against itself cannot stand. I believe that this government cannot endure permanently half slave and half free. I do not expect the house to fall. I do not expect the Union to dissolve; but I do expect it will cease to be divided. It will become all one thing or all the other. Either the opponents of slavery will arrest the further spread of it, and place it where the public mind will rest in the belief that it is in the course of ultimate extinction ; or its advocates will push it forward, until it shall become alike lawful in all the States, old as well as new, North as well as South." That was my sentiment at that time. In connection with it, I said, " we are now far into the fifth year, since a policy was inaugurated with the avowed object and confident promise of putting an end to slavery agitation. Under the operation of the policy, that agitation has not only not ceased, but has constantly augmented." I now say to you here that we are advanced still farther into the sixth year since that policy of Judge Douglas—that Popular Sovereignty of his, for quieting the slavery question—was made the national policy. Fifteen months more have been added since I uttered that sentiment, and I call upon you, and all other right-minded men, to say whether that fifteen months have belied or corroborated my words

While I am here upon this subject, I cannot but express gratitude that this true view of this element of discord among us—as I believe it is—is attracting more and more attention. I do not believe that Gov. Seward uttered that sentiment because I had done so before, but because he reflected upon this subject and saw the truth of it. Nor do I believe, because Gov. Seward or I uttered it, that Mr. Hickman of Pennsylvania, in different language, since that time, has declared his belief in the utter antagonism which exists between the principles of liberty and slavery. You see we are multiplying. Now, while I am speaking of Hickman, let me say, I know but little about him. I have never seen him, and know scarcely anything about the man ; but I will say this much of him : Of all the anti-Lecompton Democracy that have been brought to my notice, he alone has the true, genuine ring of the metal. And now, without endorsing anything else he has said, I will ask this audience to give three cheers for Hickman. [The audience responded with three rousing cheers for Hickman.]

Another point in the copyright essay to which I would ask your attention, is rather a feature to be extracted from the whole thing, than from any express declaration of it at any point. It is a general feature of that document, and indeed, of all of Judge Douglas's discussions of this question, that the territories of the United States and the States of the Union are exactly alike—that there is no difference between them at all —that the Constitution applies to the territories precisely as it does to the States—and that the United States government, under the Constitution, may not do in a State what it may not do in a territory, and what it must do in a State, it must do in a territory. Gentlemen, is that a true view of the case? It is necessary for this squatter sovereignty ; but is it true ?

Let us consider. What does it depend upon? It depends altogether upon the proposition that the States must, without the interference of the general government, do all those things that pertain *exclusively* to themselves—that are local in their nature, that have no connection with the general government. After Judge Douglas has established this proposition, which nobody disputes or ever has disputed, he proceeds to assume, without proving it, that slavery is one of those little, unimportant, trivial matters, which are of just about as much consequence as the question would be to me, whether my neighbor should raise horned cattle or plant tobacco; that there is no moral question about it, but that it is altogether a matter of dollars and cents; that when a new territory is opened for settlement, the first man who goes into it may plant there a thing which, like the Canada-thistle, or some other of those pests of the soil, cannot be dug out by the millions of men who will come thereafter; that it is one of those little things that it is so trivial in its nature that it has no effect upon anybody save the few men who first plant upon the soil; that it is not a thing which in any way affects the family of communities composing these States, nor any way endangers the general government. Judge Douglas ignores altogether the very well-known fact, that we have never had a serious menace to our political existence, except it sprang from this thing, which he chooses to regard as only upon a par with onions and potatoes.

Turn it, and contemplate it in another view. He says, that according to his popular sovereignty, the general government may give to the territories governors, judges, marshals, secretaries, and all the other chief men to govern them, but they must not touch upon this other question. Why? The question of who shall be governor of a territory for a year or two, and pass away, without his track being left upon the soil, or an act which he did for good or for evil being left behind, is a question of vast national magnitude. It is so much opposed in its nature to locality, that the nation itself must decide it; while this other matter of planting slavery upon a soil—a thing which, once planted, cannot be eradicated by the succeeding millions who have as much right there as the first comers, or if eradicated, not without infinite difficulty and a long struggle—he considers the power to prohibit it, as one of these little, local, trivial things, that the nation ought not to say a word about; that it affects nobody save the few men who are there.

Take these two things and consider them together, present the question of planting a State with the institution of slavery by the side of a question of who shall be governor of Kansas for a year or two, and is there a man here—is there a man on earth, who would not say the governor question is the little one, and the slavery question is the great one? I ask any honest Democrat if the small, the local, and the trivial and temporary question is not, who shall be governor ? While the durable, the important, and the mischievous one is, shall this soil be planted with slavery ?

This is an idea, I suppose, which has arisen in Judge Douglas's mind from his peculiar structure. I suppose the institution of slavery really looks small to him. He is so put up by nature that a lash upon his back would hurt him, but a lash upon anybody else's back does not hurt him. That is the build of the man, and consequently he looks upon the matter of slavery in this unimportant light.

Judge Douglas ought to remember when he is endeavoring to force this policy upon the American people, that while he is put up in that way a good many are not. He ought to remember that there was once in this country a man by the name of Thomas Jefferson, supposed to be a Democrat—a man whose principles and policy are not very prevalent among Democrats to-day, it is true ; but that man did not take exactly this view of the insignificance of the element of slavery of which our friend Judge Douglas does. In contemplation of this thing, we all know he was led to exclaim, " I tremble for my country when I remember that God is just !" We know how he looked upon it when he thus expressed himself. There was danger to this country—danger of the avenging justice of God in that little unimportant popular sovereignty question of Judge Douglas. He supposed there was a question of God's eternal justice wrapped up in the enslaving of any race of men, or any man, and that those who did so brave the arm of Jehovah—that when a nation thus dared the Almighty, every friend of that nation had cause to dread his wrath. Choose ye between Jefferson and Douglas as to what is the true view of this element among us.

There is another little difficulty about this matter of treating the territories and States alike in all things, to which I ask your attention, and I shall leave this branch of the case. If there is no difference between them, why not make the territories States at once ? What is the reason that Kansas was not fit to come into the Union when it was organized into a territory, in Judge Douglas's view ? Can any of you tell any reason why it should not have come into the Union at once ? They are fit, as he thinks, to decide upon the slavery question —the largest and most important with which they could pos-

sibly deal—what could they do by coming into the Union that
they are not fit to do, according to his view, by staying out
of it? Oh, they are not fit to sit in Congress and decide
upon the rates of postage, or questions of *ad valorem* or specific duties on foreign goods, or live-oak timber contracts ; they
are not fit to decide these vastly important matters, which are
national in their import, but they are fit, "from the jump,"
to decide this little negro question. But, gentlemen, the
case is too plain ; I occupy too much time on this head,
and I pass on.

Near the close of the copyright essay, the Judge, I think,
comes very near kicking his own fat into the fire. I did not
think, when I commenced these remarks, that I would read
from that article, but I now believe I will :

"This exposition of the history of these measures, show
conclusively that the authors of the Compromise Measures of
1850 and of the Kansas-Nebraska act of 1854, as well as the
members of the Continental Congress of 1774, and the
founders of our system of government subsequent to the Revolution, regarded the people of the territories and colonies as
political communities which were entitled to a free and exclusive power of legislation in their provisional legislatures, where
their representation could alone be preserved, in all cases of
taxation and internal polity."

When the Judge saw that putting in the word "slavery"
would contradict his own history, he put in what he knew
would pass as synonymous with it : "internal polity." Whenever we find *that* in one of his speeches, the substitute is used
in this manner ; and I can tell you the reason. It would be
too bald a contradiction to say slavery, but "internal polity"
is a general phrase, which would pass in some quarters, and
which he hopes will pass with the reading community for the
same thing.

"This right pertains to the people collectively, as a law-
abiding and peaceful community, and not in the isolated individuals who may wander upon the public domain in violation
of the law. It can only be exercised where there are inhabitants sufficient to constitute a government, and capable of per-
forming its various functions and duties, a fact to be ascertained and determined by"—who do you think? Judge
Douglas says "By Congress!"

12

" Whether the number shall be fixed at ten, fifteen or twenty thousand inhabitants, does not affect the principle."

Now I have only a few comments to make. Popular sovereignty, by his own words, does not pertain to the few persons who wander upon the public domain in violation of law. We have his words for that. When it does pertain to them, is when they are sufficient to be formed into an organized political community, and he fixes the minimum for that at 10,000, and the maximum at 20,000. Now I would like to know what is to be done with the 9,000? Are they all to be treated, until they are large enough to be organized into a political community, as wanderers upon the public land in violation of law? And if so treated and driven out, at what point of time would there ever be ten thousand? If they were not driven out, but remained there as trespassers upon the public land in violation of the law, can they establish slavery there? No—the Judge says popular sovereignty don't pertain to them then. Can they exclude it then? No, popular sovereignty don't pertain to them then. I would like to know, in the case covered by the essay, what condition the people of the territories are in before they reach the number of ten thousand?

But the main point I wish to ask attention to is, that the question as to when they shall have reached a sufficient number to be formed into a regular organized community, is to be decided " by Congress." Judge Douglas says so. Well, gentlemen, that is about all we want. No, that is all the Southerners want. That is what all those who are for slavery want. They do not want Congress to prohibit slavery from coming into the new territories, and they do not want popular sovereignty to hinder it; and as Congress is to say when they are ready to be organized, all that the South has to do is to get Congress to hold off. Let Congress hold off until they are ready to be admitted as a State, and the South has all it wants in taking slavery into and planting it in all the territories that we now have, or hereafter may have. In a word, the whole thing, at a dash of the pen, is at last put in the power of Congress; for if they do not have this popular sovereignty until Congress organizes them, I ask if it at last does not come from Congress? If, at last, it amounts to anything at all,

Congress gives it to them. I submit this rather for your reflection than for comment. After all that is said, at last by a dash of the pen, everything that has gone before is undone, and he puts the whole question under the control of Congress. After fighting through more than three hours, if you undertake to read it, he at last places the whole matter under the control of that power which he had been contending against, and arrives at the result directly contrary to what he had been laboring to do. He at last leaves the whole matter to the control of Congress.

There are two main objects, as I understand it, of this Harper's Magazine essay. One was to show, if possible, that the men of our revolutionary times were in favor of his popular sovereignty; and the other was to show that the Dred Scott decision had not entirely squelched out of this popular sovereignty. I do not propose, in regard to this argument drawn from the history of former times, to enter into a detailed examination of the historical statements he has made. I have the impression that they are inaccurate in a great many instances. Sometimes in positive statement, but very much more inaccurate by the suppression of statements that really belong to the history. But I do not propose to affirm that this is so to any very great extent; or to enter into a very minute examination of his historical statements. I avoid doing so upon this principle—that if it were important for me to pass out of this lot in the least period of time possible, and I came to that fence and saw, by a calculation of my known strength and agility that I could clear it at a bound, it would be folly for me to stop and consider whether I could or not crawl through a crack. So I say of the whole history, contained in his essay, where he endeavored to link the men of the Revolution to popular sovereignty. It only requires an effort to leap out of it—a single bound to be entirely successful. If you read it over you will find that he quotes here and there from documents of the revolutionary times, tending to show that the people of the colonies were desirous of regulating their own concerns in their own way, that the British government should not interfere; that at one time they struggled with the British government to be permitted to exclude the African slave-trade; if not directly, to be permitted to exclude it indirectly by taxation sufficient to discourage and destroy it.

From these and many things of this sort, Judge Douglas argues that they were in favor of the people of our own territories excluding slavery if they wanted to, or planting it there if they wanted to, doing just as they pleased from the time they settled upon the territory. Now, however his history may apply, and whatever of his argument there may be that is sound and accurate or unsound and inaccurate, if we can find out what these men did themselves do upon this very question of slavery in the territories, does it not end the whole thing? If after all this labor and effort to show that the men of the Revolution were in favor of his popular sovereignty and his mode of dealing with slavery in the territories, we can show that these very men took hold of that subject, and dealt with it, we can see for ourselves *how* they dealt with it. It is not a matter of argument or inference, but we know what they thought about it.

It is precisely upon that part of the history of the country, that one important omission is made by Judge Douglas. He selects parts of the history of the United States upon the subject of slavery, and treats it as the whole, omitting from his historical sketch the legislation of Congress in regard to the admission of Missouri, by which the Missouri Compromise was established, and slavery excluded from a country half as large as the present United States. All this is left out of his history, and in nowise alluded to by him, so far as I can remember, save once, when he makes a remark, that upon his principle the Supreme Court were authorized to pronounce a decision that the act called the Missouri Compromise was unconstitutional. All that history has been left out. But this part of the history of the country was not made by the men of the Revolution.

There was another part of our political history made by the very men who were the actors in the Revolution, which has taken the name of the Ordinance of '87. Let me bring that history to your attention. In 1784, I believe, this same Mr. Jefferson drew up an ordinance for the government of the country upon which we now stand ; or rather a frame or draft of an ordinance for the government of this country, here in Ohio, our neighbors in Indiana, us who live in Illinois, our neighbors in Wisconsin and Michigan. In that ordinance, drawn up not only for the government of that territory, but for the territories south of the Ohio river, Mr. Jefferson expressly provided for the prohibition of slavery. Judge Douglas says, and perhaps is right, that that provision was lost from that ordinance. I believe that is true. When the vote was taken upon it, a majority of all present in the Congress of the Confederation voted for it; but there were so many absentees that those voting for it did not make the clear majority necessary, and it was lost. But three years after that the Congress of the Confederation were together again, and they adopted a new ordinance for the government of this northwest territory, not contemplating territory south of the river, for the States owning that territory had hitherto refrained from giving it to the general government; hence they made the ordinance to apply only to what the government owned. In that, the provision excluding slavery *was inserted and passed unanimously*, or at any rate it passed and became a part of the law of the land. Under that ordinance we live. First here in Ohio you were a territory, then an enabling act was passed, authorizing you to form a constitution and State government, provided it was republican and not in conflict with the ordinance of '87. When you framed your constitution and presented it for admission, I think you will find the legislation upon the subject will show that, "whereas you had formed a constitution that was republican, and not in conflict with the ordinance of '87," therefore, you were admitted upon equal footing with the original States. The same process in a few years was gone through with in Indiana, and so with Illinois, and the same substantially with Michigan and Wisconsin.

Not only did that ordinance prevail, but it was constantly looked to whenever a step was taken by a new territory to become a State. Congress always turned their attention to it, and in all their movements upon this subject, they traced their course by that ordinance of '87. When they admitted new States, they advertised them of this ordinance as a part of the legislation of the country. They did so, because they had traced the ordinance of '87 throughout the history of this country. Begin with the men of the Revolution, and go down for sixty entire years, and until the last scrap of that territory comes into the Union in the form of the State of Wisconsin—everything was made to conform with the ordinance of '87, excluding slavery from that vast extent of country.

I omitted to mention in the right place that the Constitution of the United States was in process of being framed when that ordinance was made by the Congress of the Confederation ; and one of the first acts of Congress itself, under the new Constitution itself, was to give force to that ordinance by putting power to carry it out in the hands of the new officers under the Constitution, in the place of the old ones, who had been legislated out of existence by the change in the government from the Confederation to the Constitution. Not only so, but I believe Indiana once or twice, if not Ohio, petitioned the general government for the privilege of suspending that provision and allowing them to have slaves. A report made by Mr. Randolph, of Virginia, himself a slaveholder, was directly against it, and the action was to refuse them the privilege of violating the ordinance of '87.

This period of history, which I have run over briefly, is, I presume, as familiar to most of this assembly as any other part of the history of our country. I suppose that few of my hearers are not as familiar with that part of history as I am, and I only mention it to recall your attention to it at this time. And hence I ask, how extraordinary a thing it is that a man who has occupied a position upon the floor of the Senate of the United States, who is now in his third term, and who looks to see the government of this whole country fall into his own hands, pretending to give a truthful and accurate history of the slavery question in this country, should so entirely ignore the whole of that portion of our history—the most important of all. Is it not a most extraordinary spectacle, that a man should stand up and ask for any confidence in his statements, who sets out as he does with portions of history, calling upon the people to believe that it is a true and fair representation, when the leading part, and controlling feature, of the whole history is carefully suppressed ?

But the mere leaving out is not the most remarkable feature of this most remarkable essay. His proposition is to establish that the leading men of the Revolution were for his great principle of non-intervention by the government in the question of slavery in the territories ; while history shows that they decided in the cases actually brought before them, in ex-

actly the contrary way, and he knows it. Not only did they
so decide at that time, but they stuck to it during sixty years,
through thick and thin, as long as there was one of the revolutionary heroes upon the stage of political action. Through
their whole course, from first to last, they clung to freedom.
And now he asks the community to believe that the men of
the Revolution were in favor of his great principle, when we
have the naked history that they themselves dealt with this
very subject-matter of his principle, and utterly repudiated his
principle, acting upon a precisely contrary ground. It is as
impudent and absurd as if a prosecuting attorney should stand
up before a jury, and ask them to convict A. as the murderer
of B., while B. was walking alive before them.

I say again, if Judge Douglas asserts that the men of the
Revolution acted upon principles by which, to be consistent
with themselves, they ought to have adopted his popular sovereignty, then, upon consideration of his own argument, he had
a right to make you believe that they understood the principles of government, but misapplied them—that he has arisen
to enlighten the world as to the just application of this principle. He has a right to try to persuade you that he understands their principles better than they did, and, therefore, he
will apply them now, not as they did, but as they ought to have
done. He has a right to go before the community, and try to
convince them of this ; but he has no right to attempt to impose
upon any one the belief that these men themselves approved
of his great principle. There are two ways of establishing
a proposition. One is, by trying to demonstrate it upon reason ; and the other is, to show that great men in former
times have thought so and so, and thus to pass it by the
weight of pure authority. Now, if Judge Douglas will demonstrate somehow that this is popular sovereignty—the right
of one man to make a slave of another, without any right in
that other, or any one else to object—demonstrate it as Euclid
demonstrated propositions—there is no objection. But when
he comes forward, seeking to carry a principle by bringing to
it the authority of men who themselves utterly repudiate that
principle, I ask that he shall not be permitted to do it.

I see, in the Judge's speech here, a short sentence in these
words : " Our fathers, when they formed this government under which we live, understood this question just as well and

even better than we do now." That is true; I stick to that. I will stand by Judge Douglas in that to the bitter end. And now, Judge Douglas, come and stand by me, and truthfully show how they acted, understanding it better than we do. All I ask of you, Judge Douglas, is to stick to the proposition that the men of the Revolution understood this subject better than we do now, *and with that better understanding they acted better than you are trying to act now.*

I wish to say something now in regard to the Dred Scott decision, as dealt with by Judge Douglas. In that "memorable debate" between Judge Douglas and myself, last year, the Judge thought fit to commence a process of catechising me, and at Freeport I answered his questions, and propounded some to him. Among others propounded to him was one that I have here now. The substance, as I remember it, is, "Can the people of a United States territory, under the Dred Scott decision, in any lawful way, against the wish of any citizen of the United States, exclude slavery from its limits, prior to the formation of a State constitution?" He answered that they could lawfully exclude slavery from the United States territories, notwithstanding the Dred Scott decision. There was something about that answer that has probably been a trouble to the Judge ever since.

The Dred Scott decision expressly gives every citizen of the United States a right to carry his slaves into the United States territories. And now there was some inconsistency in saying that the decision was right, and saying, too, that the people of the territory could lawfully drive slavery out again. When all the trash, the words, the collateral matter, was cleared away from it—all the chaff was fanned out of it, it was a bare absurdity—*no less than that a thing may be lawfully driven away from where it has a lawful right to be.* Clear it of all the verbiage, and that is the naked truth of his proposition —that a thing may be lawfully driven from the place where it has a lawful right to stay. Well, it was because the Judge couldn't help seeing this, that he has had so much trouble with it; and what I want to ask your especial attention to, just now, is to remind you, if you have not noticed the fact, that the Judge does not any longer say that the people can exclude slavery. He does not say so in the copyright essay; he did not say so in the speech that he made here; and, so far as

I know, since his re-election to the Senate, he has never said, as he did at Freeport, that the people of the territories can exclude slavery. He desires that you, who wish the territories to remain free, should believe that he stands by that position, but he does not say it himself. He escapes to some extent the absurd position I have stated by changing his language entirely. What he says now is something different in language, and we will consider whether it is not different in sense, too. It is now that the Dred Scott decision, or rather the Constitution under that decision, does not carry slavery into the territories beyond the power of the people of the territories *to control it as other property.* He does not say the people can drive it out, but they can control it as other property. The language is different; we should consider whether the sense is different. Driving a horse out of this lot is too plain a proposition to be mistaken about; it is putting him on the other side of the fence. Or it might be a sort of exclusion of him from the lot if you were to kill him and let the worms devour him; but neither of these things is the same as "controlling him as other property." That would be to feed him, to pamper him, to ride him, to use and abuse him, to make the most money out of him "as other property;" but please you, what do the men who are in favor of slavery want more than this? What do they really want, other than that slavery, being in the territories, shall be controlled as other property?

If they want anything else, I do not comprehend it. I ask your attention to this, first, for the purpose of pointing out the change of ground the Judge has made; and, in the second place, the importance of the change—that that change is not such as to give you gentlemen who want his popular sovereignty the power to exclude the institution or drive it out at all. I know the Judge sometimes squints at the argument that in controlling it as other property by unfriendly legislation they may control it to death, as you might in the case of a horse, perhaps, feed him so lightly and ride him so much that he would die. But when you come to legislative control, there is something more to be attended to. I have no doubt, myself, that if the territories should undertake to control slave property as other property—that is, control it in such a way that it would be the most valuable as property, and make it bear its just proportion in the way of burdens as property—really deal with it as property—the Supreme Court of the United States will say, "God speed you and amen." But I undertake to give the opinion, at least, that if the territories attempt by any direct legislation to drive the man with his slave out of the territory, or to decide that his slave is free because of his being taken in there, or to tax him to such an extent that he cannot keep him there, the Supreme Court will unhesitatingly decide all such legislation unconstitutional, as long as that Supreme Court is constructed as the Dred Scott Supreme Court is. The first two things they have already decided, except that there is a little quibble among lawyers between the words *dicta* and decision. They have already decided a negro cannot be made free by territorial legislation.

What is that Dred Scott decision? Judge Douglas labors to show that it is one thing, while I think it is altogether different. It is a long opinion, but it is all embodied in this short statement: "The Constitution of the United States forbids Congress to deprive a man of his property, without due process of law; the right of property in slaves is distinctly and expressly affirmed in that Constitution; therefore, if Congress shall undertake to say that a man's slave is no longer his slave, when he crosses a certain line into a territory, that is depriving him of his property without due process of law, and is unconstitutional." There is the whole Dred Scott decision. They add that if Congress cannot do so itself, Congress cannot confer any power to do so, and hence any effort by the territorial legislature to do either of these things is absolutely decided against. It is a foregone conclusion by that court.

Now, as to this indirect mode by "unfriendly legislature," all lawyers here will readily understand that such a proposition cannot be tolerated for a moment, because a legislature cannot indirectly do that which it cannot accomplish directly. Then I say any legislature to control this property, as property, for its benefit as property, would be hailed by this Dred Scott Supreme Court and fully sustained; but any legislation driving slave property out, or destroying it as property, directly or indirectly, will, most assuredly, by that court, be held unconstitutional.

Judge Douglas says if the Constitution carries slavery into the territories, beyond the power of the people of the territo-

ies to control it as other property, then it follows logically
that every one who swears to support the Constitution of the
United States, must give that support to that property which
it needs. And if the Constitution carries slavery into the
territories, beyond the power of the people to control it as
other property, then it also carries it into the States, because
the Constitution is the supreme law of the land. Now, gentlemen, if it were not for my excessive modesty I would say
that I told that very thing to Judge Douglas quite a year ago.
This argument is here in print, and if it were not for my
modesty as I said, I might call your attention to it. If you
read it, you will find that I not only made that argument, but
made it better than he has made it since.

There is, however, this difference. I say now, and said
then, there is no sort of question that the Supreme Court *has*
decided that it is the right of the slaveholder to take his slave
and hold him in the territory ; and saying this, Judge Douglas himself admits the conclusion. He says if that is so, this
consequence will follow ; and because this consequence would
follow, his argument is, the decision cannot, therefore, be that
way—" that would spoil my Popular Sovereignty, and it cannot be possible that this great principle has been squelched out
in this extraordinary way. It might be, if it were not for the
extraordinary consequences of spoiling my humbug."

Another feature of the Judge's argument about the Dred
Scott case is, an effort to show that that decision deals altogether in declarations of negatives ; that the Constitution does
not affirm anything as expounded by the Dred Scott decision,
but it only declares a want of power—a total absence of
power, in reference to the territories. It seems to be his purpose to make the whole of that decision to result in a mere
negative declaration of a want of power in Congress to do
anything in relation to this matter in territories. I know the
opinion of the Judges states that there is a total absence of
power ; but that is, unfortunately, not all it states ; for the
Judges add that the right of property in a slave is distinctly
and expressly affirmed in the Constitution. It does not stop
at saying that the right of property in a slave is recognized in
the Constitution, is declared to exist somewhere in the Constitution, but says it is *affirmed* in the Constitution. Its language is equivalent to saying that it is embodied and so

woven into that instrument that it cannot be detached without breaking the Constitution itself. In a word, it is part of the Constitution.

Douglas is singularly unfortunate in his effort to make out that decision to be altogether negative, when the express language at the vital part is that this is distinctly affirmed in the Constitution. I think myself, and I repeat it here, that this decision does not merely carry slavery into the territories, but by its logical conclusion it carries it into the States in which we live. One provision of that Constitution is, that it shall be the supreme law of the land—I do not quote the language— any constitution or law of any State to the contrary, notwithstanding. This Dred Scott decision says that the right of property in a slave is affirmed in that Constitution, which is the supreme law of the land, any State constitution or law notwithstanding. Then I say that to destroy a thing which is distinctly affirmed and supported by the supreme law of the land, even by a State constitution or law, is a violation of that supreme law, and there is no escape from it. In my judgment there is no avoiding that result, save that the American people shall see that constitutions are better construed than our Constitution is construed in that decision. They must take care that it is more faithfully and truly carried out than it is there expounded.

I must hasten to a conclusion. Near the beginning of my remarks, I said that this insidious Douglas popular sovereignty is the measure that now threatens the purpose of the Republican party, to prevent slavery from being nationalized in the United States. I propose to ask your attention for a little while to some propositions in affirmance of that statement. Take it just as it stands, and apply it as a principle; extend and apply that principle elsewhere, and consider where it will lead you. I now put this proposition, that Judge Douglas' popular sovereignty applied will re-open the African slave-trade; and I will demonstrate it by any variety of ways in which you can turn the subject or look at it.

The Judge says that the people of the territories have the right, by his principle, to have slaves, if they want them. Then I say that the people in Georgia have the right to buy slaves in Africa, if they want them, and I defy any man on earth to show any distinction between · the two things—to

show that the one is either more wicked or more unlawful ;
to show, on original principles, that one is better or worse
than the other ; or to show by the Constitution, that one
differs a whit from the other. He will tell me, doubtless, that
there is no constitutional provision against people taking
slaves into the new territories, and I tell him +hat there is
equally no constitutional provision against buying slaves in
Africa. He will tell you that a people, in the exercise of
popular sovereignty, ought to do as they please about that
thing, and have slaves if they want them ; and I tell you that
the people of Georgia are as much entitled to popular sovereignty and to buy slaves in Africa, if they want them, as the
people of the territory are to have slaves if they want them.
I ask any man, dealing honestly with himself, to point out a
distinction.

I have recently seen a letter of Judge Douglas', in which,
without stating that to be the object, he doubtless endeavors
to make a distinction between the two. He says he is unalterably opposed to the repeal of the laws against the African
slave-trade. And why ? He then seeks to give a reason that
would not apply to his popular sovereignty in the territories.
What is that reason ? " The abolition of the African slave-
trade is a compromise of the Constitution !" I deny it.
There is no truth in the proposition that the abolition of the
African slave-trade is a compromise of the Constitution. No
man can put his finger on anything in the Constitution, or on
the line of history, which shows it. It is a mere barren assertion, made simply for the purpose of getting up a distinction between the revival of the African slave-trade and his
" great principle."

At the time the Constitution of the United States was
adopted it was expected that the slave-trade would be abolished. I should assert, and insist upon that, if Judge Douglas denied it. But I know that it was equally expected that
slavery would be excluded from the territories, and I can show
by history, that in regard to these two things, public opinion
was exactly alike, while in regard to positive action, there was
more done in the Ordinance of '87 to resist the spread of
slavery than was ever done to abolish the foreign slave-trade.
Lest I be misunderstood, I say again that at the time of the
formation of the constitution, public expectation was that the

slave-trade would be abolished, but no more so than the spread of slavery in the territories should be restrained. They stand alike, except that in the ordinance of '87 there was a mark left by public opinion, showing that it was more committed against the spread of slavery in the territories than against the foreign slave-trade.

Compromise! What word of compromise was there about it. Why, the public sense was then in favor of the abolition of the slave-trade ; but there was at the time a very great commercial interest involved in it, and extensive capital in that branch of trade. There were doubtless the incipient stages of improvement in the South in the way of farming, dependent on the slave-trade, and they made a proposition to Congress to abolish the trade after allowing it twenty years, a sufficient time for the capital and commerce engaged in it to be transferred to other channels. They made no provision that it should be abolished in twenty years ; I do not doubt that they expected it would be ; but they made no bargain about it. The public sentiment left no doubt in the minds of any that it would be done away. I repeat, there is nothing in the history of those times in favor of that matter being a *compromise* of the Constitution. It was the public expectation at the time, manifested in a thousand ways, that the spread of slavery should also be restricted.

Then I say if this principle is established, that there is no wrong in slavery, and whoever wants it has a right to have it, is a matter of dollars and cents, a sort of question as to how they shall deal with brutes,—that between us and the negro here there is no sort of question, but that at the South the question is between the negro and the crocodile. That is all. It is a mere matter of policy ; there is a perfect right according to interest to do just as you please—when this is done, where this doctrine prevails, the miners and sappers will have formed public opinion for the slave-trade. They will be ready for Jeff. Davis and Stephens, and other leaders of that company, to sound the bugle for the revival of the slave-trade, for the second Dred Scott decision, for the flood of slavery to be poured over the free States, while we shall be here tied down and helpless, and run over like sheep.

It is to be part and parcel of this same idea, to say to men who want to adhere to the Democratic party, who have always belonged to that party, and are only looking about for some excuse to stick to it, but nevertheless hate slavery, that Douglas's popular sovereignty is as good a way as any to oppose slavery. They allow themselves to be persuaded easily, in accordance with their previous dispositions, into this belief, that it is about as good a way of opposing slavery as any, and we can do that without straining our old party ties or breaking up old political associations. We can do so without being called negro-worshippers. We can do that without being subjected to the jibes and sneers that are so readily thrown out in place of argument, where no argument can be found. So let us stick to this popular sovereignty—this insidious popular sovereignty. Now let me call your attention to one thing that has really happened, which shows this gradual and steady debauching of public opinion, this course of preparation for the revival of the slave-trade, for the territorial slave-code, and the new Dred Scott decision, that is to carry slavery into the free States. Did you ever, five years ago, hear of anybody in the world saying that the negro had no share in the Declaration of National Independence ; that it· did not mean negroes at all ; and when·"all men" were spoken of, negroes were not included ?

I am satisfied that five years ago that proposition was not put upon paper by any living being anywhere. I have been unable at any time to find a man in an audience who would declare that he had ever known of anybody saying so five years ago. But last year there was not a Douglas popular sovereign in Illinois who did not say it. Is there one in Ohio but declares his firm belief that the Declaration of Independence did not mean negroes at all ? I do not know how this is ; I have not been here much ; but I presume you are very much alike everywhere. Then I suppose that all now express the belief that the Declaration of Independence never did mean negroes. I call upon one of them to say that he said it five years ago.

If you think that now, and did not think it then, the next thing that strikes me is to remark that there has been a *change* wrought in you, and a very significant change it is, being no less than changing the negro, in your estimation, from the rank of a man to that of a brute. They are taking him down, and placing him, when spoken of, among reptiles and crocodiles, as Judge Douglas himself expresses it.

Is not this change wrought in your minds a very important change ? Public opinion in this country is everything. In a nation like ours this popular sovereignty and squatter sovereignty have already wrought a change in the public mind to the extent I have stated. There is no man in this crowd who can contradict it.

Now, if you are opposed to slavery honestly, as much as anybody, I ask you to note that fact, and the like of which is to follow, to be plastered on, layer after layer, until very soon you are prepared to deal with the negro everywhere as with the brute. If public sentiment has not been debauched already to this point, a new turn of the screw in that direction is all that is wanting ; and this is constantly being done by the teachers of this insidious popular sovereignty. You need but one or two turns further until your minds, now ripening under these teachings, will be ready for all these things, and you will receive and support, or submit to, the slave trade, revived with all its horrors, a slave code enforced in our territories, and a new Dred Scott decision to bring slavery up into the very heart of the free North. This, I must say, is but carrying out those words prophetically spoken by Mr. Clay, many, many years ago—I believe more than thirty years, when he told an audience that if they would repress all tendencies to liberty and ultimate emancipation, they must go back to the era of our independence and muzzle the cannon which thundered its annual joyous return on the Fourth of July ; they must blow out the moral lights around us ; they must penetrate the human soul and eradicate the love of liberty ; but until they did these things, and others eloquently enumerated by him, they could not repress all tendencies to ultimate emancipation.

I ask attention to the fact that in a pre-eminent degree these popular sovereigns are at this work ; blowing out the moral lights around us ; teaching that the negro is no longer a man but a brute ; that the Declaration has nothing to do with him ; that he ranks with the crocodile and the reptile ; that man, with body and soul, is a matter of dollars and cents. I suggest to this portion of the Ohio Republicans, or Democrats, if there be any present, the serious consideration of this fact, that there is now going on among you a steady process of debauching public opinion on this subject. With this, my friends, I bid you adieu.

SPEECH OF MR. LINCOLN,

At Cincinnati, Ohio, *September*, 1859.

My Fellow-citizens of the State of Ohio: This is the first time in my life that I have appeared before an audience in so great a city as this. I therefore—though I am no longer a young man—make this appearance under some degree of embarrassment. But I have found that when one is embarrassed, usually the shortest way to get through with it is to quit talking or thinking about it, and go at something else.

I understand that you have had recently with you my very distinguished friend, Judge Douglas, of Illinois, and I understand, without having had an opportunity (not greatly sought to be sure) of seeing a report of the speech that he made here, that he did me the honor to mention my humble name. I suppose that he did so for the purpose of making some objection to some sentiment at some time expressed by me. I should expect, it is true, that Judge Douglas had reminded you, or informed you, if you had never before heard it, that I had once in my life declared it as my opinion that this government cannot " endure permanently half slave and half free ; that a house divided against itself cannot stand," and, as I had expressed it, I did not expect the house to fall ; that I did not expect the Union to be dissolved ; but that I did expect that it would cease to be divided ; that it would become all one thing or all the other ; that either the opposition of slavery would arrest the further spread of it, and place it where the public mind would rest in the belief that it was in the course of ultimate extinction ; or the friends of slavery will push it forward until it becomes alike lawful in all the States, old or new, free as well as slave. I did, fifteen months ago, express that opinion, and upon many occasions Judge Douglas has denounced it, and has greatly, intentionally or unintentionally, misrepresented my purpose in the expression of that opinion.

I presume, without having seen a report of his speech, that he did so here. I presume that he alluded also to that opinion in different language, having been expressed at a subsequent time by Governor Seward of New-York, and that he took the two in a lump and denounced them ; that he tried to point out

that there was something couched in this opinion which led
to the making of an entire uniformity of the local institutions
of the various States of the Union, in utter disregard of the
different States, which in their nature would seem to require
a variety of institutions, and a variety of laws, conforming to
the differences in the nature of the different States.

Not only so; I presume he insisted that this was a declaration of war between the free and slave States—that it was the
sounding to the onset of continual war between the different
States, the slave and free States.

This charge, in this form, was made by Judge Douglas, on,
I believe, the 9th of July, 1858, in Chicago, in my hearing.
On the next evening, I made some reply to it. I informed
him that many of the inferences he drew from that expression
of mine were altogether foreign to any purpose entertained by
me, and in so far as he should ascribe these inferences to me,
as my purpose, he was entirely mistaken ; and in so far as he
might argue that whatever might be my purpose, actions, conforming to my views, would lead to these results, he might
argue and establish if he could ; but, so far as purposes were
concerned, he was totally mistaken as to me.

When I made that reply to him—when I told him, on the
question of declaring war between the different States of the
Union, that I had not said that I did not expect any peace
upon this question until slavery was exterminated ; that I had
only said I expected peace when that institution was put where
the public mind should rest in the belief that it was in course
of ultimate extinction ; that I believed from the organization
of our government, until a very recent period of time, the institution had been placed and continued upon such a basis ;
that we had had comparative peace upon that question
through a portion of that period of time, only because the
public mind rested in that belief in regard to it, and that when
we returned to that position in relation to that matter, I supposed we should again have peace as we previously had. I
assured him, as I now assure you, that I neither then had, nor
have, nor never had, any purpose in any way of interfering
with the institution of slavery, where it exists. I believe we
have no power, under the Constitution of the United States,
or rather under the form of government under which we live,
to interfere with the institution of slavery, or any other of the

institutions of our sister States, be they free or slave States. I declared then, and I now re-declare, that I have as little inclination to interfere with the institution of slavery where it now exists, through the instrumentality of the general government, or any other instrumentality, as I believe we have no power to do so. I accidentally used this expression : I had no purpose of entering into the slave States to disturb the institution of slavery ! So, upon the first occasion that Judge Douglas got an opportunity to reply to me, he passed by the whole body of what I had said upon that subject, and seized upon the particular expression of mine, that I had no purpose of entering into the slave States to disturb the institution of slavery. "Oh, no," said he, "he (Lincoln) won't enter into the slave States to disturb the institution of slavery ; he is too prudent a man to do such a thing as that ; he only means that he will go on to the line between the free and slave States, and shoot over at them. This is all he means to do. He means to do them all the harm he can, to disturb them all he can, in such a way as to keep his own hide in perfect safety."

Well, now, I did not think, at that time, that that was either a very dignified or very logical argument ; but so it was. I had to get along with it as well as I could.

It has occurred to me here to-night, that if I ever do shoot over the line at the people on the other side of the line into a slave State, and purpose to do so, keeping my skin safe, that I have now about the best chance I shall ever have. I should not wonder that there are some Kentuckians about this audience ; we are close to Kentucky ; and whether that be so or not, we are on elevated ground, and by speaking distinctly, I should not wonder if some of the Kentuckians would hear me on the other side of the river. For that reason I propose to address a portion of what I have to say to the Kentuckians.

I say, then, in the first place, to the Kentuckians, that I am what they call, as I understand it, a "Black Republican." I think slavery is wrong, morally and politically. I desire that it should be no further spread in these United States, and I should not object if it should gradually terminate in the whole Union. While I say this for myself, I say to you Kentuckians, that I understand you differ radically with me upon this proposition ; that you believe slavery is a good thing ; that slavery is right ; that it ought to be extended and per-

petuated in this Union. Now, there being this broad difference between us, I do not pretend in addressing myself to
you, Kentuckians, to attempt proselyting you ; that would be
a vain effort. I do not enter upon it. I only propose to try
to show you that you ought to nominate for the next Presidency, at Charleston, my distinguished friend, Judge Douglas.
In all that there is a difference between you and him, I understand he is sincerely for you, and more wisely for you, than
you are for yourselves. I will try to demonstrate that proposition. Understand now, I say that I believe he is as sincerely for you, and more wisely for you, than you are for
yourselves.

What do you want more than anything else to make successful your views of slavery—to advance the outspread of it,
and to secure and perpetuate the nationality of it ? What do
you want more than anything else ? What is needed absolutely ? What is indispensable to you ? Why ! if I may be
allowed to answer the question, it is to retain a hold upon the
North—it is to retain support and strength from the free
States. If you can get this support and strength from the
free States you can succeed. If you do not get this support
and this strength from the free States, you are in the minority,
and you are beaten at once.

If that proposition be admitted—and it is undeniable—then
the next thing I say to you is, that Douglas of all the men in
this nation is the only man that affords you any hold upon the
free States ; that no other man can give you any strength in
the free States. This being so, if you doubt the other branch
of the proposition, whether he is for you—whether he is really
for you, as I have expressed it, I propose asking your attention for a while to a few facts.

The issue between you and me, understand, is, that I think
slavery is wrong, and ought not to be outspread, and you
think it is right and ought to be extended and perpetuated.
[A voice, " Oh, Lord."] That is my Kentuckian I am talking to now.

I now proceed to try to show you that Douglas is as sincerely for you and more wisely for you than you are for yourselves.

In the first place we know that in a government like this,
in a government of the people, where the voice of all the men

of that country, substantially, enters into the execution—or administration rather—of the government, in such a government, what lies at the bottom of all of it, is public opinion. I lay down the proposition, that Judge Douglas is not only the man that promises you in advance a hold upon the North, and support in the North, but that he constantly moulds public opinion to your ends ; that in every possible way he can, he constantly moulds the public opinion of the North to your ends ; and if there are a few things in which he seems to be against you—a few things which he says that appear to be against you, and a few that he forbears to say which you would like to have him say—you ought to remember that the saying of the one, or the forbearing to say the other, would lose his hold upon the North, and, by consequence, would lose his capacity to serve you.

Upon this subject of moulding public opinion, I call your attention to the fact—for a well-established fact it is—that the Judge never says your institution of slavery is wrong ; he never says it is right, to be sure, but he never says it is wrong. There is not a public man in the United States, I believe, with the exception of Senator Douglas, who has not, at some time in his life, declared his opinion whether the thing is right or wrong ; but Senator Douglas never declares it is wrong. He leaves himself at perfect liberty to do all in your favor which he would be hindered from doing if he were to declare the thing to be wrong. On the contrary, he takes all the chances that he has for inveigling the sentiment of the North, opposed to slavery, into your support, by never saying it is right. This you ought to set down to his credit. You ought to give him full credit for this much, little though it be, in comparison to the whole which he does for you.

Some other things I will ask your attention to. He said upon the floor of the United States Senate, and he has repeated it as I understand a great many times, that he does not care whether slavery is "voted up or voted down." This again shows you, or ought to show you, if you would reason upon it, that he does not believe it to be wrong, for a man may say, when he sees nothing wrong in a thing, that he does not care whether it be voted up or voted down ; but no man can logically say that he cares not whether a thing goes up or goes down, which to him appears to be wrong. You therefore have a demonstration in this, that to Judge Douglas's mind your favorite institution which you would have spread out, and made perpetual, is no wrong.

Another thing he tells you, in a speech made at Memphis, in Tennessee, shortly after the canvass in Illinois, last year. He there distinctly told the people, that there was a " line drawn by the Almighty across this continent, on the one side of which the soil must always be cultivated by slaves ;" that he did not pretend to know exactly where that line was, but that there was such a line. I want to ask your attention to that proposition again ; that there is one portion of this continent where the Almighty has designed the soil shall always be cultivated by slaves ; that its being cultivated by slaves at that place is right ; that it has the direct sympathy and authority of the Almighty. Whenever you can get these Northern audiences to adopt the opinion that slavery is right on the other side of the Ohio ; whenever you can get them, in pursuance of Douglas's views, to adopt that sentiment, they will very readily make the other argument, which is perfectly logical, that that which is right on that side of the Ohio, cannot be wrong on this, and that if you have that property on that side of the Ohio, under the seal and stamp of the Almighty, when by any means it escapes over here, it is wrong to have constitutions and laws " to devil" you about it. So Douglas is moulding the public opinion of the North, first to say that the thing is right in your State over the Ohio river, and hence to say that that which is right there is not wrong here, and that all laws and constitutions here, recognizing it as being wrong, are themselves wrong, and ought to be repealed and abrogated. He will tell you, men of Ohio, that if you choose here to have laws against slavery, it is in conformity to the idea that your climate is not suited to it, that your climate is not suited to slave labor, and therefore you have constitutions and laws against it.

Let us attend to that argument for a little while and see if it be sound. You do not raise sugar-cane (except the new-fashioned sugar-cane, and you won't raise that long), but they do raise it in Louisiana. You don't raise it in Ohio because you can't raise it profitably, because the climate don't suit it. They do raise it in Louisiana because there it is profitable. Now, Douglas will tell you that is precisely the slavery ques-

tion. That they do have slaves there because they are profitable, and you don't have them here because they are not
profitable. If that is so, then it leads to dealing with the one
precisely as with the other. Is there then anything in the
constitution or laws of Ohio against raising sugar-cane? Have
you found it necessary to put any such provision in your law?
Surely not! No man desires to raise sugar-cane in Ohio; but,
if any man did desire to do so, you would say it was a tyrannical law that forbids his doing so, and whenever you
shall agree with Douglas, whenever your minds are brought to
adopt his arguments, as surely you will have reached the
conclusion, that although slavery is not profitable in Ohio,
if any man wants it, it is wrong to him not to let him have
it.

In this matter Judge Douglas is preparing the public mind
for you of Kentucky, to make perpetual that good thing in
your estimation, about which you and I differ.

In this connection let me ask your attention to another
thing. I believe it is safe to assert that five years ago, no living
man had expressed the opinion that the negro had no share in
the Declaration of Independence. Let me state that again :
five years ago no living man had expressed the opinion that
the negro had no share in the Declaration of Independence. If there is in this large audience any man who ever
knew of that opinion being put upon paper as much as five
years ago, I will be obliged to him now or at a subsequent time
to show it.

If that be true, I wish you then to note the next fact; that
within the space of five years Senator Douglas, in the argument of this question, has got his entire party, so far as I
know, without exception, to join in saying that the negro has
no share in the Declaration of Independence. If there be
now in all these United States one Douglas man that does not
say this, I have been unable upon any occasion to scare him
up. Now, if none of you said this five years ago, and all of
you say it now, that is a matter that you Kentuckians ought to
note. That is a vast change in the Northern public sentiment upon that question.

Of what tendency is that change? The tendency of that
change is to bring the public mind to the conclusion that when
men are spoken of, the negro is not meant; that when negroes

are spoken of, brutes alone are contemplated. That change in public sentiment has already degraded the black man in the estimation of Douglas and his followers from the condition of a man of some sort, and assigned to him the condition of a brute. Now, you Kentuckians ought to give Douglas credit for this. That is the largest possible stride that can be made in regard to the perpetuation of your thing of slavery.

A voice—" Speak to Ohio men and not to Kentuckians !"

Mr. Lincoln—I beg permission to speak as I please.

In Kentucky, perhaps, in many of the slave States certainly, you are trying to establish the rightfulness of slavery by reference to the Bible. You are trying to show that slavery existed in the Bible times by Divine ordinance. Now, Douglas is wiser than you, for your own benefit, upon that subject. Douglas knows that whenever you establish that slavery was right by the Bible, it will occur that that slavery was the slavery of the *white* man—of men without reference to color—and he knows very well that you may entertain that idea in Kentucky as much as you please, but you will never win any Northern support upon it. He makes a wiser argument for you ; he makes the argument that the slavery of the *black* man, the slavery of the man who has a skin of a different color from your own, is right. He thereby brings to your support Northern voters who could not for a moment be brought by your own argument of the Bible-right of slavery. Will you not give him credit for that? Will you not say that in this matter he is more wisely for you than you are for yourselves ?

Now, having established with his entire party this doctrine —having been entirely successful in that branch of his efforts in your behalf, he is ready for another.

At this same meeting at Memphis, he declared that, while in all contests between the negro and the white man, he was for the white man, in all questions between the negro and the crocodile he was for the negro. He did not make that declaration accidentally at Memphis. He made it a great many times in the canvass in Illinois last year (though I don't know that it was reported in any of his speeches there), but he frequently made it. I believe he repeated it at Columbus, and I should not wonder if he repeated it here. It is, then, a deliberate way of expressing himself upon that subject. It is a matter of mature deliberation with him thus to express himself upon that point of his case. It, therefore, requires some deliberate attention.

The first inference seems to be, that if you do not enslave the negro you are wronging the white man in some way or other; and that whoever is opposed to the negro being enslaved, is, in some way or other, against the white man. Is not that a falsehood? If there was a necessary conflict between the white man and the negro, I should be for the white man as much as Judge Douglas; but I say there is no such necessary conflict. I say that there is room enough for us all to be free, and that it not only does not wrong the white man that the negro should be free, but it positively wrongs the mass of the white men that the negro should be enslaved; that the mass of white men are really injured by the effects of slave labor in the vicinity of the fields of their own labor.

But I do not desire to dwell upon this branch of the question more than to say that this assumption of his is false, and I do hope that that fallacy will not long prevail in the minds of intelligent white men. At all events, you ought to thank Judge Douglas for it. It is for your benefit it is made.

The other branch of it is, that in a struggle between the negro and the crocodile, he is for the negro. Well, I don't know that there is any struggle between the negro and crocodile, either. I suppose that if a crocodile (or as we old Ohio river boatmen used to call them, alligators) should come across a white man he would kill him if he could, and so he would a negro. But what, at last, is this proposition? I believe that it is a sort of proposition in proportion, which may be stated thus: "As the negro is to the white man, so is the crocodile to the negro; and as the negro may rightfully treat the crocodile as a beast or reptile, so the white man may rightfully treat the negro as a beast or a reptile." That is really the "knip" of all that argument of his.

Now, my brother Kentuckians, who believe in this, you ought to thank Judge Douglas for having put that in a much more taking way than any of yourselves have done.

Again, Douglas's *great principle*, "popular sovereignty," as he calls it, gives you, by natural consequence, the revival of the slave-trade whenever you want it. If you question this, listen awhile, consider awhile, what I shall advance in support of that proposition.

13

He says that it is the sacred right of the man who goes into the territories to have slavery if he wants it. Grant that for argument's sake. Is it not the sacred right of the man who don't go there equally to buy slaves in Africa, if he wants them? Can you point out the difference? The man who goes into the territories of Kansas and Nebraska, or any other new territory, with the sacred right of taking a slave there which belongs to him, would certainly have no more right to take one there than I would, who own no slave, but who would desire to buy one and take him there. You will not say—you, the friends of Judge Douglas—that the man who does not own a slave, has an equal right to buy one and take him to the territory, as the other does?

A voice—" I want to ask a question. Don't foreign nations interfere with the slave-trade?"

Mr. Lincoln—Well! I understand it to be a principle of Democracy to whip foreign nations whenever they interfere with us.

Voice—" I only asked for information. I am a Republican myself."

Mr. Lincoln—You and I will be on the best terms in the world, but I do not wish to be diverted from the point I was trying to press.

I say that Douglas's popular sovereignty, establishing his sacred right in the people, if you please, if carried to its logical conclusion, gives equally the sacred right to the people of the States or the territories themselves to buy slaves, wherever they can buy them cheapest; and if any man can show a distinction, I should like to hear him try it. If any man can show how the people of Kansas have a better right to slaves because they want them, than the people of Georgia have to buy them in Africa, I want him to do it. I think it cannot be done. If it is "popular sovereignty" for the people to have slaves because they want them, it is popular sovereignty for them to buy them in Africa, because they desire to do so.

I know that Douglas has recently made a little effort—not seeming to notice that he had a different theory—has made an effort to get rid of that. He has written a letter, addressed to somebody I believe who resides in Iowa, declaring his opposition to the repeal of the laws that prohibit the African slave-trade. He bases his opposition to such repeal upon the ground that these laws are themselves one of the compromises of the Constitution of the United States. Now it would be very interesting to see Judge Douglas or any of his friends turn to the Constitution of the United States and point out that compromise, to show where there is any compromise in the Constitution, or provision in the Constitution, express or implied, by which the administrators of that Constitution are under any obligation to repeal the African slave-trade. I know, or at least I think I know, that the framers of that Constitution did expect that the African slave-trade would be abolished at the end of twenty years, to which time their prohibition against its being abolished extended. I think there is abundant contemporaneous history to show that the framers of the Constitution expected it to be abolished. But while they so expected, they gave nothing for that expectation, and they put no provision in the Constitution requiring it should be so abolished. The migration or importation of such persons as the States shall see fit to admit shall not be prohibited, but a certain tax might be levied upon such importation. But what was to be done after that time? The Constitution is as silent about that as it is silent, personally, about myself. There is absolutely nothing in it about that subject—there is only the expectation of the framers of the Constitution that the slave-trade would be abolished at the end of that time, and they expected it would be abolished, owing to public sentiment, before that time, and they put that provision in, in order that it should not be abolished before that time, for reasons which I suppose they thought to be sound ones, but which I will not now try to enumerate before you.

But while they expected the slave-trade would be abolished at that time, they expected that the spread of slavery into the new territories should also be restricted. It is as easy to prove that the framers of the Constitution of the United States expected that slavery should be prohibited from extending into the new territories, as it is to prove that it was expected that the slave-trade should be abolished. Both these things were expected. One was no more expected than the other, and one was no more a compromise of the Constitution than the other. There was nothing said in the Constitution in regard to the spread of slavery into the territories. I grant that, but there was something very important said about it by the same generation of men in the adoption of the old ordinance of '87, through the influence of which you here in Ohio, our neighbors in Indiana, we in Illinois, our neighbors in Michigan and Wisconsin are happy, prosperous, teeming millions of free men. That generation of men, though not to the full extent members of the Convention that framed the Constitution, were to some extent members of that Convention, holding seats at the same time in one body and the other, so that if there was any compromise on either of these subjects, the strong evidence is that that compromise was in favor of the restriction of slavery from the new territories.

But Douglas says that he is unalterably opposed to the repeal of those laws ; because, in his view, it is a compromise of the Constitution. You Kentuckians, no doubt, are somewhat offended with that! You ought not to be! You ought to be patient! You ought to know that if he said less than that, he would lose the power of "lugging" the Northern States to your support. Really, what you would push him to do would take from him his entire power to serve you. And you ought to remember how long, by precedent, Judge Douglas holds himself obliged to stick by compromises. You ought to remember that by the time you yourselves think you are ready to inaugurate measures for the revival of the African slave-trade, that sufficient time will have arrived, by precedent, for Judge Douglas to break through that compromise. He says now nothing more strong than he said in 1849, when he declared in favor of the Missouri compromise—that precisely four years and a quarter after he declared that compromise to be a sacred thing, which "no ruthless hand would ever dare to touch," he, himself, brought forward the measure ruthlessly to destroy it. By a mere calculation of time it will only be four years more until he is ready to take back his profession about the sacredness of the compromise abolishing the slave-trade. Precisely as soon as you are ready to have his services in that direction, by fair calculation, you may be sure of having them.

But you remember and set down to Judge Douglas's debt, or discredit, that he, last year, said the people of territories can, in spite of the Dred Scott decision, exclude your slaves from those territories ; that he declared by " unfriendly legislation," the extension of your property into the new territories may be cut off in the teeth of the decision of the Supreme Court of the United States.

He assumed that position at Freeport, on the 27th of August, 1858. He said that the people of the territories can exclude slavery in so many words. You ought, however, to bear in mind that he has never said it since. You may hunt in every speech that he has since made, and he has never used that expression once. He has never seemed to notice that he is stating his views differently from what he did then; but, by some sort of accident, he has always really stated it differently. He has always since then declared that "the Constitution does not carry slavery into the territories of the United States beyond the power of the people legally to control it, as other property." Now, there is a difference in the language used upon that former occasion and in this latter day. There may or may not be a difference in the meaning, but it is worth while considering whether there is not also a difference in meaning.

What is it to exclude? Why, it is to drive it out. It is in some way to put it out of the territory. It is to force it across the line, or change its character, so that as property it is out of existence. But what is the controlling it "as other property?" Is controlling it as other property the same thing as destroying it, or driving it away? I should think not. I should think the controlling of it as other property would be just about what you in Kentucky should want. I understand the controlling of property means the controlling of it for the benefit of the owner of it. While I have no doubt the Supreme Court of the United States would say "God speed" to any of the territorial legislatures that should thus control slave property, they would sing quite a different tune, if by the pretence of controlling it they were to undertake to pass laws which virtually excluded it, and that upon a very well known principle to all lawyers, that what a legislature cannot directly do, it cannot do by indirection; that as the legislature has not the power to drive slaves out, they have no power by indirection, by tax, or by imposing burdens in any way on that property, to effect the same end, and that any attempt to do so would be held by the Dred Scott court unconstitutional.

Douglas is not willing to stand by his first proposition that they can exclude it, because we have seen that that proposition amounts to nothing more or less than the naked absurdity, that you may lawfully drive out that which has a lawful right to remain. He admitted at first that the slave might be lawfully taken into the territories under the Constitution of the United States, and yet asserted that he might be lawfully driven out. That being the proposition, it is the absurdity I have stated. He is not willing to stand ∕in the face of that direct, naked, and impudent absurdity; he has, therefore, modified his language into that of being " *controlled as other property.*"

The Kentuckians don't like this in Douglas! I will tell you where it will go. He now swears by the court. He was once a leading man in Illinois to break down a court, because it had made a decision he did not like. But he now not only swears by the court, the courts having got to working for you, but he denounces all men that do not swear by the courts, as unpatriotic, as bad citizens. When one of these acts of unfriendly legislation shall impose such heavy burdens as to, in effect, destroy property in slaves in a territory, and show plainly that there can be no mistake in the purpose of the Legislature to make them so burdensome, this same Supreme Court will decide that law to be unconstitutional, and he will be ready to say for your benefit, "I swear by the court; I give it up;" and while that is going on he has been getting all his men to swear by the courts, and to give it up with him. In this again he serves you faithfully, and as I say, more wisely than you serve yourselves.

Again: I have alluded in the beginning of these remarks to the fact, that Judge Douglas has made great complaint of my having expressed the opinion that this government " cannot endure permanently half slave and half free." He has complained of Seward for using different language, and declaring that there is an "irrepressible conflict" between the principles of free and slave labor. [A voice—"He says it is not original with Seward. That it is original with Lincoln."] I will attend to that immediately, sir. Since that time, Hickman, of Pennsylvania, expressed the same sentiment. He has never denounced Mr. Hickman: why? There is a little chance, notwithstanding that opinion in the mouth of Hickman, that he may yet be a Douglas man. That is the dif-

ference! It is not unpatriotic to hold that opinion, if a man
is a Douglas man.

But neither I nor Seward, nor Hickman, is entitled to the
enviable or unenviable distinction of having first expressed
that idea. The same idea was expressed by the Richmond
Enquirer, in Virginia, in 1856—quite two years before it was
expressed by the first of us. And while Douglas was plu-
ming himself, that in his conflict with my humble self, last
year, he had "squelched out" that fatal heresy, as he delighted to call it, and had suggested that if he only had had a
chance to be in New-York and meet Seward, he would have
"squelched" it there also, it never occurred to him to breathe
a word against Pryor. I don't think that you can discover
that Douglas ever talked of going to Virginia to "squelch"
out that idea there. No. More than that, that same
Roger A. Pryor was brought to Washington city and made
the editor of the *par excellence* Douglas paper, after making
use of that expression, which, in us, is so unpatriotic and
heretical. From all this, my Kentucky friends may see that
this opinion is heretical in his view only when it is expressed
by men suspected of a desire that the country shall all become
free, and not when expressed by those fairly known to entertain the desire that the whole country shall become slave.
When expressed by that class of men, it is in nowise offensive
to him. In this, again, my friends of Kentucky, you have
Judge Douglas with you.

There is another reason why you Southern people ought to
nominate Douglas at your Convention at Charleston. That
reason is the wonderful capacity of the man; the power he
has of doing what would seem to be impossible. Let me call
your attention to one of these apparently impossible things.

Douglas had three or four very distinguished men of the
most extreme anti-slavery views of any men in the Republican
party, expressing their desire for his re-election to the Senate
last year. That would, of itself, have seemed to be a little
wonderful; but that wonder is heightened when we see that
Wise, of Virginia, a man opposed to them, a man who believes
in the Divine right of slavery, was also expressing his desire
that Douglas should be re-elected; that another man that may
be said to be kindred to Wise, Mr. Breckinridge, the Vice-
President, and of your own State, was also agreeing with the

anti-slavery men in the North, that Douglas ought to be re-elected. Still, to heighten the wonder, a Senator from Kentucky, who I have always loved with an affection as tender and endearing as I have ever loved any man; who was opposed to the anti-slavery men for reasons which seemed sufficient to him, and equally opposed to Wise and Breckinridge, was writing letters into Illinois to secure the re-election of Douglas. Now that all these conflicting elements should be brought, while at daggers' point, with one another, to support him, is a feat that is worthy for you to note and consider. It is quite probable that each of these classes of men thought, by the re-election of Douglas, their peculiar views would gain something; it is probable that the anti-slavery men thought their views would gain something; that Wise and Breckinridge thought so too, as regards their opinions; that Mr. Crittenden thought that his views would gain something, although he was opposed to both these other men. It is probable that each and all of them thought that they were using Douglas, and it is yet an unsolved problem whether he was not using them all. If he was, then it is for you to consider whether that power to perform wonders, is one for you lightly to throw away.

There is one other thing that I will say to you in this relation. It is but my opinion; I give it to you without a fee. It is my opinion that it is for you to take him or be defeated; and that if you do take him you may be beaten. You will surely be beaten if you do not take him. We, the Republicans and others forming the opposition of the country, intend to "stand by our guns," to be patient and firm, and in the long run to beat you whether you take him or not. We know that before we fairly beat you, we have to beat you both together. We know that you are "all of a feather," and that we have to beat you altogether, and we expect to do it. We don't intend to be very impatient about it. We mean to be as deliberate and calm about it as it is possible to be, but as firm and resolved as it is possible for men to be. When we do as we say, beat you, you perhaps want to know what we will do with you.

I will tell you, so far as I am authorized to speak for the opposition, what we mean to do with you. We mean to treat you, as near as we possibly can, as Washington, Jefferson, and

Madison treated you. We mean to leave you alone, and in no way to interfere with your institution ; to abide by all and every compromise of the Constitution, and, in a word, coming back to the original proposition, to treat you, so far as degenerated men (if we have degenerated) may, according to the examples of those noble fathers—Washington, Jefferson, and Madison. We mean to remember that you are as good as we ; that there is no difference between us other than the difference of circumstances. We mean to recognize and bear in mind always that you have as good hearts in your bosoms as other people, or as we claim to have, and treat you accordingly. We mean to marry your girls when we have a chance —the white ones I mean, and I have the honor to inform you that I once did have a chance in that way.

I have told you what we mean to do. I want to know, now, when that thing takes place, what do you mean to do. I often hear it intimated that you mean to divide the Union whenever a Republican, or anything like it, is elected President of the United States. [A voice—"That is so."] "That is so," one of them says ; I wonder if he is a Kentuckian? [A voice—"He is a Douglas man."] Well, then, I want to know what you are going to do with your half of it ? Are you going to split the Ohio down through, and push your half off a piece ? Or are you going to keep it right alongside of us outrageous fellows ? Or are you going to build up a wall some way between your country and ours, by which that movable property of yours can't come over here any more, to the danger of your losing it ? Do you think you can better yourselves on that subject, by leaving us here under no obligation whatever to return those specimens of your movable property that come hither ? You have divided the Union because we would not do right with you, as you think, upon that subject ; when we cease to be under obligations to do anything for you, how much better off do you think you will be ? Will you make war upon us and kill us all ? Why, gentlemen, I think you are as gallant and as brave men as live ; that you can fight as bravely in a good cause, man for man, as any other people living ; that you have shown yourselves capable of this upon various occasions ; but man for man, you are not better than we are, and there are not so many of you as there are of us. You will never make much of a hand at whipping us.

If we were fewer in numbers than you, I think that you could whip us ; if we were equal it would likely be a drawn battle ; but being inferior in numbers, you will make nothing by attempting to master us.

But perhaps I have addressed myself as long, or longer, to the Kentuckians than I ought to have done. Inasmuch as I have said that whatever course you take we intend in the end to beat you. I propose to address a few remarks to our friends, by way of discussing with them the best means of keeping that promise, that I have in good faith made.

It may appear a little episodical for me to mention the topic of which I shall speak now. It is a favorable proposition of Douglas's that the interference of the general government, through the ordinance of '87, or through any other act of the general government, never has made or ever can make a Free State ; that the ordinance of '87 did not make Free States of Ohio, Indiana or Illinois. That these States are free upon his "great principle" of popular sovereignty, because the people of those several States have chosen to make them so. At Columbus, and probably here, he undertook to compliment the people, that they themselves have made the State of Ohio free, and that the ordinance of '87 was not entitled in any degree to divide the honor with them. I have no doubt that the people of the State of Ohio did make her free according to their own will and judgment, but let the facts be remembered.

In 1802, I believe, it was you who made your first Constitution, with the cause prohibiting slavery, and you did it I suppose very nearly unanimously ; but you should bear in mind that you—speaking of you as one people—that you did so, unembarrassed by the actual presence of the institution among you ; that you made it a Free State, not with the embarrassment upon you of already having among you many slaves, which if they had been here, and you had sought to make a Free State, you would not know what to do with. If they had been among you, embarrassing difficulties, most probably, would have induced you to tolerate a slave constitution instead of a free one, as indeed these very difficulties have constrained every people on this continent who have adopted slavery.

Pray what was it that made you free ? What kept yoɪ

free ?   Did you not find your country free when you came to
decide that Ohio should be a Free State?   It is important to
inquire by what reason you found it so?   Let us take an
illustration between the States of Ohio and Kentucky.   Kentucky is separated by this river Ohio, not a mile wide.   A
portion of Kentucky, by reason of the course of the Ohio, is
further north than this portion of Ohio in which we now
stand.   Kentucky is entirely covered with slavery—Ohio is
free from it.   What made that difference ?   Was it climate?
No !   A portion of Kentucky was further north than this portion of Ohio.   Was it soil ?   No ?   There is nothing in the
soil of the one more favorable to slave labor than the other.
It was not climate or soil that caused one side of the line to
be entirely covered with slavery and the other side free of it.
What was it ?   Study over it.   Tell us, if you can, in all the
range of conjecture, if there be any thing you can conceive of
that made that difference, other than that there was no law
of any sort keeping it out of Kentucky, while the ordinance
of '87 kept it out of Ohio.   If there is any other reason than
this, I confess that it is wholly beyond my power to conceive
of it.   This, then, I offer to combat the idea that that ordinance has never made any State free.

I don't stop at this illustration.   I come to the State of Indiana ; and what I have said as between Kentucky and Ohio,
I repeat as between Indiana and Kentucky ; it is equally applicable.   One additional argument is applicable also to
Indiana.   In her territorial condition she more than once
petitioned Congress to abrogate the ordinance entirely, or at
least so far as to suspend its operation for a time, in order
that they should exercise the "popular sovereignty" of having slaves if they wanted them.   The men then controlling
the general government, imitating the men of the Revolution,
refused Indiana that privilege.   And so we have the evidence
that Indiana supposed she could have slaves, if it were not for
that ordinance ; that she besought Congress to put that barrier out of the way ; that Congress refused to do so, and it all
ended at last in Indiana being a free State.   Tell me not,
then, that the ordinance of '87 had nothing to do with
making Indiana a free State, when we find some men chafing
against and only restrained by that barrier.

Come down again to our State of Illinois.   The great

northwest territory, including Ohio, Indiana, Illinois, Michigan, and Wisconsin, was acquired first, I believe, by the British government, in part at least, from the French. Before the establishment of our independence it became a part of Virginia, enabling Virginia after to transfer it to the general government. There were French settlements in what is now Illinois, and at the same time there were French settlements in what is now Missouri—in the tract of country that was not purchased till about 1803. In these French settlements negro slavery had existed for many years—perhaps more than a hundred, if not as much as two hundred years—at Kaskaskia, in Illinois, and at St. Genevieve, or Cape Girardeau, perhaps, in Missouri. The number of slaves was not very great, but there was about the same number in each place. They were there when we acquired the territory. There was no effort made to break up the relation of master and slave, and even the ordinance of 1787 was not so enforced as to destroy slavery in Illinois; nor did the ordinance apply to Missouri at all.

What I want to ask your attention to, at this point, is that Illinois and Missouri came into the Union about the same time, Illinois in the latter part of 1818, and Missouri, after a struggle, I believe sometime in 1820. They had been filling up with American people about the same period of time; their progress enabling them to come into the Union about the same time. At the end of ten years, in which they had been so preparing (for it was about that period of time), the number of slaves in Illinois had actually decreased; while in Missouri, beginning with very few, at the end of that ten years there were about ten thousand. This being so, and it being remembered that Missouri and Illinois are, to a certain extent, in the same parallel of latitude—that the northern half of Missouri and the southern half of Illinois are in the same parallel of latitude—so that climate would have the same effect upon one as upon the other, and that in the soil there is no material difference, so far as bears upon the question of slavery being settled upon one or the other—there being none of those natural causes to produce a difference in filling them, and yet there being a broad difference in their filling up, we are led again to inquire what was the cause of that difference?

It is most natural to say that in Missouri there was no law to keep that country from filling up with slaves, while in Illinois there was the ordinance of '87. The ordinance being there, slavery decreased during that ten years—the ordinance not being in the other, it increased from a few to ten thousand. Can any body doubt the reason of the difference ?

I think all these facts most abundantly prove that my friend Judge Douglas's proposition, that the ordinance of '87, or the national restriction of slavery, never had a tendency to make a free State, is a fallacy—a proposition without the shadow or substance of truth about it.

Douglas sometimes says that all the States (and it is part of this same proposition I have been discussing) that have become free, have become so upon his " great principle ;" that the State of Illinois itself came into the Union as a slave State, and that the people, upon the " great principle " of popular sovereignty, have since made it a free State. Allow me but a little while to state to you what facts there are to justify him in saying that Illinois came into the Union as a slave State.

I have mentioned to you that there were a few old French slaves there. They numbered, I think, one or two hundred. Besides that, there had been a territorial law for indenturing black persons. Under that law, in violation of the ordinance of '87, but without any enforcement of the ordinance to overthrow the system, there had been a small number of slaves introduced as indentured persons. Owing to this the clause for the prohibition of slavery was slightly modified. Instead of running like yours, that neither slavery nor involuntary servitude, except for crime, of which the party shall have been duly convicted, should exist in the State, they said that neither slavery nor involuntary servitude should thereafter be introduced, and that the children of indentured servants should be born free ; and nothing was said about the few old French slaves. Out of this fact, that the clause for prohibiting slavery was modified because of the actual presence of it, Douglas asserts again and again that Illinois came into the Union as a slave State. How far the facts sustain the conclusion that he draws, it is for intelligent and impartial men to decide. I leave it with you with these remarks, worthy of being remembered, that that little thing, those few indentured servants being there, was of itself sufficient to modify a constitution made by a people ardently desiring to have a free constitution ; showing the power of the actual presence of the institution of slavery to prevent any people, however anxious to make a free State, from making it perfectly so.

I have been detaining you longer perhaps than I ought to do.

I am in some doubt whether to introduce another topic upon which I could talk awhile. [Cries of " Go on,", and " Give us it."] It is this, then : Douglas's popular sovereignty, as a principle, is simply this : If one man chooses to make a slave of another man, neither that man or anybody else has a right to object. Apply it to a government, as he seeks to apply it, and it is this: if in a new territory, into which a few people are beginning to enter for the purpose of making their homes, they choose to either exclude slavery from their limits, or to establish it there, however one or the other may affect the persons to be enslaved, or the infinitely greater number of persons who are afterward to inhabit that territory, or the other members of the family of communities, of which they are but an incipient member, or the general head of the family of States as parent of all—however their action may affect one or the other of these, there is no power or right to interfere. That is Douglas's popular sovereignty applied. Now, I think that there is a real popular sovereignty in the world. I think a definition of popular sovereignty, in the abstract, would be about this—that each man shall do precisely as he pleases with himself, and with all those things which exclusively concern him. Applied in government, this principle would be, that a general government shall do all those things which pertain to it, and all the local governments shall do precisely as they please in respect to those matters which exclusively concern them.

Douglas looks upon slavery as so insignificant that the people must decide that question for themselves, and yet they are not fit to decide who shall be their governor, judge or secretary, or who shall be any of their officers. These are vast national matters, in his estimation, but the little matter in his estimation is that of planting slavery there. That is purely of local interest, which nobody should be allowed to say a word about.

Labor is the great source from which nearly all, if not all, human comforts and necessities are drawn. There is a difference of opinion about the elements of labor in society. Some men assume that there is a necessary connection between capital and labor, and that connection draws within it the whole of the labor of the community. They assume that nobody works unless capital excites them to work. They begin next to consider what is the best way. They say there are but two ways ; one is to hire men and to allure them to labor by their consent ; the other is to buy the men and drive them to it, and that is slavery. Having assumed that, they proceed to discuss the question of whether the laborers themselves are better off in the condition of slaves or of hired laborers, and they usually decide that they are better off in the condition of slaves.

In the first place, I say that the whole thing is a mistake. That there is a certain relation between capital and labor, I admit. That it does exist, and rightfully exist, I think is true. That men who are industrious, and sober, and honest in the pursuit of their own interests, should after a while accumulate capital, and after that should be allowed to enjoy it in peace, and also, if they should choose, when they have accumulated it, to use it to save themselves from actual labor and hire other people to labor for them, is right. In doing so they do not wrong the man they employ, for they find men who have not of their own land to work upon, or shops to work in, and who are benefited by working for others, hired laborers, receiving their capital for it. Thus a few men that own capital, hire a few others, and these establish the relation of capital and labor rightfully. A relation of which I make no complaint. But I insist that that relation after all does not embrace more than one-eighth of the labor of the country.

[The speaker proceeded to argue that the hired laborer, with his ability to become an employer, must have every precedence over him who labors under the inducement of force. He continued :]

I have taken upon myself in the name of some of you to say, that we expect upon these principles to ultimately beat them. In order to do so, I think we want and must have a national policy in regard to the institution of slavery, that acknowledges and deals with that institution as being wrong.

Whoever desires the prevention of the spread of slavery and the nationalization of that institution, yields all, when he yields to any policy that either recognizes slavery as being right, or as being an indifferent thing. Nothing will make you successful but setting up a policy which shall treat the thing as being wrong. When I say this, I do not mean to say that this general government is charged with the duty of redressing or preventing all the wrongs in the world; but I do think that it is charged with preventing and redressing all wrongs which are wrongs to itself. This government is expressly charged with the duty of providing for the general welfare. We believe that the spreading out and perpetuity of the institution of slavery impairs the general welfare. We believe—nay, we know, that that is the only thing that has ever threatened the perpetuity of the Union .itself. The only thing which has ever menaced the destruction of the government under which we live, is this very thing. To repress this thing, we think, is providing for the general welfare. Our friends in Kentucky differ from us. We need not make our argument for them, but we who think it is wrong in all its relations, or in some of them at least, must decide as to our own actions, and our own course, upon our own judgment.

I say that we must not interfere with the institution of slavery in the States where it exists, because the Constitution forbids it, and the general welfare does not require us to do so. We must not withhold an efficient fugitive slave law because the Constitution requires us, as I understand it, not to withhold such a law. But we must prevent the out-spreading of the institution, because neither the Constitution nor general welfare requires us to extend it. We must prevent the revival of the African slave-trade, and the enacting by Congress of a territorial slave code. We must prevent each of these things being done by either congresses or courts. The people of these United States are the rightful masters of both congresses and courts, not to overthrow the Constitution, but to overthrow the men who pervert the Constitution.

To do these things we must employ instrumentalities. We must hold conventions; we must adopt platforms, if we conform to ordinary custom; we must nominate candidates, and we must carry elections. In all these things, I think that we ought to keep in view our real purpose, and in none do anything that stands adverse to our purpose. If we shall adopt a platform that fails to recognize or express our purpose, or elect a man that declares himself inimical to our purpose, we not only take nothing by our success, but we tacitly admit that we act upon no other principle than a desire to have "the loaves and fishes," by which, in the end, our apparent success is really an injury to us.

I know that this is very desirable with me, as with everybody else, that all the elements of the Opposition shall unite in the next Presidential election, and in all future time. I am anxious that that should be, but there are things seriously to be considered in relation to that matter. If the terms can be arranged, I am in favor of the Union. But suppose we shall take up some man and put him upon one end or the other of the ticket, who declares himself against us in regard to the prevention of the spread of slavery—who turns up his nose and says he is tired of hearing anything more about it, who is more against us than against the enemy, what will be the issue? Why, he will get no slave States after all—he has tried that already until being beat is the rule for him. If we nominate him upon that ground, he will not carry a slave State, and not only so, but that portion of our men who are highstrung upon the principle we really fight for, will not go for him, and he won't get a single electoral vote anywhere, except, perhaps, in the State of Maryland. There is no use in saying to us that we are stubborn and obstinate, because we won't do some such thing as this. We cannot do it. We cannot get our men to vote it. I speak by the card, that we cannot give the State of Illinois in such case by fifty thousand. We would be flatter down than the "Negro Democracy" themselves have the heart to wish to see us.

After saying this much, let me say a little on the other side. There are plenty of men in the slave States that are altogether good enough for me to be either President or Vice-President, provided they will profess their sympathy with our purpose, and will place themselves on the ground that our men, upon principle, can vote for them. There are scores of them, good men in their character for intelligence and talent and integrity. If such a one will place himself upon the right ground, I am for his occupying one place upon the next Republican or Opposition ticket. I will heartily go for him. But, unless he does so place himself, I think it a matter of perfect nonsense to attempt to bring about a union upon any other basis ; that if a union be made, the elements' will scatter so that there can be no success for such a ticket, nor anything like success. The good old maxims of the Bible are applicable, and truly applicable, to human affairs ; and in this, as in other things, we may say here, that he who is not for us is against us ; he who gathereth not with us scattereth. I should be, glad to have some of the many good, and able, and noble men of the South to place themselves where we can confer upon them the high honor of an election upon one or the other end of our ticket. It would do my soul good to do that thing. It would enable us to teach them that, inasmuch as we select one of their own number to carry out our principles, we are free from the charge that we mean more than we say.

But, my friends, I have detained you much longer than I expected to do. I believe I may do myself the compliment to say that you have stayed and heard me with great patience, for which I return you my most sincere thanks.

SPEECH OF MR. LINCOLN,

AT THE COOPER INSTITUTE, NEW-YORK, *February* 27, 1860.

MR. PRESIDENT AND FELLOW-CITIZENS OF NEW-YORK : The facts with which I shall deal this evening are mainly old and familiar ; nor is there anything new in the general use I shall make of them. If there shall be any novelty, it will be in the mode of presenting the facts, and the inferences and observations following that presentation.

In his speech, last autumn, at Columbus, Ohio, as reported in *The New-York Times,* Senator Douglas said :

"Our fathers, when they framed the government under which we live, understood this question just as well as, and even better than, we do now."

I fully endorse this, and I adopt it as a text for this discourse. I so adopt it because it furnishes a precise and an agreed starting point for a discussion between Republicans and that wing of the Democracy headed by Senator Douglas. It simply leaves the inquiry : " What was the understanding those fathers had of the question mentioned ?"

What is the frame of government under which we live ? The answer must be : " The Constitution of the United States." That Constitution consists of the original, framed in 1787 (and under which the present government first went into operation), and twelve subsequently framed amendments, the first ten of which were framed in 1789.

Who were our fathers that framed the Constitution ? I suppose the " thirty-nine" who signed the original instrument may be fairly called our fathers who framed that part of the present government. It is almost exactly true to say they framed it, and it is altogether true to say they fairly represented the opinion and sentiment of the whole nation at that time. Their names, being familiar to nearly all, and accessible to quite all, need not now be repeated.

I take these " thirty-nine," for the present, as being " our fathers who framed the government under which we live."

What is the question which, according to the text, those fathers understood just as well, and even bet.er than we do now ?

It is this : Does the proper division of local from federal authority, or anything in the Constitution, forbid our federal government to control as to slavery in our federal territories ?

Upon this, Douglas holds the affirmative, and Republicans the negative. This affirmative and denial form an issue ; and this issue—this question—is precisely what the text declares our fathers understood better than we.

Let us now inquire whether the " thirty-nine," or any of them, ever acted upon this question ; and if they did, how they acted upon it—how they expressed that better understanding.

In 1784—three years before the Constitution—the United States then owning the Northwestern Territory, and no other— the Congress of the Confederation had before them the question of prohibiting slavery in that territory ; and four of the " thirty-nine" who afterward framed the Constitution were in that Congress, and voted on that question. Of these, Roger

Sherman, Thomas Mifflin, and Hugh Williamson, voted for
the prohibition—thus showing that, in their understanding, no
line dividing local from federal authority, nor anything else,
properly forbade the federal government to control as to
slavery in federal territory. The other of the four—James
McHenry—voted against the prohibition, showing that, for
some cause, he thought it improper to vote for it.

In 1787, still before the Constitution, but while the Convention was in session framing it, and while the northwestern
territory still was the only territory owned by the United
States—the same question of prohibiting slavery in the territory again came before the Congress of the Confederation ;
and three more of the " thirty-nine" who afterward signed the
Constitution, were in that Congress, and voted on the question. They were William Blount, William Few, and Abraham Baldwin ; and they all voted for the prohibition—thus
showing that, in their understanding, no line dividing local
from federal authority, nor anything else, properly forbids the
federal government to control as to slavery in federal territory. This time the prohibition became a law, being part of
what is now well known as the Ordinance of '87.

The question of federal control of slavery in the territories,
seems not to have been directly before the Convention which
framed the original Constitution ; and hence it is not recorded
that the " thirty-nine" or any of them, while engaged on that
instrument, expressed any opinion on that precise question.

In 1789, by the first Congress which sat under the Constitution, an act was passed to enforce the Ordinance of '87,
including the prohibition of slavery in the northwestern territory. The bill for this act was reported by one of the
" thirty-nine," Thomas Fitzsimmons, then a member of the
House of Representatives from Pennsylvania. It went through
all its stages without a word of opposition, and finally passed
both branches without yeas and nays, which is equivalent to
a unanimous passage. In this Congress there were sixteen of
the " thirty-nine" fathers who framed the original Constitution. They were John Langdon, Nicholas Gilman, Wm. S.
Johnson, Roger Sherman, Robert Morris, Thos. Fitzsimmons,
William Few, Abraham Baldwin, Rufus King, William Pat-
terson, George Clymer, Richard Bassett, George Reed, Pierce
Butler, Daniel Carroll, James Madison.

This shows that, in their understanding, no line dividing local from federal authority, nor anything in the Constitution, properly forbade Congress to prohibit slavery in the federal territory ; else both their fidelity to correct principle, and their oath to support the Constitution, would have constrained them to oppose the prohibition.

Again, George Washington, another of the " thirty-nine," was then President of the United States, and, as such, approved and signed the bill, thus completing its validity as a law, and thus showing that, in his understanding, no line dividing local from federal authority, nor anything in the Constitution, forbade the federal government to control as to slavery in federal territory.

No great while after the adoption of the original Constitution, North Carolina ceded to the federal government the country now constituting the State of Tennessee ; and a few years later Georgia ceded that which now constitutes the States of Mississippi and Alabama. In both deeds of cession it was made a condition by the ceding States that the federal government should not prohibit slavery in the ceded country. Besides this, slavery was then actually in the ceded country. Under these circumstances, Congress, on taking charge of these countries, did not absolutely prohibit slavery within them. But they did not interfere with it—take control of it—even there, to a certain extent. In 1798, Congress organized the territory of Mississippi. In the act of organization they prohibited the bringing of slaves into the territory, from any place without the United States, by fine, and giving freedom to slaves so brought. This act passed both branches of Congress without yeas and nays. In that Congress were three of the " thirty-nine" who framed the original Constitution. They were John Langdon, George Read, and Abraham Baldwin. They all, probably, voted for it. Certainly they would have placed their opposition to it upon record, if, in their understanding, any line dividing local from federal authority, or anything in the Constitution, properly forbade the federal government to control as to slavery in federal territory.

In 1803, the federal government purchased the Louisiana country. Our former territorial acquisitions came from certain of our own States ; but this Louisiana country was acquired from a foreign nation. In 1804, Congress gave a territorial organization to that part of it which now constitutes the State of Louisiana. New-Orleans, lying within that part, was an old and comparatively large city. There were other considerable towns and settlements, and slavery was extensively and thoroughly intermingled with the people. Congress did not, in the territorial act, prohibit slavery; but they did interfere with it—take control of it—in a more marked and extensive way than they did in the case of Mississippi. The substance of the provision therein made, in relation to slaves, was:

First. That no slaves should be imported into the territory from foreign parts.

Second. That no slave should be carried into it who had been imported into the United States since the first day of May, 1798.

Third. That no slave should be carried into it, except by the owner, and for his own use as a settler; the penalty in all the cases being a fine upon the violator of the law, and freedom to the slave.

This act also was passed without yeas and nays. In the Congress which passed it, there were two of the "thirty-nine." They were Abraham Baldwin and Jonathan Dayton. As stated in the case of Mississippi, it is probable they both voted for it. They would not have allowed it to pass without recording their opposition to it, if, in their understanding, it violated either the line proper dividing local from federal authority or any provision of the Constitution.

In 1819–'20, came and passed the Missouri question. Many votes were taken, by yeas and nays, in both branches of Congress, upon the various phases of the general question. Two of the "thirty-nine"—Rufus King and Charles Pinckney—were members of that Congress. Mr. King steadily voted for slavery prohibition and against all compromises, while Mr. Pinckney as steadily voted against slavery prohibition and against all compromises. By this Mr. King showed that, in his understanding, no line dividing local from federal authority, nor anything in the Constitution, was violated by Congress prohibiting slavery in federal territory; while Mr. Pinckney, by his votes, showed that in his understanding there was some sufficient reason for opposing such prohibition in that case.

The cases I have mentioned are the only acts of the " thirty-nine," or of any of them, upon the direct issue, which I have been able to discover.

To enumerate the persons who thus acted as being four in 1784, three in 1787, seventeen in 1789, three in 1798, two in 1804, and two in 1819–'20—there would be thirty-one of them. But this would be counting John Langdon, Roger Sherman, William Few, Rufus King, and George Read, each twice, and Abraham Baldwin four times. The true number of those of the " thirty-nine" whom I have shown to have acted upon the question, which, by the text they understood better than we, is twenty-three, leaving sixteen not shown to have acted upon it in any way.

Here, then, we have twenty-three out of our " thirty-nine" fathers who framed the government under which we live, who have, upon their official responsibility and their corporal oaths, acted upon the very question which the text affirms they " understood just as well, and even better than we do now ;" and twenty-one of them—a clear majority of the whole " thirty-nine"—so acting upon it as to make them guilty of gross political impropriety, and wilful perjury, if, in their understanding, any proper division between local and federal authority, or anything in the Constitution they had made themselves and sworn to support, forbade the federal government to control as to slavery in the federal territories. Thus the twenty one acted ; and as actions speak louder than words, so actions under such responsibility speak still louder.

Two of the twenty-three voted against Congressional prohibition of slavery in the federal territories, in the instances in which they acted upon the question. But for what reasons they so voted is not known. They may have done so because they thought a proper division of local from federal authority, or some provision or principle of the Constitution, stood in the way ; or they may, without any such question, have voted against the prohibition on what appeared to them to be sufficient grounds of expediency. No one who has sworn to support the Constitution can conscientiously vote for what he understands to be an constitutional measure, however expedient he may think it ; but one may and ought to vote against a measure which he deems unconstitutional, if, at the same time, he deems it inexpedient. It, therefore, would be unsafe to set down even the two who voted against the prohibition, as having done so because, in their understanding, any proper division of local from federal authority, or anything in the Constitution, forbade the federal government to control as to slavery in federal territory.

The remaining sixteen of the " thirty-nine," so far, as I have discovered, have left no record of their understanding upon the direct question of federal control of slavery in the federal territories. But there is much reason to believe that their understanding upon that question would not have appeared different from that of their twenty-three compeers, had it been manifested at all.

For the purpose of adhering rigidly to the text, I have purposely omitted whatever understanding may have been manifested, by any person, however distinguished, other than the thirty-nine fathers who framed the original Constitution ; and, for the same reason, I have also omitted whatever understanding may have been manifested by any of the " thirty-nine" even, on any other phase of the general question of slavery. If we should look into their acts and declarations on those other phases, as the foreign slave-trade, and the morality and policy of slavery generally, it would appear to us that on the direct question of federal control of slavery in federal territories, the sixteen, if they had acted at all, would probably have acted just as the twenty-three did. Among that sixteen were several of the most noted anti-slavery men of those times — as Dr. Franklin, Alexander Hamilton, and Gouverneur Morris—while there was not one now known to have been otherwise, unless it may be John Rutledge, of South Carolina.

The sum of the whole is, that of our " thirty-nine" fathers who framed the original Constitution, twenty-one—a clear majority of the whole—certainly understood that no proper division of local from federal authority, nor any part of the Constitution, forbade the federal government to control slavery in the federal territories, while all the rest probably had the same understanding. Such, unquestionably, was the understanding of our fathers who framed the original Constitution; and the text affirms that they understood the question better than we.

But, so far, I have been considering the understanding of

the question manifested by the framers of the original Constitution.   In and by the original instrument, a mode was provided for amending it ; and, as I have already stated, the present frame of government under which we live consists of that original, and twelve amendatory articles framed and adopted since.   Those who now insist that federal control of slavery in federal territories violates the Constitution, point us to the provisions which they suppose it thus violates ; and, as I understand, they all fix upon provisions in these amendatory articles, and not in the original instrument.   The Supreme Court, in the Dred Scott case, plant themselves upon the fifth amendment, which provides that " no person shall be deprived of property without due process of law ;" while Senator Douglas and his peculiar adherents plant themselves upon the tenth amendment, providing that " the powers not granted by the Constitution are reserved to the States respectively, and to the people."

Now, it so happens that these amendments were framed by the first Congress which sat under the Constitution—the identical Congress which passed the act already mentioned, enforcing the prohibition of slavery in the northwestern territory.   Not only was it the same Congress, but they were the identical, same individual men who, at the same session, and at the same time within the session, had under consideration, and in progress toward maturity, these constitutional amendments, and this act prohibiting slavery in all the territory the nation then owned.   The constitutional amendments were introduced before, and passed after the act enforcing the Ordinance of '87 ; so that during the whole pendency of the act to enforce the Ordinance, the constitutional amendments were also pending.

That Congress, consisting in all of seventy-six members, including sixteen of the framers of the original Constitution, as before stated, were pre-eminently our fathers who framed that part of the government under which we live, which is now claimed as forbidding the federal government to control slavery in the federal territories.

It is not a little presumptuous in any one at this day to affirm that the two things which that Congress deliberately framed and carried to maturity at the same time, are absolutely inconsistent with each other ?   And does not such affir-

14

mation become impudently absurd when coupled with the other affirmation, from the same month, that those who did the two things alleged to be inconsistent understood whether they really were inconsistent better than we—better than he who affirms that they are inconsistent?

It is surely safe to assume that the "thirty-nine" framers of the original Constitution, and the seventy-six members of the Congress, which framed the amendments thereto, taken together, do certainly include those who may be fairly called " our fathers who framed the governments under which we live." And so assuming, I defy any man to show that any one of them ever, in his whole life, declared that, in his understanding, any proper division of local from federal authority, or any part of the Constitution, forbade the federal government to control as to slavery in the federal territories. I go a step further. I defy any one to show that any living man in the whole world ever did, prior to the beginning of the present century (and I might almost say prior to the beginning of the last half of the present century), declare that, in his understanding, any proper division of local from federal authority, or any part of the Constitution, forbade the federal government to control as to slavery in the federal territories. To those who now so declare, I give, not only " our fathers who framed the government under which we live," but with them all other living men within the century in which it was framed, among whom to search, and they shall not be able to find the evidence of a single man agreeing with them.

Now, and here, let me guard a little against being misunderstood. I do not mean to say we are bound to follow implicitly in whatever our fathers did. To do so, would be to discard all the lights of current experience—to reject all progress—all improvement. What I do say is, that if we would supplant the opinions and policy of our fathers in any case, we should do so upon evidence so conclusive, and argument so clear, that even their great authority, fairly considered and weighed, cannot stand ; and most surely not in a case whereof we ourselves declare they understood the question better than we.

If any man, at this day, sincerely believes that a proper division of local from federal authority, or any part of the Constitution, forbids the federal government to control as to slavery in the federal territories, he is right to say so, and to enforce his position by all truthful evidence and fair argument which he can. But he has no right to mislead others, who have less access to history and less leisure to study it, into the false belief that " our fathers who framed the government under which we live," were of the same opinion—thus substituting falsehood and deception for truthful evidence and fair argument. If any man at this day sincerely believes " our fathers, who framed the government under which we live," used and applied principles, in other cases, which ought to have led them to understand that a proper division of local from federal authority or some part of the Constitution, forbids the federal government to control as to slavery in the federal territories, he is right to say so. But he should, at the same time, brave the responsibility of declaring that, in his opinion, he understands their principles better than they did themselves ; and especially should he not shirk that responsibility by asserting that they " understood the question just as well, and even better, than we do now."

But enough. Let all who believe that " our fathers, who framed the government under which we live, understood this question just as well, and even better than we do now," speak as they spoke, and act as they acted upon it. This is all Republicans ask—all Republicans desire—in relation to slavery. As those fathers marked it, so let it be again marked, as an evil not to be extended, but to be tolerated and protected only because of, and so far as its actual presence among us makes that toleration and protection a necessity. Let all the guarantees those fathers gave it, be, not grudgingly, but fully and fairly maintained. For this Republicans contend, and with this, so far as I know or believe, they will be content.

And now, if they would listen—as I suppose they will not —I would address a few words to the Southern people.

I would say to them : You consider yourselves a reasonable and a just people ; and I consider that in the general qualities of reason and justice you are not inferior to any other people. Still, when you speak of us Republicans, you do so only to denounce us as reptiles, or, at the best, as no better than outlaws. You will grant a hearing to pirates or murderers, but nothing like it to " Black Republicans." In all your contentions with one another, each of you deems an unconditional

condemnation of " Black Republicanism" as. the first thing to
be attended to. Indeed, such condemnation of us seems to be
an indispensable pre-requisite—license, so to speak—among
you to be admitted or permitted to speak at all.

Now, can you, or not, be prevailed upon to pause and to
consider whether this is quite just to us, or even to yourselves ?

Bring forward your charges and specifications, and then be
patient long enough to hear us deny or justify.

You say we are sectional. We deny it. That makes an
issue ; and the burden of proof is upon you. You produce
your proof; and what is it ? Why, that our party has no
existence in your section—gets no votes in your section. The
fact is substantially true ; but does it prove the issue ? If it
does, then in case we should, without change of principle, begin to get votes in your section, we should thereby cease to be
sectional. You cannot escape this conclusion ; and yet, are
you willing to abide by it ? If you are, you will probably
soon find that we have ceased to be sectional, for we shall get
votes in your section this very year. You will then begin to
discover, as the truth plainly is, that your proof does not touch
the issue. The fact that we get no votes in your section is a
fact of your making, and not of ours. And if there be fault
in that fact, that fault is primarily yours, and remains so until
you show that we repel you by some wrong principle or practice. If we do repel you by any wrong principle or practice,
the fault is ours ; but this brings you to where you ought to
have started—to the discussion of the right or wrong of our
principle. If our principle, put in practice, would wrong
your section for the benefit of ours, or for any other object,
then our principle, and we with it, are sectional, and are justly
opposed and denounced as such. Meet us, then, on the question of whether our principle, put in practice, would wrong
your section ; and so meet it as if it were possible that something may be said on our side. Do you accept the challenge ?
No ? Then you really believe that the principle which our
fathers who framed the government under which we live
thought so clearly right as to adopt it, and endorse it again and
again, upon their official oaths, is, in fact so clearly wrong as
to demand your condemnation without a moment's consideration.

Some of you delight to flaunt in our faces the warning against sectional parties given by Washington in his Farewell Address. Less than eight years before Washington gave that warning, he had, as President of the United States, approved and signed an act of Congress enforcing the prohibition of slavery in the northwestern territory, which act embodied the policy of the government upon that subject, up to and at the very moment he penned that warning ; and about one year after he penned it he wrote Lafayette that he considered that prohibition a wise measure, expressing in the same connection his hope that we should some time have a confederacy of free States.

Bearing this in mind, and seeing that sectionalism has since arisen upon this same subject, is that warning a weapon in your hands against us, or in our hands against you ? Could Washington himself speak, would he cast the blame of that sectionalism upon us, who sustain his policy, or upon you who repudiate it ? We respect that warning of Washington, and we commend it to you, together with his example pointing to the right application of it.

But you say you are conservative—eminently conservative —while we are revolutionary, destructive, or something of the sort. What is conservatism ? Is it not adherence to the old and tried, against the new and untried ? We stick to, contend for, the identical old policy on the point in controversy which was adopted by our fathers who framed the government under which we live ; while you with one accord reject, and scout, and spit upon that old policy, and insist upon substituting something new. True, you disagree among yourselves as to what that substitute shall be. You have considerable variety of new propositions and plans, but you are unanimous in rejecting and denouncing the old policy of the fathers. Some of you are for reviving the foreign slave-trade ; some for a Congressional slave-code for the territories ; some for Congress forbidding the territories to prohibit slavery within their limits ; some for maintaining slavery in the territories through the judiciary ; some for the " gurreat purrinciple" that " if one man would enslave another, no third man should object," fantastically called " popular sovereignty ;" but never a man among you in favor of federal prohibition of slavery in federal territories, according to the practice of our fathers who framed the government under which we live. Not one of your various plans can show a precedent or an advocate in the century within which our government originated. Consider, then, whether your claim of conservatism for yourselves, and your charge of destructiveness against us, are based on the most clear and stable foundations.

Again, you say we have made the slavery question more prominent than it formerly was. We deny it. We admit that it is more prominent, but we deny that we made it so. It was not we, but you, who discarded the old policy of the fathers. We resisted, and still resist, your innovation; and thence comes the greater prominence of the question. Would you have that question reduced to its former proportions? Go back to that old policy. What has been will be again, under the same conditions. If you would have the peace of the old times, re-adopt the precepts and policy of the old times.

You charge that we stir up insurrections among your slaves. We deny it; and what is your proof? Harper's Ferry! John Brown!! John Brown was no Republican; and you have failed to implicate a single Republican in his Harper's Ferry enterprise. If any member of our party is guilty in that matter, you know it or you do not know it. If you do know it, you are inexcusable to not designate the man, and prove the fact. If you do not know it, you are inexcusable to assert it, and especially to persist in the assertion after you have tried and failed to make the proof. You need not be told that persisting in a charge which one does not know to be true, is simply malicious slander.

Some of you admit that no Republican designedly aided or encouraged the Harper's Ferry affair; but still insist that our doctrines and declarations necessarily lead to such results. We do not believe it. We know we hold to no doctrine, and make no declarations, which were not held to and made by our fathers who framed the government under which we live. You never dealt fairly by us in this affair. When it occurred, some important State elections were near at hand, and you were in evident glee with the belief that, by charging the blame upon us, you could get an advantage of us in those elections. The elections came, and your expectations were not quite fulfilled. Every Republican man knew that, as to himself at least, your charge was a slander, and he was not much inclined by it to cast his vote in your favor. Republican doctrines and declarations are accompanied with a continual protest against any interference whatever with your slaves, or with you about your slaves. Surely, this does not encourage them to revolt. True, we do, in common with our fathers, who framed the government under which we live, declare our belief that slavery is wrong; but the slaves do not hear us declare even this. For anything we say or do, the slaves would scarcely know there is a Republican party. I believe they would not, in fact, generally know it but for your misrepresentations of us, in their hearing. In your political contests among yourselves, each faction charges the other with sympathy with black republicanism ; and then, to give point to the charge, defines black republicanism to simply be insurrection, blood and thunder among the slaves.

Slave insurrections are no more common now than they were before the Republican party was organized. What induced the Southampton insurrection, twenty-eight years ago, in which, at least, three times as many lives were lost as at Harper's Ferry ? You can scarcely stretch your very elastic fancy to the conclusion that Southampton was got up by black republicanism. In the present state of things in the United States, I do not think a general, or even a very extensive slave insurrection, is possible. The indispensable concert of action cannot be attained. The slaves have no means of rapid communication ; nor can incendiary free men, black or white, supply it. The explosive materials are everywhere in parcels; but there neither are, nor can be supplied, the indispensable connecting trains.

Much is said by Southern people about the affection of slaves for their masters and mistresses ; and a part of it, at least, is true. A plot for an uprising could scarcely be devised and communicated to twenty individuals before some one of them, to save the life of a favorite master or mistress, would divulge it. This is the rule ; and the slave revolution in Hayti was not an exception to it, but a case occurring under peculiar circumstances. The gunpowder-plot of British history, though not connected with slaves, was more in point. In that case, only about twenty were admitted to the secret ; and yet one of them, in his anxiety to save a friend, betrayed the plot to that friend, and, by consequence, averted the calamity. Occasional poisonings from the kitchen, and open or stealthy assassinations in the field, and local revolts extending to a score or so, will continue to occur as the natural results of slavery; but no general insurrection of slaves, as I think, can happen in this country for a long time. Whoever much fears, or much hopes, for such an event, will be alike disappointed.

In the language of Mr. Jefferson, uttered many years ago, " It is still in our power to direct the process of emancipation and deportation, peaceably, and in such slow degrees, as that the evil will wear off insensibly ; and their places be, *pari passu*, filled up by free white laborers. If, on the contrary, it is left to force itself on, human nature must shudder at the prospect held up."

Mr. Jefferson did not mean to say, nor do I, that the power of emancipation is in the federal government. He spoke of Virginia ; and, as to the power of emancipation, I speak of the slaveholding States only.

The federal government, however, as we insist, has the power of restraining the extension of the institution—the power to insure that a slave insurrection shall never occur on any American soil which is now free from slavery.

John Brown's effort was peculiar. It was not a slave insurrection. It was an attempt by white men to get up a revolt among slaves, in which the slaves refused to participate. In fact, it was so absurd that the slaves, with all their ignorance, saw plainly enough it could not succeed. That affair, in its philosophy, corresponds with the many attempts, related in history, at the assassination of kings and emperors. An enthusiast broods over the oppression of a people till he fancies himself commissioned by Heaven to liberate them. He ventures the attempt, which ends in little else than in his own execution. Orsini's attempt on Louis Napoleon, and John Brown's attempt at Harper's Ferry, were, in their philosophy, precisely the same. The eagerness to cast blame on old England in the one case, and on New England in the other, does not disprove the sameness of the two things.

And how much would it avail you, if you could, by the use of John Brown, Helper's book, and the like, break up the Republican organization ? Human action can be modified

to some extent, but human nature cannot be changed. There
is a judgment and a feeling against slavery in this nation,
which cast at least a million and a half of votes. You cannot
destroy that judgment and feeling—that sentiment—by breaking up the political organization which rallies around it. You
can scarcely scatter and disperse an army which has been
formed into order in the face of your heaviest fire, but if you
could, how much would you gain by forcing the sentiment
which created it out of the peaceful channel of the ballot-
box, into some other channel? What would that other channel probably be? Would the number of John Browns be
lessened or enlarged by the operation?

But you will break up the Union rather than submit to a
denial of your constitutional rights.

That has a somewhat reckless sound; but it would be pal-
liated, if not fully justified, were we proposing, by the mere
force of numbers, to deprive you of some right, plainly written
down in the Constitution. But we are proposing no such
thing.

When you make these declarations, you have a specific and
well-understood allusion to an assumed constitutional right
of yours to take slaves into the federal territories, and to hold
them there as property. But no such right is specifically
written in the Constitution. That instrument is literally
silent about any such right. We, on the contrary, deny that
such a right has any existence in the Constitution, even by
implication.

Your purpose, then, plainly stated, is, that you will destroy
the government, unless you be allowed to construe and enforce the Constitution as you please, on all points in dispute
between you and us. You will rule or ruin in all events.

This, plainly stated, is your language to us. Perhaps you
will say the Supreme Court has decided the disputed constitutional question in your favor. Not quite so. But waiving
the lawyer's distinction between dictum and decision, the
courts have decided the question for you in a sort of way.
The courts have substantially said, it is your constitutional
right to take slaves into the federal territories, and to hold
them there as property.

When I say the decision was made in a sort of way, I mean
it was made in a divided court by a bare majority of the

14*

Judges, and they not quite agreeing with one another in the reasons for making it ; that it is so made as that its avowed supporters disagree with one another about its meaning, and that it was mainly based upon a mistaken statement of fact—the statement in the opinion that " the right of property in a slave is distinctly and expressly affirmed in the Constitution."

An inspection of the Constitution will show that the right of property in a slave is not distinctly and expressly affirmed in it. Bear in mind the Judges do not pledge their judicial opinion that such right is impliedly affirmed in the Constitution ; but they pledge their veracity that it is distinctly and expressly affirmed there—" distinctly" that is, not mingled with anything else—" expressly" that is, in words meaning just that, without the aid of any inference, and susceptible of no other meaning.

If they had only pledged their judicial opinion that such right is affirmed in the instrument by implication, it would be open to others to show that neither the word "slave" nor "slavery" is to be found in the Constitution, nor the word "property" even, in any connection with language alluding to the things slave, or slavery, and that wherever in that instrument the slave is alluded to, he is called a " person ;" and wherever his master's legal right in relation to him is alluded to, it is spoken of as " service or labor due," as a " debt" payable in service or labor. Also, it would be open to show, by contemporaneous history, that this mode of alluding to slaves and slavery, instead of speaking of them, was employed on purpose to exclude from the Constitution the idea that there could be property in man.

To show all this is easy and certain.

When this obvious mistake of the Judges shall be brought to their notice, is it not reasonable to expect that they will withdraw the mistaken statement, and reconsider the conclusion based upon it ?

And then it is to be remembered that " our fathers, who framed the government under which we live"—the men who made the Constitution—decided this same constitutional question in our favor, long ago—decided it without a division among themselves, when making the decision ; without division among themselves about the meaning of it after it was made, and so far as any evidence is left, without basing it upon any mistaken statement of facts.

Under all these circumstances, do you really feel yourselves
justified to break up this government, unless such a court decision as yours is shall be at once submitted to as a conclusive
and final rule of political action ?

But you will not abide the election of a Republican President. In that supposed event, you say, you will destroy the
Union ; and then, you say, the great crime of having destroyed it will be upon us !

That is cool. A highwayman holds a pistol to my ear, and
mutters through his teeth, " Stand and deliver, or I shall kill
you, and then you will be a murderer !"

To be sure, what the robber demanded of me—my money
—was my own ; and I had a clear right to keep it ; but it
was no more my own than my vote is my own ; and the threat
of death to me, to extort my money, and the threat of destruction to the Union, to extort my vote, can scarcely be distinguished in principle.

A few words now to Republicans. It is exceedingly desirable that all parts of this great confederacy shall be at peace,
and in harmony, one with another. Let us Republicans do
our part to have it so. Even though much provoked, let us
do nothing through passion and ill temper. Even though the
Southern people will not so much as listen to us, let us calmly
consider their demands, and yield to them if, in our deliberate
view of our duty, we possibly can. Judging by all they say
and do, and by the subject and nature of their controversy
with us, let us determine, if we can, what will satisfy them ?

Will they be satisfied if the territories be unconditionally
surrendered to them ? We know they will not. In all their
present complaints against us, the territories are scarcely mentioned. Invasions and insurrections are the rage now. Will
it satisfy them if, in the future, we have nothing to do with
invasions and insurrections ? We know it will not. We so
know because we know we never had anything to do with invasions and insurrections ; and yet this total abstaining does
not exempt us from the charge and the denunciation.

The question recurs, what will satisfy them ? Simply this :
We must not only let them alone, but we must, somehow,
convince them that we do let them alone. This, we know by
experience, is no easy task. We have been so trying to convince them, from the very beginning of our organization, but

with no success. In all our platforms and speeches we have
constantly protested our purpose to let them alone ; . but this
has had no tendency to convince them. Alike unavailing to
convince them is the fact that they have never detected a man
of us in any attempt to disturb them.

These natural, and apparently adequate means all failing,
what will convince them? This, and this only : cease to call
slavery *wrong*, and join them in calling it *right*. And this
must be done thoroughly—done in *acts* as well as in *words*.
Silence will not be tolerated—we must place ourselves avow-
edly with them. Douglas's new sedition law must be enacted
and enforced, suppressing all declarations that slavery is
wrong, whether made in politics, in presses, in pulpits, or in
private. We must arrest and return their fugitive slaves with
greedy pleasure. We must pull down our Free-State constitutions. The whole atmosphere must be disinfected from all
taint of opposition to slavery, before they will cease to believe that all their troubles proceed from us.

I am quite aware they do not state their case precisely in
this way. Most of them would probably say to us, " Let us
alone, do nothing to us, and say what you please about slavery." But we do let them alone—have never disturbed them
—so that, after all, it is what we say, which dissatisfies them.
They will continue to accuse us of doing, until we cease saying.

I am also aware they have not, as yet, in terms, demanded
the overthrow of our Free-State constitutions. Yet those
constitutions declare the wrong of slavery, with more solemn
emphasis, than do all other sayings against it ; and when all
these other sayings shall have been silenced, the overthrow of
these constitutions will be demanded, and nothing be left to
resist the demand. It is nothing to the contrary, that they do
not demand the whole of this just now. Demanding what
they do, and for the reason they do, they can voluntarily stop
nowhere short of this consummation. Holding, as they do,
that slavery is morally right, and socially elevating, they cannot cease to demand a full national recognition of it, as a legal
right, and a social blessing.

Nor can we justifiably withhold this, on any ground, save
our conviction that slavery is wrong. If slavery is right, all
words, acts, laws, and constitutions against it, are themselves

wrong, and should be silenced, and swept away. If it is right, we cannot justly object to its nationality—its universality ; if it is wrong, they cannot justly insist upon its extension —its enlargement. All they ask, we could readily grant, if we thought slavery right ; all we ask, they could as readily grant, if they thought it wrong. Their thinking it right, and our thinking it wrong, is the precise fact upon which depends the whole controversy. Thinking it right, as they do, they are not to blame for desiring its full recognition, as being right ; but, thinking it wrong, as we do, can we yield to them ? Can we cast our votes with their view, and against our own ? In view of our moral, social, and political responsibilities, can we do this ?

Wrong as we think slavery is, we can yet afford to let it alone where it is, because that much is due to the necessity arising from its actual presence in the nation ; but can we, while our votes will prevent it, allow it to spread into the national territories, and to overrun us here in these free States ?

If our sense of duty forbids this, then let us stand by our duty, fearlessly and effectively. Let us be diverted by none of those sophistical contrivances wherewith we are so industriously plied and belabored—contrivances such as groping for some middle ground between the right and the wrong, vain as the search for a man who should be neither a living man nor a dead man—such as a policy of "don't care" on a question about which all true men do care—such as Union appeals beseeching true Union men to yield to disunionists, reversing the divine rule, and calling, not the sinners, but the righteous to repentance—such as invocations to Washington, imploring men to unsay what Washington said, and undo what Washington did.

Neither let us be slandered from our duty by false accusations against us, nor frightened from it by menaces of destruction to the government, nor of dungeons to ourselves. Let us have faith that right makes might, and in that faith, let us, to the end, dare to do our duty, as we understand it.

THE WAR WITH MEXICO,

IN THE HOUSE OF REPRESENTATIVES,

January 12th, 1848.

On the resolutions referring the President's Message to the various Standing Committees

Mr. LINCOLN addressed the Committee as follows:

MR. CHAIRMAN: Some, if not all, the gentlemen on the other side of the House, who have addressed the Committee within the last two days, have spoken rather complainingly, if I have rightly understood them, of the vote given a week or ten days ago, declaring that the war with Mexico was unnecessarily and unconstitutionally commenced by the President. I admit that such a vote should not be given in mere party wantonness, and that the one given is justly censurable, if it have no other or better foundation. I am one of those who joined in that vote; and I did so under my best impression of the *truth* of the case. How I got this impression, and how it may possibly be removed, I will now try to show. When the war began, it was my opinion that all those who, because of knowing too *little*, or because of knowing too *much*, could not conscientiously approve the conduct of the President (in the beginning of it), should, nevertheless, as good citizens and patriots, remain silent on that point, at least till the war should be ended. Some leading Democrats, including Ex-President Van Buren, have taken this same view, as I understand them; and I adhered to it and acted upon it, until since I took my seat here; and I think I should still adhere to it, were it not that the President and his friends would not allow it to be so. Besides, the continual effort of the President to argue every silent vote given for supplies into an endorsement of the justice and wisdom of his conduct, besides that singularly candid paragraph in his late message, in which he tells us that Congress, with great unanimity (only two in the Senate, and fourteen in the House dissenting), had declared that " by the act of the Republic of Mexico a state

of war exists between that government and the United States ;"
when the same journals that informed him of this, also informed him that, when that declaration stood disconnected
from the question of supplies, sixty-seven 'in the House, and
not fourteen, merely, voted against it; besides this open attempt to prove, by telling the *truth*, what he could not prove
by telling the *whole truth*, demanding of all who will not submit to be misrepresented, in justice to themselves, to speak
out. Besides all this, one of my colleagues [Mr. RICHARD-
SON] at a very early day in the session, brought in a set of
resolutions, expressly endorsing the original justice of the war
on the part of the President. Upon these resolutions when
they shall be put upon their passage, I shall be *compelled* to
vote; so that I cannot be silent, if I would. Seeing this, I
went about preparing myself to give the vote understandingly,
when it should come. I carefully examined the President's
messages, to ascertain what he himself had said and proved
upon the point. The result of this examination was to make
the impression, that, taking for true all the President states as
facts, he falls far short of proving his justification ; and that the
President would have gone farther with his proof, if it had
not been for the small matter that the *truth* would not permit
him. Under the impression thus made, I gave the vote before
mentioned, I propose now to give concisely the process of the
examination I made, and how I reached the conclusion I
did.

The President, in his first message of May, 1846, declares
that the soil was ours, on which hostilities were commenced
by Mexico ; and he repeats that declaration, almost in the
same language, in each successive annual message—thus showing that he esteems that point a highly essential one. In the
importance of that point, I entirely agree with the President.
To my judgment, it is the very point upon which he should be
justified or condemned. In his message of December, 1846,
it seems to have occurred to him, as is certainly true, that
title, ownership to soil, or anything else, is not a simple fact,
but is a conclusion following one or more simple facts ; and
that it was incumbent upon him to present the facts from
which he concluded the soil was ours on which the first blood
of the war was shed.

Accordingly, a little below the middle of page twelve, in the

message last referred to, he enters upon that task, forming an
issue and introducing testimony, extending the whole to a little below the middle of page fourteen.   Now I propose to try
to show that the whole of this issue and evidence is from
beginning to end, the sheerest deception.   The issue, as he
presents it, is in these words, " But there are those who,
conceding all this to be true, assume the ground that the true
western boundary of Texas is the Nueces, instead of the Rio
Grande; and that, therefore, in marching our army to the
east bank of. the latter river, we passed the Texan line and
invaded the territory of Mexico."   Now, this issue is made
up of two affirmatives, and no negative.   The main deception
of it is, that it assumes as true that one river or the other is
necessarily the boundary, and cheats the superficial thinker
entirely out of the idea that possibly the boundary is somewhere *between* the two, and not actually at either.   A further
deception is, that it will be in *evidence*, which a true issue
would exclude.   A true issue made by the President would
be about as follows :   " I say the soil *was ours* on which the
first blood was shed ; there are those who say it *was not.*"
   I now proceed to examine the President's evidence as applicable to such an issue.   When that evidence is analyzed, it is
all included in the following propositions :
   1. That the Rio Grande was the western boundary of Louisiana as we purchased it of France in 1803.
   2. That the Republic of Texas always *claimed* the Rio
Grande as her western boundary.
   3. That by various acts she had claimed it *on paper.*
   4. That Santa Anna in his treaty with Texas recognized
the Rio Grande as her boundary.
   5. That Texas *before*, and the United States *after* annexation, had *exercised* jurisdiction *beyond* the Nueces, *between* the
two rivers.
   6. That our Congress understood the boundary of Texas to
extend beyond the Nueces.
   Now for each of these in its turn :
   His first item is, that the Rio Grande was. the western
boundary of Louisiana as we purchased it from France in
1803 ; and seeming to expect this to be disputed, he argues
over the amount of nearly a page to prove it true ; at the end
of which he lets us know that, by the treaty of 1819, we sold

to Spain the whole country from the Rio Grande eastward to the Sabine. Now, admitting, for the present, that the Rio Grande was the boundary of Louisiana, what, under heaven, had that to do with the *present* boundary between us and Mexico? How, Mr. Chairman, the line that once divided your land from mine can *still* be the boundary between us *after* I have sold the land to you, is to me, beyond all comprehension. And how any man, with an honest purpose only of proving the truth, could even have *thought* of introducing such a fact to prove such an issue, is equally incomprehensible. The outrage upon common *rights* of seizing as our own what we have once sold, merely because it *was* ours *before* we sold it, is only equalled by the outrage on common *sense* of any attempt to justify it.

The President's next piece of evidence is, that " the Republic of Texas always *claimed* this river [Rio Grande] as her western boundary." That is not true in fact. Texas *has* claimed it, but she has not *always* claimed it. There is, at least, one distinguished exception. Her State constitution— the Republic's most solemn and well-considered act—that which may, without impropriety, be called her last will and testament, revoking all others—makes no such claim. But suppose she had always claimed it ; has not Mexico always claimed the contrary? So that there is but *claim* against *claim*, leaving nothing proved until we get back of the claims, and find which has the better *foundation.*

Though not in the order in which the President presents his evidence, I now consider that class of his statements, which are in substance nothing more than Texas has, by various acts of her Convention and Congress, claimed the Rio Grande as her boundary—*on paper.* I mean here what he says about the fixing of the Rio Grande as her boundary in her old constitution (not her State constitution), about forming congressional districts, counties, etc. Now, all of this is but naked *claim*, and what I have already said about claims is strictly applicable to this. If I should claim your land by word of mouth, that certainly would not make it mine ; and if I were to claim it by a deed which I had made myself, and with which you had had nothing to do, the claim would be quite the same in substance, or rather, in utter nothingness.

I next consider the President's statement, that *Santa Anna*, in his *treaty* with Texas, recognized the Rio Grande as the western boundary of Texas. Besides the position so often taken, that Santa Anna, while a prisoner-of-war—a captive—*could not* bind Mexico by a treaty, which I deem conclusive; besides this, I wish to say something in relation to this treaty, so called by the President, with Santa Anna. If any man would like to be amused by a sight at that *little* thing, which the President calls by that *big* name, we can have it by turning to *Niles' Register*, volume 50, page 336. And if any one should suppose that *Niles' Register* is a curious repository of so mighty a document as a solemn treaty between nations, I can only say that I learned to a tolerable degree of certainty, by inquiry at the State Department, that the President himself never saw it anywhere else.

By-the-way, I believe I should not err if I were to declare, that during the first ten years of the existence of that document, it was never by anybody *called* a treaty; that it was never so called till the President, in his extremity, attempted, by so calling it, to wring something from it in justification of himself in connection with the Mexican wars.

It has none of the distinguishing features of a treaty. It does not call itself a treaty. Santa Anna does not therein assume to bind Mexico ; he assumes only to act as the President, commander-in-chief of the Mexican army and navy, and stipulates that the then present hostilities should cease, and that he would not *himself*, take up arms, nor *influence* the Mexican people to take up arms, against Texas, during the existence of the war of Independence. He did not recognize the independence of Texas ; he did not assume to put an end to the war, but clearly indicated his expectation of its continuance ; he did not say one word about boundary, and most probably never thought of it. It is stipulated therein that the Mexican forces should evacuate the territory of Texas, *passing to the other side of the Rio Grande;* and in another article it is stipulated, that to prevent collision between the armies, the Texan should not approach nearer than within five leagues—of what is not said—but clearly, from the object stated, it is of the Rio Grande. Now, if this is a treaty recognizing the Rio Grande as the boundary of Texas, it contains a singular feature of stipulating that Texas shall not go within five leagues of *her own* boundary.

Next comes the evidence of Texas before annexation, and
the United States afterward, *exercising* jurisdiction *beyond* the
Nueces, and *between* the two rivers. This actual *exercise* of jurisdiction is the very class or quality of evidence we want. It
is excellent, so far as it goes ; but does it go far enough ? He
tells us it went *beyond* the Nueces, but he does not tell us it
went to the Rio Grande. He tells us jurisdiction was exercised *between* the two rivers, but he does not tell us it was exercised over *all* the territory between them. Some simple-
minded people think it *possible* to cross one river and go *beyond*
it, without going *all the way* to the next ; that jurisdiction may
be exercised *between* two rivers without covering *all* the country between them. I know a man, not very unlike myself,
who exercises jurisdiction over a piece of land between the
Wabash and the Mississippi, and yet so far is this from being
all there is between those rivers, that it is just one hundred
and fifty-two feet long by fifty wide, and no part of it much
within a hundred miles of either. He has a neighbor between
him and the Mississippi—that is, just across the street, in that
direction—whom, I am sure, he could neither *persuade* nor
force to give up his habitation ; but which, nevertheless, he
could certainly annex, if it were to be done by merely standing on his own side of the street and *claiming* it, or even setting down and writing a *deed* for it.

But next, the President tells us, the Congress of the United
States *understood* the State of Texas they admitted into the
Union, to extend *beyond* the Nueces. Well, I suppose they
did—I certainly so understood it—but how *far* beyond ?
That Congress did *not* understand it to extend clear to the Rio
Grande is quite certain by the fact of their joint resolutions
for admission, expressly leaving all questions of boundary to
future adjustment. And, it may be added, that Texas herself
is proved to have had the same understanding of it that our
Congress had, by the fact of the exact conformity of her new
constitution to those resolutions.

I am now through the whole of the President's evidence ;
and it is a singular fact, that if any one should declare the
President sent the army into a settlement of Mexican people,
who had never submitted, by consent or force, to the authority
of Texas or the United States, and that *there*, and *thereby*, the
first blood of the war was shed, there is not one word in all

the President has said which would either admit or deny the declaration. In this strange omission chiefly consists the deception of the President's evidence; an omission which, it does seem to me, could scarcely have occurred but by design. My way of living leads me to be about the courts of justice; and there I have sometimes seen a good lawyer, struggling for his client's neck, in a desperate case, employ every artifice to work around, befog, and cover up with many words, some position pressed upon him by the prosecution, which he *dared* not admit, and yet *could* not deny. Party bias may help to make it appear so; but, with all the allowance I can make for such a bias, it still does appear to me that just such, and from just such necessity, is the President's struggles in this case.

Sometime after my colleague [Mr. Richardson] introduced the resolutions I have mentioned, I introduced a preamble, resolution, and interrogatories, intended to draw the President out, if possible, on this hitherto untrodden ground. To show their relevancy, I propose to state my understanding of the true rule for ascertaining the boundary between Texas and Mexico. It is, that *wherever* Texas was *exercising* jurisdiction was hers; and *wherever* Mexico was exercising jurisdiction was hers; and that *whatever* separated the actual exercise of jurisdiction of the one from that of the other, was the true boundary between them. If, as is probably true, Texas was exercising jurisdiction along the western bank of the Nueces, and Mexico was exercising it along the eastern bank of the Rio Grande, then *neither* river was the boundary, but the uninhabited country between the two was. The extent of our territory in the region depended, not upon any *treaty-fixed* boundary (for no treaty had attended it), but on revolution. Any people, anywhere, being inclined, and having the power, have the right to rise up and shake off the existing government, and form a new one that suits them better. This is a most valuable, a most sacred right—a right which, we hope and believe, is to liberate the world. Nor is this right confined to cases in which the whole people of an existing government may choose to exercise it. Any portion of such people that *can*, *may* revolutionize, and make their *own* of so much of the territory as they inhabit. More than this, a *majority* of any portion of such people may revolutionize, putting down a *minority*, intermingled with or near about them, who may oppose their movements. Such minority was precisely the case of the Tories in our own Revolution. It is a quality of revolutions not to go by *old* lines or *old* laws; but to break up both, and make new ones. As to the country now in question, we bought it of France in 1803, and sold it to Spain in 1819, according to the President's statement. After this, all Mexico, including Texas, revolutionized against Spain; and still later, Texas revolutionized against Mexico. In my view, just so far as she carried her revolution, by obtaining the *actual*, willing or unwilling, submission of the people, *so far* the country was hers, and no farther.

Now, sir, for the purpose of obtaining the very best evidence as to whether Texas had actually carried her revolution to the place where the hostilities of the present war commenced, let the President answer the interrogatories I proposed, as before mentioned, or some other similar ones. Let him answer fully, fairly, and candidly. Let him answer with *facts*, and not with argument. Let him remember he sits where Washington sat; and, so remembering, let him answer as Washington. As a nation *should* not, and the Almighty *will* not, be evaded, so let him attempt no evasion, no equivocation. And if, so answering, he can show that the soil was ours where the first blood of the war was shed—that it was not within an inhabited country, or, if within such, that the inhabitants had submitted themselves to the civil authority of Texas, or of the United States, and that the same is true of the site of Fort Brown—then am I with him for his justification. In that case I shall be most happy to reverse the vote I gave the other day. I have a selfish motive for desiring that the President may do this; I expect to give some votes, in connection with the war, which, without his so doing, will be of doubtful propriety, in my own judgment, which will be free from the doubt if he does so. But if he *cannot* or *will not* do this—if, on any pretence, or no pretence, he shall refuse or omit it—then I should be fully convinced of what I more than suspect already, that he is deeply conscious of being in the wrong; that he feels the blood of this war, like the blood of Abel, is crying to Heaven against him; that he ordered Gen. Taylor into the midst of a peaceful Mexican settlement, purposely to bring on a war; that originally having some strong motive—what, I will not stop now to give my opinion concerning—to involve the two countries in a war, and trusting to escape scrutiny by fixing the public gaze upon the exceeding brightness of military glory, this attractive rainbow that rises in showers of blood—that serpent's eye that charms to destroy—he plunged into it, and has swept *on* and *on*, till, disappointed in his calculation of the ease with which Mexico might be subdued, he now finds himself, he knows not where. How like the half insane mumbling of a fever dream, is the whole war part of the late message! At one time telling us that Mexico has nothing whatever that we can get but territory : at another, showing us how we can support the war by levying contributions on Mexico. At one time urging the national honor, the security of the future, the prevention of foreign interference, and even the good of Mexico herself, as among the objects of the two; at another, telling us that, "To reject indemnity by refusing to accept a cession of territory, would be to abandon all our just demands and to wage the war, bearing all its expenses, without a *purpose or definite object.*"

So, then, the national honor, security of the future, and everything but territorial indemnity, may be considered the *no purposes* and *indefinite* objects of the war, but, having it now settled that territorial indemnity is the only object, we are urged to seize by legislation here, all that he was content to take a few months ago, and the whole province of Lower California to boot, and to still carry on the war—to take *all* we are fighting for, and *still* fight on. Again, the President is resolved, under all circumstances, to have full territorial indemnity for the expenses of the war, but he forgets to tell us how we are to get the excess, after those expenses shall have surpassed the value of the *whole* of the Mexican territory. So, again, he insists that the separate national existence of Mexico shall be maintained ; but he does not tell us *how* this can be done after we shall have taken *all* her territory. Lest the questions I here suggest, be considered speculative merely, let me be indulged a moment in trying to show they are not.

The war has gone on some twenty months ; for the expenses of which, together with an inconsiderable old score, the President now claims about one half of the Mexican territory, and that by far the better half, so far as concerns our ability to make anything out of it. *It* is comparatively uninhabited ; so that we could establish land offices in it, and raise some money in that way. But the other half is already in-habited, as I understand it, tolerably densely for the nature of the country ; and all its lands, or all that are valuable, already appropriated as private property. How, then, are we to make anything out of these lands with this incumbrance on them, or how remove the incumbrance? I suppose no one will say we should kill the people, or drive them out, or make slaves of them, or even confiscate their property? How, then, can we make much out of this part of the territory ? If the prose-cution of the war has, in expenses, already equalled the *better* half of the country, how long its future prosecution will be in equalling the less valuable half is not a *speculative*, but a *practi-cal* question, pressing closely upon us ; and yet it is a question which the President seems never to have thought of.

As to the mode of terminating the war and securing peace, the President is equally wandering and indefinite. First, it is to be done by a more vigorous prosecution of the war in the vital parts of the enemy's country ; and, after apparently talk-ing himself tired on this point, the President drops down into a half despairing tone, and tells us, that " with a people dis-tracted and divided by contending factions, and a government subject to constant changes, by successive revolutions. *the con-tinued success of our arms may fail to obtain a satisfactory peace.*" Then he suggests the propriety of wheedling the Mexican peo-ple to desert the counsels of their own leaders, and, trusting in our protection, to set up a government from which we can secure a satisfactory peace, telling us that " *this may become the only mode of obtaining such a peace.*" But soon he falls into doubt of this too, and then drops back on the already half-abandoned ground of " more vigorous prosecution." All this shows that the President is in no wise satisfied with his own positions. First, he takes up one, and, in attempting to argue us *with* it, he argues himself *out* of it ; then seizes another and goes through the same process ; and then, confused at being able to think of nothing new, he snatches up the old one again, which he has some time before cast off. His mind, tasked beyond his power, is running hither and thither like some tortured creature on a burning surface, finding no posi-tion on which it can settle down and be at ease.

Again, it is a singular omission in this message, that it no-where intimates *when* the President expects the war to terminate. At its beginning, General Scott was, by this same President, driven into disfavor, if not disgrace, for intimating that peace could not be conquered in less than three or four months. But now, at the end of twenty months, during which time our arms have given us the most splendid successes—every department, and every part, land and water, officers and privates, regulars and volunteers, doing all that men *could* do, and hundreds of things which it had ever before been thought that man could *not* do ; after all this, this same President gives us a long message without showing us that, *as to the end,* he has himself even an imaginary conception. As I have before said, he knows not where he is. He is a bewildered, confounded, and miserably perplexed man. God grant he may be able to show there is not something about his conscience more painful than all his mental perplexity !

INTERNAL IMPROVEMENTS.

HOUSE OF REPRESENTATIVES.

June 20th, 1848.

In Committee of the Whole on the state of the Union, on the Civil and Diplomatic Appropriation Bill,

Mr. LINCOLN said:

Mr. CHAIRMAN : I wish at all times and in no way to practise any fraud upon the House or the Committee, and I also desire to do nothing which may be very disagreeable to any of the members. I therefore state, in advance, that my object in taking the floor is to make a speech on the general subject of internal improvements, and if I am out of order in doing so, I give the Chair an opportunity of so deciding, and I will take my seat.

The CHAIR : I will not undertake to anticipate what the gentleman may say on the subject of internal improvements. He will, therefore, proceed in his remarks, and if any question of order shall be made, the Chair will then decide it.

Mr. Lincoln : At an early day of this session the President
sent us what may be properly called an internal-improvement
veto message. The late Democratic Convention which sat at
Baltimore, and which nominated Gen. Cass for the Presidency, adopted a set of resolutions, now called the Democratic
platform, among which is one in these words :

" That the Constitution does not confer upon the general
government the power to commence and carry on a general
system of internal improvements."

General Cass, in his letter accepting the nomination, adds
this language :

" I have carefully read the resolutions of the Democratic
National Convention, laying down the platform of our political
faith, and I adhere to them as firmly as I approve them cor-
dially."

These things, taken together, show that the question of internal improvements is now more distinctly made—has become
more intense, than at any former period. It can no longer be
avoided. The veto message and the Baltimore resolutions I
understand to be, in substance, the same thing ; the latter
being the mere general statement, of which the former is the
amplification—the bill of particulars. While I know there
are many Democrats, on this floor and elsewhere, who disap-
prove that message, I understand that all who shall vote for
Gen. Cass will thereafter be counted as having approved it, as
having endorsed all its doctrines. I suppose all, or nearly all,
the Democrats will vote for him. Many of them will do so,
not because they like his position on this question, but because
they prefer him, being wrong in this, to another whom they
consider further wrong on other questions. In this way the
internal improvement Democrats are to be, by a sort of forced
consent carried over, and arrayed against themselves on this
measure of policy. General Cass, once elected, will not
trouble himself to make a constitutional argument, or, perhaps, any argument at all, when he shall veto a river or harbor bill. He will consider it a sufficient answer to all Democratic murmurs, to point to Mr. Polk's message and the
" Democratic platform." This being the case, the question
of improvements is very near a final crisis ; and the friends of
the policy must now battle, and battle manfully, or surrender
all. In this view, humble as I am, I wish to review, and con-

15

test, as well I may, the general positions of this veto message. When I say *general* positions, I mean to exclude from consideration so much as relate to the present embarrassed state of the treasury, in consequence of the Mexican war.

Those general positions are: That internal improvements ought not to be made by the general government.

1. Because they would overwhelm the treasury.

2. Because while their *burdens* would be general, their *benefits* would be *local* and *partial*, involving an obnoxious inequality; and

3. Because they would be unconstitutional.

4. Because the States may do enough by the levy and collection of tonnage duties; or, if not,

5. That the Constitution may be amended.

"Do nothing at all, lest you do something wrong," is the sum of these positions—is the sum of this message—and this, with the exception of what is said about constitutionality, applying as forcibly to making improvements by State authority, as by the national authority. So that we must abandon the improvements of the country altogether, by any and every authority, or we must resist and repudiate the doctrines of the message. Let us attempt the latter.

The first position is, that a system of internal improvement would overwhelm the treasury.

That in such a system there is a *tendency* to undue expansion, is not to be denied. Such tendency is found in the nature of the subject. A member of Congress will prefer voting for a bill which contains an appropriation for his district, to voting for one which does not; and when a bill shall be expanded till every district is provided for, that it will be too greatly expanded is obvious. But is this any more true in Congress than in a State legislature? If a member of Congress must have an appropriation for his district, so a member of a legislature must have one for his county; and if one will overwhelm the national treasury, so the others will overwhelm the State treasury. Go where we will, the difficulty is the same. Allow it to drive us from the halls of Congress, and it will just as easily drive us from the State legislatures. Let us, then, grapple with it, and test its strength. Let us, judging the future by the past, ascertain whether there may not be, in the discretion of Congress, a sufficient power to limit and re-

strain this expansive tendency within reasonable and proper
bounds.   The President himself values the evidence of the
past.   He tells us, that at a certain point of our history, more
than two hundred millions of dollars had been *applied for*, to
make improvements ; and this he does to prove that the treasury would be overwhelmed by such a system.   Why did he
not tell us how much was *granted ?*   Would not that have been
better evidence ?   Let us turn to it, and see what it proves.
In the Message the President tells us, that " during the four
succeeding years, embraced by the administration of President
Adams, the power not only to appropriate money, but to apply it, under the direction and authority of the general government, as well to the construction of roads as to the improvement of rivers and harbors, was fully asserted and exercised."
This, then, was the period of greatest enormity.   These, if
any, must be the days of the two hundred millions.   And how
much do you suppose was really expended for improvements
during that four years ?   Two hundred millions ?   One hundred ?   Fifty ?   Ten ?   Five ?   No, sir ; less than two millions.   As shown by authentic documents, the expenditures
on improvements during 1825, 1826, 1827, and 1828,
amounted to $1,879,000 01.   These four years were the period
of Mr. Adams's administration, nearly and substantially.   This
fact shows, that when the power to make improvements was
" fully maintained and exercised," the Congresses *did* keep
within reasonable limits ; and what *has* been done, it seems
to me, *can* be done again.

Now for the second position of the Message, namely, that
the burdens of the improvements would be *general*, while their
benefits would be *local* and *partial*, involving an obnoxious inequality.   That there is some degree of truth in this position I
will not deny.   No commercial object of government patronage can be so exclusively *general* as not to be of some peculiar
local advantage ; but, on the other hand, nothing is so *local* as not
to be of some general advantage.   The navy, as I understand it,
was established, and is maintained at a great annual expense,
partly to be ready for war, when war shall come, but partly,
also, and perhaps chiefly, for the protection of our commerce
on the high seas.   The latter object is, as far as I can see, in
principle, the same as internal improvements.   The driving of
a pirate from the track of commerce, on the broad ocean, and

the removing of a snag from its more narrow path in the Mississippi river, cannot, I think, be distinguished in principle. Each is done to save life and property, and for nothing else. The navy, then, is the most general in its benefits of all this class of objects ; and yet the navy is of some peculiar advantage to Charleston, Baltimore, Philadelphia, New-York, and Boston, beyond what it is to the interior towns of Illinois. The next most general object I can think of, would be the improvement of the Mississippi river and its tributaries. They touch thirteen of our States—Pennsylvania, Virginia, Kentucky, Tennessee, Mississippi, Louisiana, Arkansas, Missouri, Illinois, Indiana, Ohio, Wisconsin, and Iowa. Now, I suppose it will not be denied, that these thirteen States are a little more interested in improvements on that great river than the remaining seventeen. These instances of the navy and the Mississippi river, show clearly that there is something of local advantage in the most general objects. But the converse is true. Nothing is so *local* as not be of some *general* benefit. Take, for instance, the Illinois and Michigan canal—considered apart from its effects, it is perfectly local ; every inch of it is within the State of Illinois. That canal was first opened for business last April. In a very few days we were all gratified to learn, among other things, that sugar had been carried through the canal from New-Orleans to Buffalo, in New-York. This sugar took this route, doubtless, because it was cheaper than the old route. Supposing the benefit in the reduction of the cost of carriage to be shared between the buyer and seller, the result is, that the New-Orleans merchant sold his sugar a little *dearer*, and the people of Buffalo sweetened their coffee a little *cheaper* than before—a benefit resulting *from* the canal, not to Illinois where the canal *is*, but to Louisiana and New-York, where it is *not*. In other transactions Illinois will, of course, have her share, and perhaps the larger share too, in the benefits of the canal ; but the instance of the sugar clearly shows, that the *benefits* of an improvement are, by no means, confined to the locality of the improvement itself.

The just conclusion from all this is, that if the nation refuse to make improvements of the more general kind, because their benefits may be somewhat local, a State may, for the same reason, refuse to make an improvement of a local kind, because its benefits may be somewhat general. A State may well say to the nation, "If you will do nothing for me, I will do nothing for you." Thus it is seen, that if this argument of "inequality" is sufficient anywhere, it is sufficient everywhere, and puts an end to improvement altogether. I hope and believe, that if the nation and the States would, in good faith, in their respective spheres, do what they could in the way of improvements, what of inequality might be produced in one place might be compensated in another, and that the sum of the whole would not be very unequal. But suppose, after all, there should be some degree of inequality: inequality is certainly never to be embraced for its own sake; but is every good thing to be discarded which may be inseparably connected with some degree of it? If so, we must discard all government. This capitol is built at the public expense, for the public benefit; but does any one doubt that it is of some peculiar local advantage to the property-holders and business people of Washington? Shall we remove it for this reason? And if so, where shall we set it down, and be free from the difficulty? To make sure of our object shall we locate it nowhere, and have Congress hold its sessions, as the loafer lodges, "in spots about?" I make no special allusion to the present President when I say there are few stronger cases of "burden to the many, and benefit to the few"—of "inequality"—than the Presidency itself is by some thought to be. An honest laborer digs coal at about seventy cents a day, while the President digs abstractions at about seventy dollars a day. The *coal* is clearly worth more than the *abstractions*, and yet what a monstrous unequality in the prices! Does the President, for this reason, wish to abolish the Presidency? He *does* not, and he *ought* not. The true rule in determining to embrace or reject anything, is not whether it have *any* evil in it, but whether it have more of evil than of good. There are few things *wholly* evil or *wholly* good. Almost everything, especially in governmental policy, is an inseparable compound of the two, so that our best judgment of the preponderance between them is continually demanded. On this principle, the President, his friends, and the world generally, act on most subjects. Why not apply it, then, upon this question? Why, as to improvements, magnify the *evil*, and stoutly refuse to see any *good* in them?

Mr. Chairman, on the third position of the message (the

constitutional question) I have not much to say. Being the
man I am, and speaking when I do, I feel that any attempt at
an original constitutional argument, I should not be, and
ought not to be listened to patiently. The ablest and best of
men have gone over the whole ground long ago. I shall attempt but little more than a brief notice of what some of
them have said   In reference to Mr. Jefferson's views, I read
from Mr. Polk's veto message :

"President Jefferson, in his message to Congress in 1806,
recommended an amendment of the Constitution, with a view
to apply an anticipated surplus in the treasury ' to the great
purposes of public education, roads, rivers, canals, and such
other objects of public improvements as it may be thought
proper to add to the constitutional enumeration of the federal powers.' " And he adds, " I suppose an amendment to
the Constitution, by consent of the States, necessary, because
the objects now recommended are not among those enumerated in the Constitution, and to which it permits the public
monies to be applied.". In 1825, he repeated, in his published
letters, the opinion that no such power has been conferred on
Congress. I introduce this, not to controvert, just now, the
constitutional opinion, but to show that on the question of
expediency, Mr. Jefferson's opinion was against the present
President—that this opinion of Mr. Jefferson, in one branch,
at least, is, in the hands of Mr. Polk, like Fingal's gun—

"Beats wide, and kicks the owner over."

But, to the constitutional question :
In 1826, Chancellor Kent first published his commentaries
on American law. He devoted a portion of one of the
lectures to the question of the authority of Congress to appropriate public moneys for internal improvements. He mentioned that the question had never been brought under judicial
consideration, and proceeds to give a brief summary of the
discussions it had undergone between the legislative and executive branches of the government.
He shows that the legislative branch had usually been for,
and executive *against* the power, till the period of Mr. J. Q.
Adams' administration ; at which point he considers the executive influence as withdrawn from opposition and added to the
support of the power.

In 1844 the Chancellor published a new edition of his commentaries, in which he adds some notes of what had transpired on the question since 1826. I have not time to read
the original text or the notes, but the whole may be found on
page 267 and the two or three following pages of the first volume of the edition of '44. As to what Chancellor Kent seems
to consider the sum of the whole, I read from one of the notes:
" Mr. Justice Story, in his commentaries on the Constitution
of the United States, vol. ii., page 429–440, and again, page
519–538, has stated at large the arguments for and against the
proposition that Congress have a constitutional power to lay
taxes, and to apply the power to regulate commerce, as a
means to encourage and protect domestic manufactures ; and,
without giving any opinion of his own on 'the contested doctrine, he has left the reader to draw his own conclusions. I
should think, however, from the arguments as stated, that
every mind which has taken no part in the discussions, and felt
no prejudice or territorial bias on either side of the question,
would deem the argument in favor of Congressional power
vastly superior."

It will be seen, that in this extract the power to make improvements is not directly mentioned, but by examining the
context, both of Kent and of Story, it will appear that the
power mentioned in the extract, and the power to make improvements, are regarded as identical. It is not to be denied
that many great and good men have been *against* the power ;
but it is insisted that quite as many, as great and as good,
have been *for* it ; and it is shown that, on full survey of the
whole, Chancellor Kent was of opinion that the arguments of
the latter were *vastly superior.*. This is but the opinion of a
man, but who was that man ? He was one of the ablest and
most learned lawyers of his age, or of any age. It is no dis-
paragement to Mr. Polk, nor, indeed, to any one who devotes
much time to politics, to be placed far behind Chancellor Kent
as a lawyer. His attitude was most favorable to correct
conclusions. He wrote coolly and in retirement. He was
struggling to rear a durable monument of fame, and he well
knew that *truth* and thoroughly sound reasoning were the only
sure foundations. Can the party opinion of a party Pre-ident
on a law question, as this purely is, be at all compared or
set in opposition to that of such a man, in such an attitude, as
Chancellor Kent?

This constitutional question will probably never be better settled than it is, until it shall pass under judicial consideration ; but I do think no man who is clear on this question of expediency need feel his conscience much pricked on this.

Mr. Chairman, the President seems to think that enough may be done in the way of improvements by means of tonnage dues, under State authority, with the consent of the general government. Now, I suppose this matter of tonnage duties is well enough in its own sphere. I suppose it may be efficient, and perhaps *sufficient*, to make slight improvements and repairs in harbors already in use, and not much out of repairs. But if I have any correct general idea of it, it must be wholly inefficient for any generally beneficent purposes of improvement. I know very little, or rather nothing at all, of of the practical matters of levying and collecting tonnage duties, but I suppose that one of its principles must be, to lay a duty for the improvement of any particular harbor, *upon the tonnage coming into that harbor.* To do otherwise—to collect money at one harbor to be expended on improvements on another — would be an extremely aggravated form of that inequality which the President so much deprecates. If I be right in this, how could we make any entirely new improvements by means of tonnage duties ? How make a road, a canal, or clear a greatly obstructed river ? The idea that we could, involves the same absurdity of the Irish bull about the new boots : " I shall never git 'em on," says Patrick, " till I wears 'em a day or two, and stretch 'em a little." We shall never make a canal by tonnage duties until it shall already have been made awhile, so the tonnage can get into it.

After all, the President concludes that possibly there may be some great objects of improvement which cannot be effected by tonnage duties, and which, therefore, may be expedient for the general government to take in hand. Accordingly, he suggests, in case any such should be discovered, the propriety of amending the Constitution. Amend it for what ? If, like Mr. Jefferson, the President thought improvements *expedient*, but not constituttional, it would be natural enough for him to recommend such an amendment ; but hear what he says int his very message :

" In view of these portentous consequences, I cannot but think that this course of legislation should be arrested, even if there were nothing to forbid it in the fundamental laws of our Union."

For what, then, would *he* have the Constitution amended? With *him* it is a proposition to remove *one* impediment, merely to be met by *others*, which, in his opinion, cannot be removed—to enable Congress to do what, in his opinion, they ought not to do if they could.

[Here Mr. Meade, of Virginia, inquired if Mr. Lincoln understood the President to be opposed, on grounds of expediency, to any and every improvement.]

To which Mr. Lincoln answered: In the very part of his message of which I am now speaking, I understand him as giving some vague expressions in favor of some possible objects of improvements; but, in doing so, I understand to be directly in the teeth of his own argument·in the other parts of it. Neither the President, nor any one, can possibly specify an improvement, which shall not be liable to one or the other objections he has urged on the score of expediency. I have shown, and might show again, that no work—no object—can be so general as to dispense its benefits with precise equality; and this inequality is among the "portentous consequences" for which he declare the improvements should be arrested. No, sir; when the President intimates that something in the way of improvements may properly be done by the general government, he is shrinking from the conclusions to which his own argument would force him. He ·feels not that the improvements of this broad and goodly land are a mighty interest, and he is unwilling to confess to the people, and perhaps to himself, that he has built an argument which, when pressed to its conclusion, utterly annihilate this interest.

I have already said that no one who is satisfied of the expediency of making improvements, need be much uneasy in his conscience about its unconstitutionality. I wish now to submit a few remarks on the general proposition of amending the Constitution. As a general rule, I think we would do much better to let it alone. No slight occasion should tempt us to touch it. Better not take the first step, which may lead to a habit of altering it. Better, rather, to habituate ourselves to think it unalterable. It can scarcely be made better than it is. New provisions would introduce new difficulties, and thus create and increase still further appetite for change.

15*

No, sir ; let it stand as it is.   New hands have never touched it.   The men who made it have done their work, and have passed away)   Who shall improve on what *they* did ?

Mr. Chairman, for the purpose of reviewing this message in the least possible time, as well as for the sake of distinctness, I have analyzed its arguments as well as I could, and reduced them to the propositions I have stated.   I have now examined them in detail.   I wish to detain the committee only a little while longer, with some general remarks on the subject of improvement.   That the subject is a difficult one, cannot be denied.   Still, it is no more difficult in Congress than it is in the State legislatures, in the counties, or in the smallest municipal districts which anywhere exist.   All can recur to instances of this difficulty in the case of country roads, bridges, and the like.   One man is offended because the road passes over his land ; another is offended because it does *not* pass over his ; one is dissatisfied because the bridge, for which he is taxed, crosses the river on a different road from that which leads from his house to town ; another cannot bear that the county should get in debt for these same roads and bridges ; while not a few struggle hard to have roads located over their lands, and then stoutly refuse to let them be opened, until they are first paid the damages.   Even between the different wards and streets of towns and cities, we find the same wrangling and difficulty.   Now these are no other than the very difficulties against which, and out of which, the President constructs his objections of " inequality," " speculation " and " crushing the treasury."   There is but a single alternative about them—they are *sufficient*, or they are *not*.   If sufficient, they are sufficient *out* of Congress as well as *in* it, and there is an end.   We must reject them as insufficient, or lie down and do nothing by any authority.   Then, difficulty though there be, let us meet and overcome it.

> " Attempt the end, and never come to doubt ;
> Nothing so hard, but search will find it out. "

Determine that the thing can and shall be done, and then we shall find the way.   The tendency to undue expansion is unquestionably the chief difficulty.   How to do *something*, and still not do *too much*, is the desideratum.   Let each contribute his mite in the way of suggestion.   The late Silas Wright, in a letter to the Chicago Convention, contributed his, which was worth something; and I now contribute mine, which may be worth nothing. At all events it will mislead nobody, and therefore will do no harm. I would not borrow money. I am against an overwhelming, crushing system. Suppose that at each session Congress shall first determine *how much* money can, for that year, be spared for improvements; then apportion that sum to the most important objects. So far all is easy; but how shall we determine which are the most important? On this question comes the collision of interests. I shall be slow to acknowledge that *your* harbor, or *your* river, is more important than *mine*, and *vice versa.* To clear this difficulty, let us have that same statistical information which the gentleman from Ohio (Mr. Vinton) suggested at the beginning of this session. In that information we shall have a stern, unbending basis of *facts*—a basis in no wise subject to whim, caprice, or local interest. The pre-limited amount of means will save us from doing *too much*, and the statistics will save us from doing what we do in *wrong places.* Adopt and adhere to this course, and, it seems to me, the difficulty is cleared.

One of the gentlemen from South Carolina (Mr. Rhett) very much deprecates these statistics. He particularly objects, as I understand him, to counting all the pigs and chickens in the land. I do not perceive much force in the objection. It is true, that if everything be enumerated, a portion of such statistics may not be very useful to this object. Such products of this country as are to be *consumed* where they are *produced*, need no roads and rivers, no means of transportation, and have no very proper connection with this subject. The *surplus*, that which is produced in *one* place to be consumed in *another;* the capacity of each locality to produce a *greater* surplus; the natural means of transprrtation, and their susceptibility of improvement; the hindrances, delays, and losses of life and property during transportation, and the causes of each, would be among the most valuable statistics in this connection. From these it would readily apper where a given amount of expenditure would do the most good. These statistics might be equally accessible, as they would be equally useful, to both the nation and the States. In this way, and by these means, let the nation take hold of the larger works, and the States the smaller ones, and thus, working in a meeting direction, discreetly, but steadily and firmly, what is made unequal in one place may be equalized in another, extravagance avoided, and the whole country put on that career of prosperity which shall correspond with its extent of territory, its natural resources, and the intelligence and enterprise of its people.

SKETCH

OF THE

LIFE OF HANNIBAL HAMLIN,

REPUBLICAN CANDIDATE FOR VICE-PRESIDENT.

Mr. Hamlin was born in Paris, county of Oxford, State of Maine, August 27, 1809. His father, Dr. Cyrus Hamlin, was a surgeon and physician, and a native of Massachusetts. He was clerk of the courts for several years, and subsequently sheriff of Oxford county. He was one of the leading influential citizens of his town and county, and died in 1828, aged about fifty-eight years.

Mr. Hamlin's mother was a daughter of Dea. Elijah Livermore, of the town of Livermore, Oxford county, Maine. She was a very estimable lady, and died in 1851, aged about seventy. Mr. Hamlin was fitted for college, but his father dying, he abandoned the idea of a college course, and for a while labored at home upon the old homestead farm. Before commencing the study of law, he worked in a printing office in his native town, and for more than a year conducted the *Jeffersonian,* since merged in the Oxford *Democrat,* in connection with the Hon. Horatio King. Subsequently, he studied law with the late Judge Cole, and after completing his course of study, he was admitted to the bar, and removed to Hampden, Maine, where he enjoyed an extensive practice until he voluntarily retired from it. His first entrance into public life was in 1836, when he was elected a representative from the town of Hampden to the Maine legislature. He was re-

elected in 1837, 1838, 1839, 1840, and again in 1847 He
was speaker of the house of representatives in 1837, 1839,
and 1840. In 1840 he was a candidate for Congress, but
owing to the great popularity of General Harrison, and the
remarkable success of the Whig party in that campaign, he
was defeated by a few hundred votes. In 1842 he again run
for Congress, and was elected by a large majority, and in 1844
he was also elected to the same body, by an increased vote.
By the death of the lamented Governor Fairfield, a vacancy
was created in the United States Senate, and on the 26th of
May, 1848, Mr. Hamlin was elected for four years to fill that
vacancy.

In July, 1851, he was re-elected to the Senate for six years.
In 1856, he was elected Governor of Maine, and resigned his
seat in the Senate to assume the duties of the office, January
7, 1857. On the 16th day of the same month, he was elected
by both branches of the legislature to the United States Senate for six years, and resigned the office of Governor, February 20, 1857. Until he resigned the position, he was for a
long time chairman of the committee on commerce in the
Senate.

The above brief sketch of the early life and public services
of Mr. Hamlin, while it may be a matter of interest to the
American people, is far from being all they inquire after connected with his personal history. Placed as he now is before
the people of this great country, as a candidate for the second
office in their gift, it is perfectly natural they should desire to
know something of his political history and public record

Mr. Hamlin's antecedents are democratic. On arriving at
his majority, he connected himself with the old Democratic
party, and acted with that political organization until 1856,
when, in a brief and eloquent speech in the Senate, he publicly withdrew from it, and allied himself to the Republican
party. Upon looking over Mr. Hamlin's public record in

Congress upon the slavery question, we find nothing inconsistent with his present position upon that subject. When he
first entered Congress, he manfully battled for the *right of
petition* against the gag rules introduced into that body. He
not only voted to receive the petitions of the people, but upon
more than one occasion spoke eloquently in favor of this great
constitutional right.

In 1845, while he voted against the joint resolution for the
annexation of Texas, yet he was not opposed to the measure
provided it could be brought about by negotiation and treaty,
and provided further that at least an equal portion of said
domain should be kept free territory, for the benefit of the
great laboring interests of the free States. Had his counsels,
and the counsels of Colonel Benton, Silas Wright, and other
great lights in the party, been adhered to, the Mexican war
and all its evil consequences would have been avoided.

When the " Two-Million Bill " was before the House in
1846–7, proposing to put into the hands of the President a
certain amount of money with which to negotiate a treaty of
peace with Mexico, Mr. Hamlin stood up side by side with
David Wilmot, Preston King, and other influential democrats,
in defence of the celebrated " *Proviso*," known as the " Wilmot Proviso," prepared by Judge Wilmot, yet *actually offered
by Mr. Hamlin*, in the absence of the author. For this proviso he uniformly voted and labored until it passed the House.

In the house of representatives, in Maine, at the session in
1847—to which he was elected immediately after his return
from Congress—he introduced resolutions embodying the same
sentiments, advocated them in a masterly speech, and mainly
through his influence they passed the house with only six
nays, and the senate with only one dissenting vote.

Following up his record upon this question, we find him
voting in the United States Senate in 1848, in favor of the
Jefferson Proviso for the restriction of slaveery in the bill for

the organization of a territorial government for Oregon. Still later, in 1850, he voted to insert a similar restriction in the bills giving territorial governments to Utah and New-Mexico. The proviso being defeated, he voted against the bills in strict accordance with the instructions of a *democratic* legislature in Maine.

In the same year, 1850, Mr. Hamlin made the *first* speech in the United States Senate in favor of the unconditional admission of California as a *free* State, and his speech was then considered one of the most able delivered upon that subject.

He also voted against the bill giving ten millions of dollars to Texas, for the relinquishment of lands to which she never had the slightest title. In 1854, following his own convictions of duty, he labored and voted against the repeal of the Missouri compromise, in strict conformity with the resolutions of the then democratic legislature of Maine, and then in the last Congress did all in his power to defeat the perfidious Lecompton Constitution.

We have thus given Mr. Hamlin's record upon some of the great leading questions connected with the subject of slavery during the last fourteen years, showing that upon no occasion has he ever acted or voted in any way not perfectly consistent with this record. Upon other matters, during his long Congressional career, his votes have been uniformly consistent and in perfect harmony with the character of the man. Upon all matters of financial policy, while he never has been disposed to withhold justice from honest claimants, he has sternly resisted dishonest, fraudulent claims, got up with an intention to rob the treasury. In justice to Mr. Hamlin, we should here say that no man in Congress for the last twenty years has been more faithful, or has labored more untiringly to aid poor but honest claimants upon the bounty of the government than he. There is scarcely a town in the State of Maine, where you will not find men who have been made in-

valids in their country's service, widows and orphans, who
are now living upon the little bounty obtained for their relief
through his prompt and effective influences and labors. No
honest complainant, however poor or humble, was ever coldly
turned away from the presence of Senator Hamlin. Schemes
of public plunder which frequently find their way into Congress, never obtain favor with him.

Another trait of character which has always given him
great popularity with the people, is his strict honesty and stern
moral integrity. No man can be found who will rise up and
say Hannibal Hamlin ever cheated him, politically or in any
other way. His whole life has been marked by a strict attention to every public duty incident to his official positions.

As a public speaker is is superfluous for us to speak of our
distinguished Senator. In this respect the whole country is
well informed. Few men have a more enviable reputation as
forensic debators.

Senator Hamlin's sympathies have always been strongly
with the masses. This, perhaps, accounts for his great popularity with the people. In proof of this we have only to refer to his election as Governor of Maine, in 1856. Without
solicitation on his part and against his wishes at the largest
political convention ever holden in the State, he was on the
first ballot unanimously selected the standard bearer of the
Republicans in the ensuing contest.

The Democrats, aided by the straight Whigs, had carried the
State the year before by about five thousand majority, and
both branches of the Legislature.

Senator Hamlin stumped the State from one end to the
other. Nothing but the great fight between Douglas and Lincoln ever exceeded it. It was a splendid hard-fought canvass.

The Democrats had Judge Wells their standard bearer and
all the distinguished men of their party in the field, pitted
against Hamlin and his coadjutors. Look at the result. The

Republieans swept the State and elected their distinguished leader by about *twenty thousand* majority. So highly were Governor Hamlin's services appreciated in the U. S. Senate the Legislature of Maine, with great unanimity, returned him again to that body for six years. Before he became a member of Congress, Mr. Hamlin had an extensive practice as a lawyer. Since his election to the Senate he has abandoned it, and now, when not actively engaged in his public duties, may be found, like the great and distinguished Silas Wright, at *work with his own hands* on his farm, in the rural, quiet town of Hampden, where, at his hospitable home, his numerous friends always meet a hearty welcome.

Such is a brief outline of the life and character of Hannibal Hamlin. Possessed of great legislative experience, wise in counsel, bold and determined in action, true to his friends and his country, he will be triumphantly elected to the high commendary positionso honorably filled by a long line of illustrious statesmen in the past.

1000101262

WILKES COLLEGE LIBRARY